# PSYCHOLOGY OF LANGUAGE LEARNING

# Psychology of Language Learning

*Dr. Joseph C. Mukalel*
*M.A., M.Ed., M.A. (U.K.), Ph.D.*
School of Gandhian Thought and Development Studies
Mahatma Gandhi University
Kottayam (Kerala)

DISCOVERY PUBLISHING HOUSE
NEW DELHI—110 002

First Published – 200[illegible]

Reprinted – 2024

ISBN: 978-81-7141-402-4



**Psychology of Language Learning**

*Published by:*

**DISCOVERY PUBLISHING HOUSE PVT. LTD.**

4383/4B, Ansari Road, Darya Ganj
New Delhi-110 002 (India)
*Phone*: +91-11-23279245; 23253475; 43596065
*Mobile*: +91 9811179893 / +91 9871656464
*E-mail*: discoverybooksindia@gmail.com
orderdphbooks@gmail.com
namitwasan9@gmail.com
*web*: www.discoverypublishinggroup.com

*Printed at:*
Infinity Imaging Systems
Delhi

# *Introduction*

Language teaching is a highly unified experience for any one who has shown willingness to take such a thing seriously enough. Language teaching is not the prerogative of any one discipline so far as its theoretical implications are concerned. The language teacher is required to tap resources from quite a number related of fields of studies (i) to base his teaching experience on a broad theoretical foundation, (ii) to draw proximate help for effective classroom performance, (iii) to broaden his teaching experience beyond the bounds of the classroom, and (iv) to develop for himself teaching techniques which are highly effective in a given classroom and socio-cultural context. The days are gone when the language teacher could afford to know only the general grammatical, historical and literary background of the language he is expected to teach. That was the time when language teachers could even function in the classroom without any formal training in the methodology of teaching a second or foreign language.

The knowledge of and training in the *techniques* and *methodology* of teaching second or foreign languages (English, for instance) against the Indian background is a basic concern which covers a wide variety of areas essential for present-day language teachers. After obtaining enough grounding in the methodology and techniques of language teaching with all the theoretical implications that go with such a field of enquiry, I think, the language teacher must plunge confidently into the greater details of what I may call the *psycholinguistic foundations* of language teaching which is our concern in the present work. A work of this kind introduces the language teacher to those aspects of *psychology* on the one hand, and *linguistics* on the other which pertains directly to the *language behaviour* of man. Even though in broad terms, psycholinguistics is founded on the general principles of psychology and linguistics, it has developed in recent times into a fairly independent field of thought with its ultimate roots always gathering the best of what is available from the fieids of *general psychology* and *structural linguistics*.

Again, by contrast to structural linguistics, psycholinguistics concentrates on language behaviour as such in terms of its 'functional aspects' of rather than the 'linguistic structure' which constitutes the content of language behaviour as a function. Once the *psycholinguistic foundations* are laid, and the language teacher becomes conversant with the relevant aspects and theoretical implications of language as a function, he is required to obtain greater details in what we shall call, the linguistic foundations of language teaching.

Psycholinguistics is concerned about language behaviour at several levels, and from a number of perspectives and the language teacher need to be acquainted with several of these levels and perspectives. The early phases of the child's *language acquisition* is a principal concern of the language teacher whose responsibility it is to build up further language experiences on what the child has acquired at home. The teacher must be acquainted with the intricacies of *language development* and the syntactic and semantic implications of language development in the child as a speaker-listener. The classroom, in fact, is the second arena for language development just as the home constitutes the first. The teacher is concerned about the intricate aspects of *language production*, and of *language receptions* as exercised by the speaker-listener. The classroom is the second citadel of systematic language experience just as the home constitutes the first.

The language teacher cannot afford to be misled by those theories which uphold the superiority of the *biological mechanisms* in man before everything else, especially *the mind*. The average teacher who entertains firm convictions in regard to the active and dominant role of the human mind in all aspects pertaining to human behaviour, should not experience a moment's doubt in regard to his common-sense convictions. The chapters on *Language and the Brain*, and *Language and the Mind* are geared to provide the language teacher a basis in the roles of the biological mechanisms and the mind in language behaviour. For no empirical reasons whatsoever is it possible for us to push aside the dominant role of the mind in the behaviour of man. In the chapters that follow a close attempt has been made to view together the three dimensions of human behaviour (1) the *cognitive*, (2) the *linguistic*, and (3) the *sociological*, and at the same time bring together the *semantic component* as the 'content of language' and *conceptualization* (concepts, conceptual elements and streams of concepts) as the 'content of the mind' in the parallel processes of *conceptual organization* and *imaginative organization*. The very purpose is to view together the content of human cognitive experience and the content of language experience in one and the same *representation* of reality as part of the same unified human experience. Chapters on the *sociological implications* and *Bilingualism* attempt to explicate the *sociological component* of human language behaviour.

The language teacher is further led to those aspects of language behaviour where a demarcation between *structure* and *function* is impossible to draw. Language as a unified experience is viewed from three distinct levels : (1) the *Grammar* (with a capital 'G'), (2) the usage, and (3) the use of the language which are studied from both the *vertical* (historical, temporal) and *horizontal* (dialectic, spatial) viewpoints. The chapter on *The Teacher and Usage* discusses the three intrinsic levels of language and introduce a symthetic view of the *use* part of linguistic structure and the *idiolectic* part of the speaker's performance. The final chapters include aspects of language behaviour and things which render language behaviour a most concrete experience for the classroom learner as well as the classroom practitioner. The chapter on *Errors and Error Analysis* and the following chapters on the *Choice of Teaching Methods* and the *Creative Aspects* of the teaching-learning experiences are intended to acquaint the language teacher with the *relevance* of psycholinguistics to classroom practice.

The present work begins, so to say, in a characteristic manner acquainting the language teacher with the *psycholinguistic perspectives* of language behaviour in general : the *creative*, *communicational*, *biological* and *behavioural* dimensions of human language. Language acquisition process is looked at from a variety of perspectives including most of all the conditions prevalent (i) in the *home atmosphere* ($L_1$) and (ii) in the *classroom* ($L_2$). Throughout the present work the home is considered the first citadel and the classroom is thought of as the second citadel of language acquisition. The language teacher, again is presented with the intricate process of language acquisition in terms of the *internalization* of linguistic systems, the acquisition of phonology, vocabulary, syntax and the process of socialization, semantic development having been resevered for later chapters. The process of internalization of language is treated initially in its broader sense and later chapters introduce the more specialized aspects of internalization.

Eventhough as a rule we are prone to deal with the unilingual dimension of language acquisition while discussing in relation to the home and class-room situations, in a country like India, the bilingual implications of language acquisition and production are almost inseparable. This is true especially in the urban contexts with its metropolitan or cosmopolitan atmosphere where children mostly grow up as bilinguals of one type or another. The chapter on *Bilingual Implications* discusses language acquisition so that the language teacher may draw his own morals in relation to his classroom practices to make his work most effective.

It is worthwhile to note that the dichotomy which once existed between the purely structural studies on language (*structural linguistics*) and the purely functional or developmental studies on language (*psycholinguistics*) is fast disappearing thanks to the work of the transformational generative linguists who have succeeded considerably in establishing inter-disciplinary links between linguistics and quite a number of other disciplines including mathematics and communicational engineering. Such inter-disciplinary links will have the greatest advantage of helping us view language from its truly united perspectives rather than study it in terms of dichotomous and water-tight compartments which would not in fact attain for us our theoretical and practical ends in the study of human language as such and languages in particular.

# Contents

*Introduction* V

1. Psycholinguistic Approaches to Language 1
   1. Meaning and Scope of Psycholinguistics
   2. Language as Verbal Behaviour
   3. Language as Biological Growth
   4. Language as Set of Habits
   5. Language as Creative-Behaviour
   6. Language as Communication

2. Acquisition of the First Language 13
   1. Learning Conditions of $L_1$ and $L_2$
   2. Factors Affecting the Learning of $L_1$
   3. Stages of $L_1$ Acquisition Process
   4. Internalisation of Linguistic Systems
   5. Acquiring the Phonology $L_1$
   6. Acquiring the Lexicon of $L_1$
   7. Acquiring the Syntax of $L_1$
   8. The Process of Socialization and Acquisition of Semantic Maturity

3. Language and Communication 29
   1. The Act of Communication
   2. Speaker-Listener Polarity
   3. The Processes of Encoding and Decoding
   4. Teaching Communication Skills
   5. Teleological Nature of Language
   6. The Child and Communication

4. Linguistic Competence and Performance 38
   1. Essence of Linguistic Competence

2. Essence of Performance
3. Linguistic Competence : a Process of Development
4. Relevance of Competence to the Classroom
5. Language Performance and the Classroom

5. Psychological Factors in Language Learning 60
   1. Intelligence
   2. Resourcefulness
   3. Creativity
   4. Motivation

6. Sociological Implications of Language Acquisition 71
   1. Language and Society
   2. The Child as a Learner at Home
   3. Language and the Child's Cognitive Development
   4. The Child and Socialization
   5. Socialization and the Classroom

7. Bilingualism and Its Implications 92
   1. Bilingual Competence
   2. Bilingual Swapping Process
   3. The Structure of Bilingual Skills
   4. Sociological Implications of Bilingualism
   5. Bilingual Development in Children

8. Language and the Brain 105
   1. Language and Biolinguistics
   2. Neurological Substratum of Language
   3. Biological Dependence of Language
   4. The Brain and Sense Experiences
   5. The Senses and Symbolic Behaviour

9. Language and the Mind 124
   1. The Content of the Human Mind
   2. Universals and Language Development
   3. Language and Thought
   4. Development of Symbolic Behaviour in the Child
   5. The Semantic Content of Language

10. Deviant Language Behaviour 146
   1. Physiological and Psychological Background
   2. Physiological Abnormalities

3. Psychogenic Speech Disorders
4. Deviant Language Behaviour and Home
5. Language Disorder and the Classroom

11. The Teacher and Usage 169
1. The Problem of Usage
2. The Grammar of a Language
3. Usage and Language Change
4. Usage and Linguistic Strata
5. Usage in the Classroom

12. The Phenomenon of Errors in Language 193
1. Nature of Errors in Language Behaviour
2. Errors, Grammar and Usage
3. Errors and Use
4. Error Analysis–I
5. Error Analysis–II

13. Creative Aspects of Language Learning 215
1. Creative Behaviour
2. Linguistic Creativity
3. Creative Non-verbal Behaviour
4. Aspects of Creative Classroom Learning
5. Creative Behaviour of the Teacher

*Bibliography* 233

*Index* 249

# 1
# Psycholinguistic Approaches to Language

## 1. Meaning and Scope of Psycholinguistics

Language as an observable phenomenon may be studied from its structural or functional viewpoints. Both one ways of scientifically looking at language. On the one hand, the linguist views the community involved in a process of Communication. People speak to one another; they get things done in accordance to their desires. People exchange ideas and viewpoints; and they gather information or provide others with information. In otherwords, tauto the process of language is one of give and take in which the members of the linguistic community is involved. Language is not a simple process, it is a highly dynamic, active and complex process in which several agents and components are involved. The proximate and the chief agents involved in the process of language are the *speaker* and *listener*. The speaker may be called the producing agent and the listener, the receiving agent. No process of speech can be adequately studied without these two agents who adequate the process of speech. Speech function is usually represented in the following diagram:

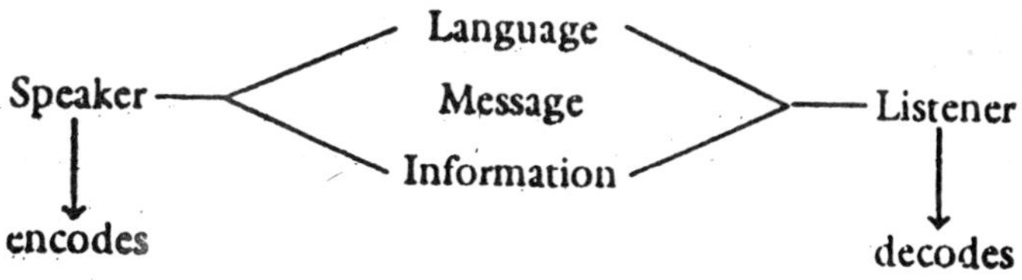

The diagram shown on page 1 takes into account the whole process of speech beginning with the speaker and the choices involved in encoding the message and the listener the message. Within this process we are in a position to isolate two things: a process and something around which the process taken place. Correspondingly, on the one hand, there is the *speech process* and on the other, the *language* itself. The speech process is not the language; the language constitutes as its content i.e. something around which the process takes places. The first, therefore, is the proper object of psycholinguistics; and the sound is the proper object of linguistics.

*Psycholinguistics* studies language as a process i.e. from its functions viewpoints involving the roles played by the speaker and the listener. The psychological background of the speaker and that of the listener, this come to bear upon the understanding of the psycholinguistic aspects of language in general. The predominant question answered is how language is acquired and produced and what elements make up these processes. Linguistics, on the other hand, studies the structural components of language as an objective verbally. This is very true especially of the structural school of linguistic which held the helm of linguistic thinking during the first half of twentieth century. The chief concern of the period was to study language as an objective, structural system. The transformational generative grammarians no longer believe in such a dichotomy between structure and function, but views language in a more unified manner giving greater scope for linguistic processes in the study of language. It is more or less a well-acknowledged fact coming back on to the traditional ways of looking at language. Whatever be the trends in present-lay linguistics, for practical purposes, it scene better to view language from these two viewpoints without making water-light compartments of these two aspects of the same speech-function.

Psycholinguistics is based on the general principles of *psychology* as the science of the behaviour of the human individual as well as on the general principles of *linguistics* as the science of language. Consequently we may talk of psycholinguistics as an applied science as well as basic science since psycholinguistics also formulates its own basic principles on language as the most complex form of human behaviour. There a number of very relevant questions which psycholinguistics attempts to answer: (1) what is the nature of the language as a verbal behaviour ? (2) To what extent is language a biological growth ? (3) What role does habit formation play in language acquisition ? (4) What is the communication-structure of language? (5) What is the essential relation between language and information ? (6) Is language purely a stimulus-response bond or is it also a creative behaviour ? (7) What role does creativity plays in linguistic acquisition and production ? (8) How do the learning conditions of the $L_1$ differ from the learning conditions of $L_2$ ? (9) What kind of internalization process takes place when language is learned ? (10) To what extent can the language acquisition process of children all over the world be held similar?

Innumerable problems of the kind given above come under the scope of psycholinguistic. By answering these questions psycholinguistics will be in a position to make headway in the understanding of the essential nature of human language. But most of there solutions cannot be reached by any sort of investigation in isolation. There are mostly interdisciplinary problems as we have examined in the case of general linguistics. In its investigations into the phenomenon of language, psycholinguistics has to proceed in co-ordination with several other field of knowledge. First and foremost the general basis is received from and continuous reference is made to *linguistics* and *psychology*. Language is on the one hand such a unified activity and on the other an object of complex nature that both a structural as well as behavioral description alone can do justice to its nature. This is how linguistics and psychology have continuous bearing on psycholinguistics. In the same manner *sociology* comes to bear upon the investigations of psycholinguistics. Sociology, concerned with the behaviour of the individual in society, helps psycholinguistics to understand the role of language in society and the role of social forces in the development of language especially at the early stages. Another very important field of enquiry is *communication engineering* which investigates into the structure of communication and the way the process of communication can be made more efficient and economical. Psycholinguistics studies language primarily as a vehicle for communication of information or intention. A co-ordinated work in these fields have been definitely yielding much valuable information with regards to the communicative structure of language, as well as it has paved way ton more advanced communication system research in psycholinguistics have several such practical and technological advantages.

## 2. Language as Verbal Behaviour

Within the system of psycholinguistics it is appropriate to view language as verbal behaviour. The notion of verbal behaviour originated with the behaviourist psychologists within the context of stimulus-response-reinforcement patterns of behavior. Man is studied exclusively from the viewpoint of his complex behavioural patterns. The behaviourist psychologists do not find anything but behaviour in man; an inner *substantiality* or a unifying inner principle is not widely accepted among the behaviourist groups. But cognitive-field theories are coming more and more towards a unifying, inner principle in man. Without getting into this controversy we may rightly say that man is dependable in terms of his behaviour.

The essential components of verbal behaviour i.e. the language behaviour view of man are *verbal stimulatis* and *verbal response*. The entire behavioral pattern of a community rests on these two components. In other words the community is involved in an interpersonal communion, which is describable in terms of stimulates-response bonds. Even though we accept the stimulus response pattern of behaviour at a basic level of explanation, we do not comply with the description of man in terms of a more organism. The verbal behaviour of man i.e. in a community takes place not exactly the way intra-human organisms interact in these groups. The patterns of verbal behaviour in man has a set of characteristics that makes it unique. The verbal behaviour has more of a teleological nature than any other form of behaviour. Man seldom speaks, without a purpose, however rudimentary the purpose may be. Man's verbal behaviour is purposeful behaviour parallel to his other forms of behaviour.

Verbal behaviour has structural and functional dimensions. It is man's behaviour, a pattern of action, proceeding from and entered around his personality. At the same time structurally it is language : a behaviour pattern consisting of language. Man work on building a house; they cut down a tree: both are behaviour. In either case man makes use of thing that one fully external to his person. But in verbal behaviour man employes something that is fully internal to his person i.e. the language. Both the structural aspects of the language he uses for communication and the behavioral modality of the manner of producing that language function at an intrinsic level.

The child growing up in the family atmosphere undergoes the family atmosphere undergoes language experience along with several other aspects of the child's psychophysiological growth. Language development as the inculcation of the child's verbal behaviour is a stretched and continuous one lasting not only for a few years, but in, fact, for life. The child takes his own time in course of this psychophysiological growth to pick up and master the language. There is no undue, artificial hurry in the process. The verbal behaviour develops and gets established along with other patterns of behaviour like walking but we may say that it takes the longest period as part of personality development. Any retardation in either is said to affect the other especially at the early phase of the development of verbal behaviour. The development of verbal behaviour as part of personality development, therefore, is aided by the intensity of the child's overall experience. The features of this experience have a direct bearing on the way the child is going to handle his language.

All these bear upon the fact that the child learns his language chiefly as behaviour. Learning the first and foremost way to communicate himself, for the child, is not different from other ways of self-assertion, liaison with the family and satisfaction of his needs. The fact that the native child learns his language as an integral part of his overall behavioral pattern is something to be always remembered in sealing methods and techniques for the teaching of a foreign language.

## 3. Language as Biological Growth

A very controversial point in regard to the essential nature of language development is whether the biological features of language or the intellectual, creative features predominate in the process. In the foregoing chapter on the relation between linguistics and biology and biolinguistics we shall see the role of biological features like the function of the nervous system in language. A basic fact is that language is both biological and something other than that language has definite *biological substratum*, a springboard from which language takes illumined leaps, a horizon that cannot easily be fathomed.

These *biological formulations* from the basis of both language acquisition and production. In several ways language acquisition can be described as biological growth. As a seed sprouts and grows into a tree of its own species and not of another or as the embryo of a certain animal grows only into an animal of the same species, the human offspring is endowed with a set of innate biological and psychological features and specificities which form the directive principles in the growth and development of the child. The child is endowed with a set of biological organs of speech of birth. Though the intra-human animals do share in several of these biological organs and are used for meeting the primary biological needs such as eating and breathing, man do use there organs for linguistics purposes as a secondary function. Lower animals too communicate themselves somehow through variety of sounds by means of these organs.

Among the organs of speech the most neglected and the least studied is the *auditory organ*, the ears. The primary function of the ears is certainly the reception of sounds. Sounds on the other hand is meant primarily for communication of some sort of all level of existence. Therefore one may assertain that the organs of audition are perhaps the most unique of speech-organs. A part from all these biological organs of speech which are the natural endowments of the child to develop a language, there are other aspects which make language growth a biological function.

Apart from the presence of the organs of speech which are the exterior causes for the production and reception of speech, man possesses a brain and the *nervous system* which are the real biological substratum for language. In the chapter on *Language and the Brain* we shall examine in detail the role the brain plays in language production. Any damage to the organs of speech can only partially retard the production or reception of language to the extent of the damage; but a serious damage to the brain can fully retard language production an reception and render the individual speechers. The physical growth of the nervous system including the brain and of the organs of speech and auditions, is basic to the biological growth of language.

At birth the child is endowed with the capacity to learn

language, but not any one language in particular. It is not at all believed as a hereditary factor that a child can learn this or that language. As a result the biological faculties, as we may call the organs, get adjusted to and acquainted with the sound-system of the native language proper. This biological adjustment is a part of the biological growth of the language. Because of this characteristic it happens that the child will find it very difficult to programme certain sounds and sequences of sounds which belong to another language. A child from the south of India finds the Z, z, or v sounds of English difficult to pronounce. An English child finds the MK or Mb cluster of African languages a problem. This certainly is a problem of the biological growth of the language. Language is biological phenomenon with regards to several such factors mentioned above. But lots of light can be thrown into the biological nature of language if we examine language as a set of habits.

## 4. Language as a set of Habits

Controversies one carried to the extreme as to whether language learning and production processes consist nearly of habit formation and habitual processes, or it is an intellectual activity with habit formation only as the under shell. In otherwords the question is asked if language is a *set of habits* or it is a *rule-governed behaviour.* An analysis of the phenomenon tends to reveal that extreme viewers on language have their basis on some essential aspects of language. No one can rightly rule out the role of habit formation from behaviour of any kind, especially from language, and at its same time rule out the functions of language as a rule-governed, creative behaviour.

For the behaviouristic, language consists of a set of habits. Let us examine the role of habits in the production of language. Habits are said to be patterns of behaviour which are so much established in the neuromuscular system that they can be involuntarily or semi-consciously carried out. Efforts one minimized as behaviour enters the level of habits and man can carry it out without any special act of the will or without conscious attention. To understand the nature of habits fully it is good to compare two basic sets of human activities: *reflex behaviour* and *learned behaviour.* The question, then, is whether language can be described as reflex behaviour or learned behaviour. Reflexes are automatic behaviour pattern in animals, controlled by neuro-muscular activities, when there is a dust pantile in the age at once our hands shots up to help the age dispel the pantile; or man shifts the sleeping positions at night. In all such behaviour the governing factor is not the conscious attention of man, but it is the result of *neuro-muscular organization*, a feature peculiar to animals and to some extend to plants. It is a process of *biological adjustment* as a safeguard to life.

There are, on the other hand, behaviour patterns which are learned. The basis of learned activities is repetition and practice. Swimming, for man, is a learned activity, not a reflex behaviour as in case of a puppy or a kitten. Soon after they are born, if put in water, they show signs of their ability to swim. But a human child doesn't reveal any ability to swim and he has to have practice in swimming. Several skills associated to the occupations of man require continuous and labouring practice unlike reflex behaviour. Such skills we say are learned.

If so, where exactly shall we place language? It is a reflex behaviour, or is it a learned behaviour? Habits come to our aid at this juncture: when a learned activity acquires enough practice and crossed the level of conscious manipulation, we call it a *habit*. Reflexes are rudimentary habits because they requires no conscious manipulation. Out the other hand, learned behaviour to become habits when there are automatic. The fact seems, to be that language is both a reflex behaviour and a learned activity at different levels. Let's examine the *pre-linguistics phase* of language learning. The impact cries, and produces, bobbling noise. It produces random sounds. What are all these? Here we may certainly find the child reacting to its physiology and physical experiences: hunger, thirst, feeling of well-being, heat, cold etc. These are reflex behaviour patterns as no one has taught the child these acts. But the peculiar thing is that such pre-linguistic experience in fact lay the foundation for the further production of language proper. One wonders about the language development of an infant who never babbles, or has problems in doing so. Such are the reflex bases of language. Also all that we discussed in relation to language as biological growth is relevant in the consideration of language as a reflex activity.

At the same time, and on the basis of language as reflex behaviour, we find that language is a learned habit. Even though man, by nature and in virtue of his biological structure, is dispersed to learning language, he is not so in so far as any particular language is concerned. His organism, micro-muscular system and intellect are disposal to any language on earth, with the request that to master particular language man has to learn it, practice it and inculcate the habits of using the skills of the language. Man has, in other words, to raise language to the habit level by continuous use of the same. At this level no reflexes will come to his significant aid. Here, we say that language is a learned activity. Man is endowed with the physiological and intellectual facilities for learning a language; but a language is particular has to be picked up by his own effort. This is achieved through the process of internalization of the various linguistic systems as discussed in the following chapters. The internalized linguistic systems enable a child to manipulate language at an automatic level as fully formed habits. This seems to be the only way, the another feels, that language can be explained as a set of habits. Carrying the learned aspects or the reflex aspects to any extreme overlooking the other will only had to a needless controversy with regard to the essential nature of language. The pages which follow will examine the role creativity plays in language development and will examine language as a rule-governed behaviour in anticipation to a more detailed discussion we have in the final chapter on the subject.

## 5. Language as Creative Behaviour

There is ample foundation for the fact that language is a set of habits when viewed from its biological development as well as from the automatic and non-deliberate way language functions. Just because language functions at the habits listen to, write as well read without being so much conscious of what he does and how he does it, and at the same time pay full attention to the content material of the language. This is major difference between a beginner and well-versed speaker of a language; especially when it is used as a foreign language.

But language is not merely a set of habits, and language development is not a mere process of habit-formation. Language crosses the boundary of habits and enters the unfathomable horizon of creative experience. A major breakthrough which transformation generative grammar achieved in present-day linguistics is the recognition and emphasis of the creative nature of language, which though had been recognized by traditional grammars, came to be neglected for the past several decades. The role of creativity in language reinstates the status and dignity of man as man, as language is an experience uniquely proper to man.

Language is a creative phenomenon, and language acquisition is a creative experience. It will be a poor performance and an injustice done to the blooming, energetic millions of $L_1$ learners of language learning is described as trial and error process, imitation, conditioning or any form of stimulus-response connections. Certainly each of there of some time or other of the process of language learning does come into play. But it is improper to explain language acquisition chiefly and solely as any of the processes mentioned above. Instead, linguistic creativity alone will do justice to the extremely creative way the child acquires his native language.

The child lives in the natural, family atmosphere and confronts a multitude of native language material poured into his organs of condition. This situation is examined in trial in Ch. 2. Unlike the systematic, well-graded and phased language material of the classroom presented in highly controlled situations, the language which the child confronts is all confused, mixed up, and of non-controlled situations. At one time the child listens to the mother starting at the elder brother, and at another it may be heated exchange between the parents. At the same time, amidst all this complex linguistic material, the child begins the process of *internalizing* linguistic systems as explained in Ch. 2. Even though the language is confused, the child is not confused; he receives only what he wants and rejects all that is not relevant. Although the language he hears is not in any way phased and graded, he receives i.e. internalizes things only in a graded and well-combined way. This in fact, is a great secret of the $L_1$ acquisition process.

The internalized linguistic systems function like a generator. The child's intellect is able to pick and choose between language patterns and items. Internationalization, of broadly speaking sounds, the lexicon, the syntax and the semantic implications (Ch. 2) is a continuous and lasting process. It is the building up of the linguistic competence as the functional basis for all the performance which the individual is going to have in course of years. The individual does not produce stereotyped, learned-by heart-material, but sentences on a creative basis. The speaker or the writer is involved in a series of linguistic choices and as a result comes out with a sentence or sequence of sentences which is not the imitation of any sentence previously constructed. In short, it is possible and it happens that the native child utters sentences which he himself has never uttered before or he has heard others uttering. This is the essence of *linguistic creativity.* The duplicates of several sentences that a child constructs may not be found formed by any one in speaking or in writing.

It is a conditioned stimulus-response situation which controls the structural implications of the child's language, but the language is the result of a creative option from among a multitude of choices and possibilities. The child exercise on intellectual assimilation of a given situation and with conscious awareness of the situation he is able to produce utterances in his language. This is the very essence of the child's linguistic creativity.

There are observable evidence available, also with regards to the creative way a child encounters his environment. An energetic, enthusiastic child comment with several surprises in course of the day manifesting his creative use of language. No stimulus-response theory can explain the child who comes out with absolutely apt replies that shock the parents. No conditioning can explain the situation when a sentence uttered by a child in a context is the exact replica of something with which the mother scolded the child days before. This is reorganization of the verbal-context relationship a factor that doubtlessly points out to the creative use of language. Several such language behavioural features of the child are held precious by parents because the whole thing is a rewarding experience for the parents who anxiously watch the language growth of the child especially at its early phases. Creative behaviour is examined in greater details in the final chapter of the book.

## 6. Language as Communication

One of the foremost preoccupations of psycholinguistics is the communicative nature of language. Self-expression is a feature that is almost the definition of human personality. The essential sociability of man is parallel to the communicative tendency. More than anything also, linguistic considers language as inherently possessing the quality at communication. All linguistic systems are aimed at this end. For psycholinguistics, the functional aim of language is communication. The whole endeavour of this field of enquiry is to explicate this functional aim i.e. communication.

Man speak; but he does so far some purpose. However, indistinct or indefinite the purpose may be. The most explicit and outstanding purpose of language is communication. Communication has a structure (see Chapter 3). Psycholinguistic enquiries into the structure of communication. Communication involves a speaker i.e. the source, and a listener i.e. the target. Between there two distinct Polarizes there occurs an event which we call communication. Communication, consequently, is a full-fledged event involving persons, instruments and obstructions. But the chief connecting link between the two ends, and the essence of the event is the message. We may consider 'message' as the totality of all that the speaker passes on to the listener. If communication is a process involving the speaker and the listener and all that goes on between the two, against the psychological background of them both, then message is the content of the process, apart from the speaker and the listener.

In other words, message is identical with the 'language' which function as the vehicle for something. What is this something? It is referred to as 'information'. Information is the content of message borne by the language employed as the vehicle. All this boils down to the fact that information is the only worth while this from a psycholinguistic point of view that qualities language as communication. Information is the final content of the structure of communication.

Language is a symbolic behavioral system. As such, information is fed into language, if at all it can be said so. The process of conforming a given information with a set of linguistic material or a symbolic system is known as encoding. Encoding involves on the part of the speaker several choices. The process of recognizing or extracting the given information from the symbolic system or code is known as decoding. This is the fundamental structure of communication. Ther reader should be able to identify information later with the *semantic* and *conceptual* contents which we shall be introducing in later chapters.

# 2
# Acquisition of the First Language

## 1. Learning Conditions of $L_1$ and $L_2$

There is a world of difference between the child learning or rather acquiring his native language and the adult acquiring a foreign language. In our understanding of the *acquisition process* of a language these two understanding may be considered types: the learning of $L_1$ i.e. one or more languages learned in the family environment, in absolutely congenial circumstances without the cumbersome activities of the classroom. In India especially it is a usual phenomenon that a child is required to learn more than one language as its first language without any one conspicuously predominating the others. There are several possible variations among what we may call : the *mother-tongue* i.e. the language of the parents (it also happens that the parents belongs to different linguistic communities), the local language, the regional language, and the national language. It happens that a child from the very beginning comes in touch with and is compelled to learn quite a few of these varieties of language. It is not possible for us to differentiate the learning processes of those language as each of these has similar or the same *learning environment*. Therefore in the present work by $L_1$ we mean all the languages mentioned above i.e. the set of languages that a child picks up before the school-going age.

By $L_2$ we do not mean the second language which the child picks, up the second language for an Indian boy may be Hindi as the family comes to stay in a Hindi speaking region when the boy is three or four year old. By $L_2$ in the present work is meant what Robbert Lado calls, the target language or the languages the child learns at School. It may be another regional language of the country or it may be a foreign language. In this category for which we have an entirely different learning environment i.e. the classroom, we conclude a language like Hindi and a foreign language like English. Both these are learned in the classroom at the level of $L_2$. The distinction between $L_1$ and $L_2$ brought out here will be constantly referred to in the following pages. It should cause no misunderstanding the minds of the readers when English language is referred to as $L_2$ in India.

The learning conditions of $L_1$ and $L_2$, against the background discussed above, differ vastly. The learning processes at these two levels are affected and influenced by several factors, and the very *process of acquisition* differs to a great extent. The $L_1$ is picked up at home in the most natural situations, guided and controlled by those who are near and dear to the child. The $L_2$, on the other hand is learned in the most artificial situations, the overcrowded classroom, in an atmosphere of fear, anxiety and tension. The learning of the $L_1$ takes place along with other aspects of biological growth such as walking; as it is said, the child walks and talks. Language learning is an integral part of the biological growth, it is paced and controlled by forces that do not create much of tension in the child as those in the classroom. The $L_2$ learning takes place when the child's attention is scattered and pulled apart by several unrelated forces such as peer group friendships and rivalries.

More than anything else the learning of $L_2$ takes place when the $L_1$ language or languages have already taken roots. The most refined and rudimentary language habits have been fashioned on the 'tabular rasa' of the child's linguistic potencies; both physiological and mental. The $L_2$ is introduced into such an actualized setting when the child's receptive potency has been considerably determined. Over and above these limitations, the classroom has a single teacher for several dozens of pupils while at home the single child is aided by several 'teachers' in the learning of the $L_1$. A very significant aspect in the learning of the $L_1$ which has conspicuous reference to the teaching of the $L_2$ is the natural adherence to the basic *principles* of *learning* as such. The child picks up linguistic elements which are easier and more useful to practical life earlier than what is more difficult and less useful. Similarly the child picks up the words for things and action that are closer in his *experience*. Much before he learns words like *road*, *man* or *virtue*, child comes to know words such as *water*, *milk*, *bed* and *food*. In other words the learning of the $L_1$ is governed by the principles of proximity, usefulness, concreteness, particularity and interest. In today's endeavour to teach foreign languages, in spite of all efforts and good will, this is one aspect where we have miserably failed: seldom to present day textbooks and teaching materials contain things which are most useful, concrete and interesting to the children of a given level.

The characteristic difference between the learning conditions of the $L_1$ and $L_2$ from the essential background for the teaching of $L_2$ in class. *Psycholinguistics* investigates into the integral aspects of the $L_1$ learning process, consequently trying to achieve two things: knowledge of the nature of language learning process as well as insights into the teaching of $L_2$.

## 2. Factors Affecting the Learning of $L_1$

An analysis of the conditions under which $L_1$ is picked up would reveal a variety of factors that affect the native language learning process. (1) the *physical environment* influences the $L_1$ learning process. The material surroundings of a child have a lot to do with what and how he picks up a language. Much more than an adult the child gets truly involved in his material surroundings. The dog, the cat, the house, and the trees around the house have a lot to do with the way the child learns his first language. (2) The *social environment* affects $L_1$ learning greatly. The child growing up among the parents and an orphan child make a world of difference in language learning. The child whose mother goes out daily to work and the one who is always by the mother's side pick up $L_1$ quite differently however hard the former may make up for her absence. The mother, the family and the neighborhood are social elements most essential to the natural language growth of the child. Sociological factors are more determinant that anything else in the $L_1$ learning process. (3) *Physical* and *economic resources* affects $L_1$

learning process. The language development of a child from an economically backward family has all the reasons to be hampered in contrast to a child from a well-to-do family. Economic resources influence the child's contact with things and events and possibly limit the range of the child's overall experience. Economic factors determine to a child's overall experience. Economic factors determine to a great extent the feasibility of the parents to care for the language development of the child. (4) The learning of $L_1$ has the most powerful *motivations* behind it. This is a unique characteristic of the first language or language. There are compelling needs which are both *internal* as well as *external*. (a) There are several internal needs which compel the child to learn his first language as quickly and perfectly as he can. Among these internal needs the most compelling ones are the need for food, warmth and shelter. These are of physiological nature. There are also emotional needs to fulfil such as the needs for constant care, love and affection. These needs cannot at all be met unless the child masters some kind of liaison devices with the world outside. The *first language* is the most essential of such devices. (b) There are several needs and motivations which are external by nature. Social interaction, on the one fulfilment of the social urges of the child, requires mastery over a language for interaction with the members of society. There is the need for *self-expression* and *creative behaviour* which raises the human being for above the level of a sheer biological organism, requires the mastery of some languages for communication. The child not only makes use of the first language for functional purposes, but also more than anything else creativity enjoys himself by talking to the 'catty' and 'doggy'. This is an element that cannot be overlooked.

An outstanding feature of the early language learning experience is *egocentricity*. The child is highly egocentric, this egocentric attitude is reflected above all the child's language learning experience. He picks up only the language items that are absolutely essential to expressing himself. He is the centre of his entire language experience. The first language is the chief means to get things done for himself, to assert himself to the social environment and to expert maximum control over his environment. The child fees that the whole world revolves around him. The pronouns he picks up at the outset are highly reflective of this egocentric nature;

*I, me, my, mine* are said to be the earliest pronouns the child picks up, it takes time before the begins using pronouns such as *we, us our* etc. In short, language learning of the early period as well as the entire language learning experience is parallel to the development of the child's personality: it is movement from 'the dim image of the mother' to an all pervading ' vision of humanity' as such.

## 3. Stage of $L_1$ Acquisition Process

Even though accounts by psycholinguists on the first language acquisition process very greatly and there has been no absolute agreement with regards to the phases of language development in children all over the world, there has been no doubt that the language development of children is fully *phased*. It takes place in terms of various definable stages which children in any part of the world are said to undergo although the chronological correspondence may not be the same. Attempts have been made to describe the learning of language of children in terms of *operant* and *classical conditioning*. Skinner expresses the view that these early operant responses take the form of 'mands', 'tacts' or 'milk', a tact is a naming response in which the child names some aspect of his environment and is variedly *rewarded* especially by the happiness of the mother. An *echoic* response is simply a repetition of his own or an adult's utterance, the reward being self-stimulation. These responses are further corrected, shaped and modified by the mother and other members of the family and the child learns to approximate adult utterances. *Rewarding* of the correct response help consolidate these and progress towards accurate *verbal response*.

As it is often described, the speech mechanism is a crude possibility. The child is at birth endowed with the basic potentiates for language in the form of biological organs of speech as well as the inner faculties of speech co-ordination and production. These biological and mental faculties function as the substratum for language development.

The child living in and interacting with society, is continuously bombarded with the language of the society. But the earliest phases of language development do not seem to be much affected by what goes on around. The *first cry* of the infant functions as the crude starting points which makes possible all activities of the lungs and the speech organs. The earliest significant utterance of the infant are the *babbling sounds* characterized by a two-way system: of the 'ba......ba, ma....ma, pa...pa' sounds produced by the infant are conveyed to the brain centres as auditory impulses which further enable the infant to produce the same sound again. It is described as a *vocal-ear reflex*, a self-stimulating and self-reinforcing phenomenon. Society is too dim to influence articulatory functions at this phase. We may describe this as the stage of random articulation.

The mother, representing society, is the motivating force behind the next phase, usually called by psycholinguistics as *echolalia*. The same or similar articulate elements are produced by the infant as the mother. Here the ego for the first time confronts the mother i.e. society. The mother utters the word 'doll' and the infant takes pleasure in repeating the possible echo *da*. There is a double-*pronged auditory* excitement that caused by the mother as well as by the infant. *Echolalia* is thus described as an *ear-vocal reflex*: beginning with the mother's utterance and ending with the utterance by the infant. This is essentially a stage of very crude imitation, an exact imitation of the utterance by the adult being impossible for the infant. The organ for audition, the ear, plays a greater role at this phase of language development.

In the stage following we find a *conditioning* of the *articulate elements* by objects and situations. This phase is characterized by the child's naming things as they are held out to or found by the child. It is described as the stage of an intense 'naming explosion'. A conditional response is effected by the visual stimulation, the doll, with the verbal stimulus, the word doll. The sight of the doll along with the world doll enables the child to associate both and learn the word doll and remember it in connection with the thing, the doll.

In the following phase of the language process, the sight of the doll alone is enough or the child to evoke the world doll, the parent providing a visual stimulus to which the child is in a position to evoke a truly verbal response, The last stage in this process is linguistically very characteristic. Here a verbal stimulus alone can evoke a *verbal response*. Here the child has reached the realm of actual language. He is in a position to function at the level of symbolic language. The child can answer a questing; the word doll can be used in answer to a question without any visual aid. The child begins to comprehend word symbols, not merely imitate sound units. He begins manipulating language items to his own advantage. Now, he is on the way to becoming what we call 'a linguistic adult': capable of manipulating his language to meet all practical situations within the purview of the experiences of his own linguistic community. All that now remains is the intricate, idiomatic, abstract, artistic and professional language which he begins acquiring in society as a school-going child or otherwise.

## 4. Internalization of Linguistic System

The entire language learning is a process of internalization of systems. This has been clearly and systematically re-emphasized by Noam Chomsky in his works in transformational generative linguistics. This goes diametrically opposed to the stimulus-response theories where an attempt is made to explain all aspects of language process in terms of stimulus-response-reinforcement bonds. Chomsky condemns the connectionism of skinner, which adheres to an explanation to all language phenomenon by means of behaviourist principles.

Section 3 of the present chapter deals with the sequential stages of the development of a child's language, but from a *psychological perspective*. Looking at language development from a purely *linguistic perspective*, it is wholly a process of internalization: the functional aspects of language acquisition require more of a psychological description in terms of the patterns of behaviour; the structural aspects of language acquisition, on the other hand require a linguistic description in terms of the internalization of linguistic systems. *Internalization* of linguistic systems occurs at a variety of levels. The infant at the early period of linguistic development lives in a language atmosphere. He is bombarded, so to say, by the language utterances of the people around, directed at his as well as otherwise. The earliest utterance of the child (see Sec. 3) known as *random articulation* are not in fact the exact feedback of this linguistic atmosphere constantly affecting the auditory organs of the child. This random articulation, by nature a *vocal-ear reflex*, is some kind of internal process stimulated by the pleasurable experiences of the child, the main stimulus being the *reflex* itself. It is a self stimulated activity as random articulation gathers momentum.

But once the infant's auditory organ begins reacting to the

environment, the infant takes in whatever it can. At first the random articulation consists of non-distinctive sounds like those of the infrahuman animals. These cannot be considered linguistic units, rather we call the random articulation sounds pre-linguistic, but forming the very foundation of later linguistic behaviour. The first system which the child takes in or rather *internalizes* is the basic sound system of the language: the phonological system (see Section 5 of the present chapter). The elders speak in natural ways carrying on the affairs of day to day life. It is not a teaching process. The 'teachers' live; the 'pupil' learns: both happen in an automatic, involuntary fashion. At this stage from all the language material the child listens to, the only thing that he internalizes is the set of sounds. He, in otherwords, begins the process of producing the distinctive sounds which are basic to the language he begins to pick up.

While picking up the sounds units the child is getting familiar with the basic *morphological sets* of the language, yet not in a position to produce them. The internalization of the morphological units and full words takes place because much before production there is the comprehension of these items. The child follows the language of the elders even though he cannot actively communicate. With further development comes the period when the child not only follows but produces *words*, not merely imitating the elders, but after having thoroughly internalized the *relation between the word and the feature of experience* which the word represents. Meanwhile, again, the language, full fledged and natural utterances of the elders go on. So far the child has been able to pick up the distinctive sounds and then the sequences of these sounds, the words from the language store of the elders. Before mastering the words, the *distinctive sounds* are combined into some sort of non-sense units which we often hear children speak. After the words internalized are in active use, these are employed in 'non-grammatical utterances: incomplete and mixed up sentences. It takes time before further development takes place, when the child is able to produce grammatical sentences. The internalization of the basic grammar i.e. structural rules of the languages, has been taken place as a result of the child's continuous acquaintance with adult language.

The process of internalisation takes place not only at the

phonological and grammatical levels mentioned above, but also at the level of the *semantic component* of the language. Language development cannot be thought of except in essential relations to the structure of experience. Every community has sets of things, events, values and features of experience that the growing and maturing individual has to somehow undergo and confront. Language from another perspective is a *representative symbolic system* of the totality of the cultural and social experiences of a community. As such a mastery over this symbolic system, or rather an acquaintance with the system means an internalization of the features of experience in terms of sets of abstractions which we may call concepts. As the child progresses in language, in a parallel manner, as language learning is not a process of common thing linguistics items to memory, he more and more internalizes the semantics of the language in the form of meanings and meaning specifications resulting in a continuous acquaintance with the cultural and sociological and aspects of the community. In short the entire process of language learning is one of *internalization of systems*: phonological, morphological (vocabulary), systematic and semantic systems of the language.

## 5. Acquiring the Phonology of $L_1$

The first and the basic linguistic system which the child internalizes, as we have seen in the foregoing pages, is the phonology of the language. Constant acquaintance with adult language enables the child to increase his sound stock. Internalization is not a compartmentalized process in terms of the systems. It is not that the child takes in the entire sound system of the particular language and then goes on to acquire the vocabulary of the language. It is more of an overlapping process with the result that each system goes more or less parallel to others. The child produces more or less 'non-distinctive' sounds during the random articulation-phase. At the same time the child's ears are constantly fed with *adult-language* produced at varying situations at home. As all this language consists of sounds which are definable in terms of this phonetic characteristics, the child's auditory organs get acquainted with these and in course of time, as a result, the random articulation is substituted by the sounds of the language. In itself it is a gradual process and takes years before the major portion of the sounds are mastered exactly. While the acquisition of the sounds is in progress, the child is in a position, already to comprehend words, and even phrases. This is why it is impossible to demarcate the beginning and end of any one process.

The sounds produced by man to give shape to his language have unique features. They are very different from the sounds, produced in the cries of birds and animals. It has not yet been shown if the cry of an animal (e.g. the chattering of monkeys) consists of definable sounds units and a recombination of these is ever possible to these animals. The same is true of the cries of birds. These are all set, stereotyped order of sounds which do not permit any change in its usual sequence. But in case of man it is otherwise, p, b, k, g, t or d are sounds units of English language. It is a fact that requires no description that 'n' number of combinations of these sounds with the other sounds of the language are possible. A reordering of these sounds results in a variety of words in the language. This is how language has become possible at all. This *reorganization* of sounds into varieties of sequential forms is possible only with human language. This is possible because the sounds produced by man in the production of language are physically, definable in terms of the *features* of *articulation*.

At the stage of random articulation the infant produces the sounds da.....da......da..... We have explained it as a vocal-ear reflex. But when the mother holds out a doll and says *doll* the ' da.......da.....:.' sounds assume a special role. From a *non-distinctive level* these sounds are elevated to the level of *distinctive sounds* of the language and as a result the child now produces *do....do.....do..* sounds with a two-pronged correspondence. The /do :/ sounds of the one hand correspond to and are the result of the random articulation da......da.......da.......da......., and on the other, the unit corresponds to the word *doll* produced by the mother. At the present stage it is not possible for the infant to imitate the word doll; but the sounds which stand out in the word are assimilated by and are made part of the child's language.

The same happens with other phonological elements of the language. As the child's experience with adult language increases, the stock of sounds acquired thus is found to increase. In a continuous but involuntary endeavour to pick up one's own language, the native child masters one sound after another in the context of his language behaviour. But the process is so long and tedious that at the beginning very few sounds may be pronounced exactly even though semi-nonsense words are structured during the first stage. Whatever sounds units and sequences of sound are mastered are employed in words of some kind i.e. semi-nonsense words. It happens in such cases that perhaps only the mother knows what the child utters sometime's and asks for. It may be altogether unintelligible to the rest.

## 6. Acquiring the Vocabulary of $L_1$

The earliest forms uttered by the child employing the distinctive sounds which he has picked up, are non-sense words which have partial similarity to those produced by the elders. These are usually heard in the form of 'unc' for uncle, *ℓ* 'en' for hen, 'mik' for milk 'do' for doll and so on. This partial resemblance enables the elders to recognize what the child utters together with the situation in which the form is produced. A characteristic thing of this period is that while producing words of partial resemblance, the child at the same time is in a position to recognize a few hundred words which he cannot actively produce. This again helps the child establish contact with the grown up of the family. It shows that the forms of these words are some-how internalized, acquired, by the child while immaturity of the articulately organs in giving shape to the sequences hinders the child from actively producing these forms.

Individual differences affect mastery over the forms of language as it happens in all aspects of development. Constitutional as well as environmental differences, the potency for cognitive organization, opportunities for learning and practising and a large number of related factors influence the intensity of picking up words from the language the child listens to every day.

The presence of synonyms, antonyms, homophones, idioms and proverbial uses in the language of the adults causes problems for the child. Contrast and comparison from one of the basic processes with which the child picks up the *vocabulary* of the language. These occurs in day-to-day life similar or identical situations from which through contrast and comparison the child deducts both morphological aspects and vocabulary. This, again, is intensified by the use of *analogy* by the child. Traditionally analogy has been given the greatest role in language learning process. The child who is habituated to the forms *walking-walked moving-moved* and *proving-proved* produces with confidence forms like *going-goed*. Here the child is said to employ the principle of analogy. The constant recurrence of a word helps the child picks up the form and at the same time contrasts the same in the production of another word in another situation. *Drink water, drink tea* and *drink milk* make the child produce an utterance like *drink food* where he goes wrong. Here the adult interferes to correct him.

The constant familiarity with forms like: walks, *walking* and *walked, moves, moving* and *moved, names, naming* and *named*, and *looks, looking* and *looked* helps the child distinguish morphones such as: -s, -ing and -ed as some sort of separate units. Thereby the child will attempt the use of the same with word forms where he goes wrong. It is certainly not the mistake of the child, but of the language in which exceptions to a rule are far too many.

In the process of acquiring new words the child is required to fix *semantic limits, distinctions* and *restrictions*. It is a type of *contextual analysis* to isolate words and to recognize there senses. This is a process of demarcating the boundaries of linguistic units at various levels starting from sounds to semantics. The acquisition of the vocabulary of $L_1$ is governed, again, by the principles of simplicity, usefulness, proximity, particularity and concreteness. Words with these characteristics are always acquired earlier than their opposites in various degrees. The child is bound to learn to word like *bed* much earlier than *cushion* or *school*. the vocabulary which the child acquires is related first to his physiological needs, things and experiences of the family circle, experiences of the neighbourhood and then further it extends to world outside until it subsumes in a gradual manner the lexicon of the language he grows up to as adulthood.

## 7. Acquiring the Syntax of $L_1$

The process of internalization reaches its peak in the acquisition of the syntax of the language. Acquiring the basic *syntax* of the language is something stretched along from the beginning of the language learning process until the child is said to reach what is known as 'linguistic adulthood' around the age of six. The internalization of the grammar of the language, in fact, begins when the child comprehends the sentences constructed by the adults. The chief function associated with the *acquisition of syntax* is the ordering of word-elements in a sentence. From the production of non-sense utterances the child progresses to individual but correct words. But the most interesting thing is that the individual, linguistically isolated words uttered by the child are no longer semantically isolated at this stage. So to say, the isolated words are full, frozen and condensed expressions surging out of the child's maturing mind. Looking at a picture when the child utters the word '*apple*' it is a full-fledged sentence in the form of *it is an apple* frozen into the single word apple. The same happens with utterances such as *water, go, me* or *mama*, the mother who is utmost conscious of the child's needs finds no difficulty in recognizing these utterances chiefly because the child places these utterances in various *contextual setting* which enables the mother to understand the contextual setting which enables the mother to understand the utterances as: *I need water, you go away from me, give me the doll* and *please, hold me in your arms, mama*. All these are condensed into semantically compressed one-word utterances as given above.

This certainly shows that the child at this stage is able at least to recognize utterances of the above kind produced by the adults. More and more he acquires the basic patterns of the sentences of the native language with the result that in course of time communication through *phrases* and further through *short sentences* become possible on the basis of the patterns that are already internalized. In the context of *transformational generative grammar*, the factor mentioned above is the *linguistic competence* of the child the building blocks of which have been discussed in the foregoing pages. The essence of competence is the internalized linguistic systems, not only syntax in the restricted sense, but the manifold *systems of the language* beginning with the sounds to the meanings.

Linguistic competence is the 'generator' of the sentence of the native language. The acquisition of the sound system, and the vocabulary enables the child to organize the entire linguistic material he listens to in terms of the *basic patterns* of his language. As a result the child builds up a 'generator' i.e. the complex syntactic system as the resources of all the language that he is going to produce in future. A basic pattern of English such as: *I walk*, as part of the linguistic competence of the child, enables the child later to produce at the surface level sentences such as:

I walk
He walks
They walk
I am walking
You are walking
He has walked
You have walked etc.

With the internalization of each pattern, the child becomes capable of structuring 'n' number of sentences within the same pattern as the need arises. Thus the '*syntactic spectrum*' in the child's brain function like a generator enabling the speaker to produce sentences i.e. correct sentences as per the patterns that make up the tautum of the 'syntactic spectrum' any discrepancy in the formation of these patterns results in the production of wrong sentences. With the $L_1$ learner this does not happen as no such structure is formally taught, all that he picks up are by means of a *process of abstraction* from the structures produced by the adult speakers of the language. The result of such an abstraction are the *phrase-structure rules* considered basic to the transformational generative process.

## 8. The Process of Socialization and Acquisition of Semantic Maturity

The development of language and the process of socialization go so much hand that both lead towards what may be called *Semantic maturity*. The beginning of language development takes places in a highly egocentric context. As we have seen the child is the centre of a world of experiences, and these experiences are *centrifugal* in terms of the child. The earliest material which the child masters are of the egocentric nature, he picks up words only for those things that satisfy his earliest biological needs and later of things that belong to his socio-physical surroundings such as the things around and the people at home. All these elements are expected to satisfy the child's requirements in varied manner. It takes three or four years before the child begins picking up words for actual socializing *paralinguistic experiences*. The earliest pronouns are centered on as well as directed to the self; the use of *we*, *us, our, they* etc. come only much later.

Real growth of language can seldom be separated from *socialization*. Socialization may be viewed as a process in which the child at first becomes aware of the presence of 'the others', and accept 'the others' as part of his experiences. It is a movement from the self to the world at large enveloping and involving others in society in the world of the self instead of more and more becoming isolated from society. It is a widening of the individual's horizon from the narrow circle of the ego to an all embracing vision of humanity.

Language is not an isolated system in the abstract. No natural language is isolated from a given society. Every language is, in other words, representative of the *socio-cultural experiences* of a community. Consequently, if language is such, the development i.e. acquisition of language becomes an embodiment of the socio-cultural components of the particular community. Although one may visualize an abstract, isolated learning of a language by a foreign student, yet even in this context what the individual is not acquainted with are only those aspects of the people's life which are strange to and different from the native way of life. This can never be the case with the $L_1$ learner who is wholly impressed in the experiences of the native community and there is no escape from it in normal circumstances.

Learning the language, against the background given above, means an *accumulation* of greater semantic facts parallel to the accumulation of the vocabulary and expressions of the language. The proverbs, idioms, and varied expressions peculiar to the native language are the *Semantic carriers* specific to the language apart from the meaning specifications that represent the ordinary experiences of the community such as related to family life, religions life, experiences of school, those of the peer groups and further of later friendship circles as well as those of professional life.

As the individual's experiences widen and acquaintance with the reality of life increases, language too matures in a parallel manner. The end-result is what we called earlier, a *Semantic maturity* which essentially links language with the socio-cultural experiences. It can well be considered part of the individual's personality development, as semantic maturity means the broadening of the world-vision of the individual. At this level it is easy for us to find how essentially the language of a community and the individual's personality development are linked. The other words, *socialization*, as an essential aspect of the development of personality is directly linked with the development of the native language.

# 3

# Language and Communication

## 1. The Act of Communication

William Wundt on the one hand, and George Miller, on the other are said have initiated research into the communication structure of language in the modern period. Buhler, a German psychologist, was another who investigated into the structure of communication. Buhler applied the models of communication engineering to psycholinguistics and incorporated serval ideas from Gestalt psychology regarding language performance and developed what is known as 'Cybernetics', the science of combination.

Communication is an event. It is an act involving persons, instruments symbols and abstractions. Communication is an event which takes place between two agents: the speaker and the listener. These two are not at all isolated organisms, but persons with psychosocial background and purposefulness. An act of communication takes place between the *speaker* and the *listener*, in which are involved the acceptance or rejection of sets of concepts and their linguistic symbols both on the part of the listener and the speaker. [This phenomenon will be examined in a following section]. Communication has a *direction*, a *channel* and *modality*. An *act of communication* proper is directed from the speaker to the listener; the feed-back or response to the speaker is another, a distinct act of Communication in which the listener assumes the role of the speakers and there takes place a constant shift in speaker-listener roles. It is such a shift in the speaker-listener roles that makes communication a continuous chain of acts, a continuous event. The direction of Communication is, therefore, a shifting factor.

Communication, whether between two persons speaking face to face or between two people on the phone, or on the wireless, or even in a written form, takes place only in a channel. Any form of communication requires a channel, however short or distant it may be. The channel may be air, wire or the space or any medium that conducts sound. Communication in the sense we understand here, is a physical activity and requires a channel of same sort. The sound-waves travel through the channel in the direction of the listener. An act of communication, also takes place is a specific modality : as *audio modality* or *visual modality*. It is possible for the blind and the dead to communicate through what we may call *tactile modality*, through the sense of touch. But in normal circumstances the two modalities mentioned above function as the medium. In short, an acts of communication cannot adequately be described without emphasizing the direction, the channel and the modality in which communication takes places.

Communication is structural in terms of several components. It may be viewed as a structure of layers. The act of communication involves the speaker and the listener, as well as the link between the two: the *message*. We may identity the message as a system of codes in which some *information* is inlaid. Linguistically speaking, the message is the symbolic system, the language. Language, for that matter is the system of codes that links the speaker and the listener. The content of communication, thus, is the message; the content of message is the information encoded in the message. Information, in otherwords is the quintessence of communication. An act of communication can thus be measured and evaluated in terms of the amount of information encoded in the message. Linguistically, again, a speech-act which do not have some content of some information or intention cannot be considered language, for practical purposes, as such a language which does not carry out some form of communication, does not possess the symbolic implications language as such must have. Information is empirically measurable and thereby it is possible to calculate the *redundancy level* of a message. This will be examined later in detail. Redundant language as such does not bear any new information which is used chiefly along with the information for explicative or decorative purposes. This is essentially the structure of an act of communication.

## 2. The Speaker-Listener Polarity

The event of communication very much depends on two polarities i.e. the speaker and the listener. The direction, channel and the modality of communication require that the two polarities should maintain relative distance. Communication is in fact a confrontation between two individuals with a view to exchanging some *information* or getting some *intention* fulfilled. Exchanging some information or the fulfillment of some intention through communication calls for the presence of the polarities of the speaker and the listener. The speaker is equipped with the competence of a set of languages and the same is expected of the listener. This is a complex phenomenon. Communication becomes a possibility only when there is correspondence in the language-content of the two polarities. A code-system can never by interpreted unless the symbolic value of the code is known. In communication the code may be a language proper or it may be that language is further codified into another feasible system such as the *Morse* code. Possible recognition of the codes used is a perquisite in any communication.

The speaker is confronted with the need to convey some information, acquire the same, or get some intention fulfilled. There are a variety of such situations available as the context of communication. The speaker is determined linguistically, psychologically and sociologically. It is against this background that he will choose the system of code or language that he wishes to employ. It may be that the speaker is conversant with several languages, but he is expected to judge the common base between the speaker and the listener. Of all the language the speaker knows, he will select for purposes of encoding only that language which will be understood by his listener. Choosing a code which doesn't establish a liaison between the two will not serve the purpose.

The polarity between the two: the speaker and the listener makes communication all the more complex. The speaker's choice of the language, his style, his tone, the particular words employed, the explanatory or decorative words used, the jokes that are brought in at times: all these have grant implications on the success of communication. The speaker must be able to judge what the listener wants, his likes and dislikes, the preferences and prejudices, and of possible the atmosphere in which the person listener to the speaker. The seriousness of judging the listener's background as mentioned above will depend on the seriousness of the informational or intentional content of communication.

As information is the quintessence of communication, in serious circumstances, the speaker has to be cautions to avoid all sorts of redundant elements in his communication. Again, redundancy will have bearing on the level of seriousness of the communication-content. The greater the importance of the given communication, the greater the need to avoid redundancy. Redundancy consists in the employing words and expressions which have mere explicative or decorative purposes. The presence or absence of such elements will not so much affect the communication-content. The basic principle in structuring the content of communication is to encode the maximum possible information in the minimum possible language elements or codes, thereby achieving economy in communication.

The closer at hand the speaker and the listener one, the easier to make things clear in communication. There is better possibility for immediate clarification. The further the speaker-listeners are and the shorter the time available, the greater the need to take care of the structuring of communication. The number of choices involved on the part of the speaker and the keenness involved on the part of the listener render communication a serious phenomenon. Failure in communication or defects in its structuring leads to all kinds of socio-economical and political consequences.

## 3. The Processes of Encoding and Decoding

An act of communication itself is structured system, as we have examined, consisting of certain well-defined levels. It is an activity involving certain sets of behaviour on the part of the speaker and the listener. Encoding and decoding, thus, are aspects of communication which make the *transmission* of information possible. The transmission of information through the channel, from the speaker to the listener requires the relating of the message-content with adequate symbols which function as the vehicle of information, and the de-linking of both for the purpose of comprehension. Encoding, in otherwords, is the process of linking an adequate set of codes with a set of concepts with which the information is structured. On, it is the linking of a set of codes with some unit of natural language which itself symbolizes a set of concepts.

Decoding, on the other hand, is the process, by the listener or the reader, of de-linking the set of concepts from the set of codes. Or, it is the *de-linking* of the language units from the set of codes through which the language is codified. An either case i.e. in encoding as well as in decoding it is basically a matter of interaction between two components of communication : the *code* and the *content*. When any natural language functions as the code, the content is a set of concepts, when the code consists in symbols other than any natural language, the content is language proper which, in turn, functions as vehicles for concepts. Encoding and decoding are the beginning and the end of communication. Encoding is the function proper to the speaker and decoding, in turn, is the function proper to the listener. But there is the constant shift in roles: the speaker becoming the listener and the listener becoming the speaker.

Swapping of roles as speaker and listener is a characteristic feature of communication. A communication-chain is a complex net-work of several acts of communication, in which an act of communication may be considered a single unit. While swapping the roles as speaker and listener, there takes place in both polarities a complex shift between encoding and decoding. The whole process in the brain will took like a film with alternate pictures represented. Here lies the fundamental complexity in the use of language for communication. In a continuous communication-chain the speaker and the listener are faced with 'n' number of concepts, conceptual organization, words and expressions, idiomatic uses etc. will determine the success or failure, or the nature of communication.

In this context a greatly determining factor is the mutual intelligibility. In constructed code systems this intelligibility poses not much of a problem because such codes possess almost mathematical precision. Mostly in such cases there is a one to one correspondence between the code-unit and the signified in terms of language or concepts. The process of decoding in such cases is not difficult providing the decoding agents is fully trained in the system. On the other hand, in natural languages, employed directly for purposes of communication, as is usually the case, there are unsurmountable problems with regards to intelligibility. These, chiefly are due to the natural ambiguities inherent in language. Such problems considerably affect intelligibility in communication.

Problems of intelligibility too make encoding and decoding the centre factors in communication. There should be as much common ground between the speaker and the listener in language elements as well as in semantic implications for the success of communication. While encoding, this is the chief consideration i.e. to meet the listener as much as possible at his own level, and to minimize redundancy. All this will enable the listener to decode and attain optimum intelligibility.

## 4. Teaching Communication Skills

If in the context of linguistics we consider language as structured for purposes of communication, it follows that this cannot be neglected in the teaching of a foreign language. Of the two polarities we have seen earlier, the speaker is the active initiator of the act of communication; the listener is the so called 'passive' agent who recognizes or comprehends. On the basis of this distinction we speak of communication skills and skills. Speaking and writing are skills of communication, and listening and reading are skills of comprehension.

An act of communication shows that the two polarities are absolutely essential and that expression takes place in one and reception in the other. We also saw that a communication-chain is a continuous swapping of the speaker-listener roles between the two agents. Since such is the nature of language as communication, we ought to teach any foreign language in terms of the communication characteristics. Just as we have seen that the child at home uses language as part of his behavioral pattern, language is used for purposes of communication. Verbal behaviour and communication are aspects of the same phenomenon, language. For this reason, we identify language with verbal behaviour as well as with communication even though these are domains of behaviour which are not language, and there are domains of communication too which do not consist of language.

The child at home is able to pick up the $L_1$ so thoroughly and well because for his the $L_1$ is both an essential aspect of his day-to-day behaviour and it is the only means for him to communicate himself to the world-around and to satisfy his manifold needs. The teacher in the $L_2$ classroom cannot, in any manners, afford to neglect the behavioural and the communicational aspects of language. The fundamental fault with most of our foreign language teaching methods is the failure to develop techniques which will enable the $L_2$ learner to pick up those aspects of language which will help him employ what he learns in living situations and make the $L_2$ a part of his life. The present day move towards ESP, English for specific purposes attempts to meet this requirement to some extent. Whatever may be the arguments in terms of the absence of proper $L_2$ atmosphere and the need for the active use of $L_2$, it requires that $L_2$ should be taught chiefly as communication.

## 5. The Teleological Nature of Language

That language is a purposeful activity has been recognized from very early days of language study. The varied purposefulness of language as human behaviour may be described in terms of its teleological nature. The very structure of language shows that it has a definite-set of orientations. Language is essentially structured of two components : the *content* and the *expression*. The content forms the inner component; expression forms the outer layer. By content is usually meant the sets of universals which are the obstructions of persons, things, events and features of varied human experiences. The content layer of language is what forms material for semantic studies in linguistics. In otherwords the content of language corresponds to the semantics of language.

It is not possible for us to view language expect in relation to man, his nature and his varied experiences. Language does not exist outside of man, even though we are able to view it in an objective manner, independent of this man or that. The language of a community will survive in the last surviving individual even when the rest of the community perishes. Man's basic relation to language is expressed in semantics. Semantics consists in the totality of a society's varied experiences. The sum-total of the experiences is, so to say, frozen into the semantic system of the language. The past, present and even the future potentialities of a society get imprinted in the total semantic system.

When communication takes place, all that happens is an on-the-spot employment of the elements of the semantic system. A thorough acquaintance with the culture of a society means a thorough mastery over the language of the society. It is on the basis of the semantic system of the language that of any time two persons meet to communicate between them. The content of communication, the information exchanged, forms an integral piece of the semantics of the language. In other words, any form of communication is some form of communion, or confrontation between persons bearing the semantic systems of the language. It can also be said in another way that language can not be used in any form without having a bearing on its communication-structure. Whatever be the manner in which language is used, it is some form of communication, so long as it is intended to be an expression of a self directed towards another. Here in lies the teleological nature of language.

Language as a semantic system internalized by a man cannot be employed without a proximate or remote purpose. This fact is co-existent with human nature. Right from infancy to death bed man depends on the potentialities of language to communicate himself to the world around. It is the down-to-earth purposefulness of language that makes it something proper to man as man. Mankind survives overcoming all hazards that seem to threaten its survival, because, mankind can fully well trust on language through which the present day's technologically complex interaction is achieved. Language is meant not ' to hide human thoughts' but to give vent to and communicate his inner world of thoughts and there by achieve social interaction.

## 6. The Child and Communication

The communicational nature of language is most apparent in connection with the language development of the child. The language of adults assumes more and more varying degrees of aesthetic, philosophical, metaphysical, poetic and mystical dimensions all of which are not explicitly communicational by nature. But the language of the child by virtue of the child's physiological, physical and physiological predicaments develop essentially as a form of communication. The chid has no other satisfactory device to achieve to his fulfillment of his needs; the only device to achieve self-expression is language; and language is the role means to have any kind of interaction with and to control society.

The child, endeavouring to cope with the growing demands on him, finds, himself solely in an atmosphere of communication. What he listens to, the language-store on the basis of which internalization of systems takes place in him, are all not textbook or literary language but the down-to-earth language used in communication at home and outside. The communicational language of the family equips the child further to meet similar situations elsewhere. The child becomes conversant with the language of communication in day-to-day life; and this language further serves as the basis for future asthmatic, professional or technical language.

Much more than in the adult who has mastered more than one language, and possess patterns of behaviour befitting to an adult, the child who is monolingual reveals the extent to which a language functions as a communicational device. Articulatory limitations and the level of maturity pose both encoding and decoding problems for the child and decoding of the child's language for the adult. But again, verbal behaviour as communication takes place in a paralinguistic setting, and the adult is thereby helped in comprehending the child's language.

# 4
# Linguistic Competence and Performance

## 1. Essence of Linguistic Competence

A full understanding of the process of first language acquisition and the acquisition of a second language cannot be attained except in the context of the human individual's unique capacity to learn and function as a *listener-speaker*. There has always been paradoxical discussions and opinions about the predominance of man's cognitive structure in the development of *thought* on the one hand, and the development and functioning of *language* on the other. The roles of each, thought and language, and the predominance of one over the other has remained a controversial issue. Lets us take up the case of a one year old child who manifests undoubtful instances of intention with the world outside of its own cognitive realm. There are different aspects of this *interaction*. As we saw in earlier chapters the infant distinguishable phases of development before it reaches the stage of full-fledged *verbal utterance* in the conventional sense of the term. But much before the first complete grammatical sentence is produced, there is a long period of development when the utterances of the infant show a continuous growth in terms of the structural complexity starting with the non-distinctive sound elements and passing through distinctive sounds, non-sense word, lexical elements, an non-grammatical utterances until the child is in a position to produce a fully grammatical sentence. The whole thing is an 'interactional development' alongwith what we may rightly call the child's social intelligence. From the time the infant recognizes things and persons of world outside, it is trying to get forever closer to this reality which the infant recognizes to be somehow different from its own being.

The infant's interaction with the world outside of its cognitive realm, however rudimentary this interaction may be, takes place also by means of *non-verbal* aspects apart from the verbal interaction we have talked about. The child being a very dynamic individual compared to its mobile or immobile world around, finds much to do in terms of its contact with the world around. The young child manipulates everything that he can find around, turns his attention on anything that finds place in his world around, in one way or other responds to the variety of stimuli that he receives from around, and develops a constant attraction for things and persons that often come in touch with him. The most interesting aspect of this interactional development is that the child develops a parallelism between the verbal and the non-verbal aspects of the interaction. The child basically acquires language as a result of this parallelism which brings together for the child the two worlds of *language* and *features of experience*.

What has all this to do with the child's linguistic competence? Competence as the *built-in linguistic ability* is a progressively developing factor. Competence is not acquired by the native child in a day or two. By competence is meant, as we have seen, the native speaker's *ability* to produce original sentences in his language, the kind of sentences that he has neither heard nor has he himself spoken or written before it is the built in capacity to produce an infinite number of sentences employing the lexicon of his language which he has mastered or is in the process of mastering. The ensure of competence therefore lies in the individual's capacity to produce of his own an infinite number of sentences either in speech or in writing. It is the endeavour of the linguist or the psychologist who is interested in the child's acquisition of language to discover what the rudiments of such a competence are and how it enables the individual speaker to produce sentences which are grammatically and symantically in line with the sentence production rules of the language.

An enquiry into the rudiments of linguistic competence would lead us to factors that form the content of the infants early experiences. Their experiences include two major categories : (i) *linguistic experiences*, and (ii) *paralinguistic experiences* ( which we may also label as *verbal experiences* and *non-verbal experiences*). As the infant comes to recognize elements of the world outside, we may say that he enters into the *formative stage* of linguistic competence. With the sort of 'tabular rasa' of a mind he has, anything and everything affects the susceptibility of his cognitive faculty. Consequently, even before the child is in a position to utter the units of his language, his contracts with the world outside assume specified roles in the formation of his linguistic competence. All this put together we may label as the child's *pre-verbal* experiences in relation to language acquisition. The child is a product of human society, and with his own spatio-temporal limitations he becomes part of a particular community. The earliest experiences which are pre-verbal are undoubtedly the very base of the later verbal behaviour of the child. A longitudinal non-experimental study undertaken by the author (unpublished) on ten children of the age range between eight and fifteen months has shown the following characteristic feature in regard to their *pre-verbal behaviour* that has had remarkable contribution to the formation of this linguistic competence: The observation lasted for a period of three months. The babies were assigned to two people including me in groups of five. The pre-verbal; paralinguistic' patterns of behaviour were recorded in definite periods during the three months. The observers, in fact, recorded over fifty significant instances which they thought are remarkable pre-verbal behaviour that formal the earliest elements of the babies' linguistic competence. The following are some of the instances which marked the 'pre-verbal formative stage' of linguistic competence in children:

(1) Most children were observed to be responding to the parents' demands in some non-verbal way or other to the satisfaction and surprise of the parents.

(2) Most children responded to the parents' requests despite the presence of the strangers and the behaviour such as taking his doll and putting it in the hands of the parents often accompanied some sort of indistinct utterance.

(3) Most children reacted to the presence of the street vendors who would announce their arrival which was a familiar thing for the children.

(4) Most children looked at the parents with lots of expression on their face and readiness for verbal utterance when the door-bell rang.

(5) Most children picked up certain familiar and note nouns from the parts' conversation and at certain occasions even brought things like a doll to the parents' side hoping as if they would need it.

(6) Most children were in a position to substitute an alternate unit (not to brand it as a nonsense word) for a word employed by the parents in several cases. The units substituted mostly had the same or similar initial couple of sounds.

The following are some of the major conclusions which the observers drew out of the behaviour and verbal samples of the ten children:

(1) Much before the first intelligible word or utterance is produced, the child manifests patterns of behaviour which can only be the results of an *intrinsic cognitive modification* which we may call *linguistic competence.*

(2) The child at a very early age receives stimuli from the social and physical environment, and in reading to these stimuli he reveals the working of the rudimentary *cognitive structure* of which the child's linguistic competence at this stage is a formative part.

(3) The behaviour patterns of which about fifty were recorded by the investigators point to a clear pre-verbal cognitive base which will function later as the substratum of the individual's linguistic competence.

(4) At this pre-verbal phase of the child's language development his non-verbal behaviour takes predominance over his linguistic behaviour with the non-verbal behaviour of the child possessing its own symbolic significance. The child lifting the doll and pointing towards the parent at the instance the parent utters the word 'doll' is observed as symbolic behaviour which substitutes the sentences: *Take, here is the doll* or *Mummy, do you want the doll ?*

(5) Must of what a child does symbolically with linguistic value

(say, in a paralinguistic manner) escapes the notice of the parents unless the parents ( like the investigators did) carefully take not of the child's behaviour. Again, certain behaviour is conspicuously significant while others and less so. It is possible, therefore, to consider the pre-verbal linguistic behaviour in terms of a *hierarchy* which begins with the earliest recognition of the world outside and ends with the first utterance of a meaningful, grammatical sentence of the child's native language.

The pre-verbal roots of the child's linguistic competence goes much deeper than one world ordinarily expect. Linguistic competence is the speaker's ability to comprehend and produce a language in accordance to the norms of the language he is acquiring or using. Just as linguistic competence is the foundation for the production of language, it is equally so, for the comprehension of language. The child as observed gives expression to his level of competence in a more elementary and rudimentary manner as we search further back to the earlier months of the child's life. It is at this earliest period when the child is hardly five to ten months that observation has been made of very conspicuous patterns of behaviour which were undoubtedly the result of the child's elementary comprehension of adult language rather than a haphazard set of stimulus-response situations. The essence of linguistic competence this lead us back to the earliest manifestative non-verbal behaviour of the child in response to the language stimuli presented to him, and then followed by the kind of utterances that-mark the beginning of the actual use of language, both complete and incomplete utterances. An investigation into the native of competence as developed by children will not possess the necessary comprehensiveness in less the pre-verbal roots of competence are looked into. The human child is a continually developing and maturing organism, and as such his language behaviour can only be studied from that highly dynamic perspective.

## 2. Essence of Performance

By linguistic performance is usually meant (following Noam Chomsky's description of performance) the actual use of language in all its manifestations i.e. *listening, reading, speaking* and *writing.* Many may have reservations in including listening and reading as part of linguistic performance, but as we shall see things more in detail this will be made clear. If linguistic competence is the *possession* of a specific language ability ( not of the fundamental faculties and potentials for language and part of the specific gifts of man as man), then linguistic performance is the actual *operation* of this ability in terms of the four *basic skills* of language. It is in anyone of the manifestations of human language in terms of a specific operation that we discover the *performance* of language.

A fundamental question, the, if linguistic performance and the language skills can be identified i.e. are they identical ? To a mode of consideration that is extrinsic to language exercise, both seem identical because both somehow or other imply operation, function or performance. In fact unlike what we have seen as implied by performance, skills have again multiple dimensions. It is not possible to identify language skills with language performance, just as one cannot identify the skills with linguistic competence. Both competence and performance penetrate language skills as we have understood them. Just as competence and performance involve the possession and operation of the language ability, the language skills involve two things: (i) the possession of the specific skills (listening, speaking, reading and writing) and (ii) the actual operation of these skills in a given time terminating in some concrete language exercise: comprehension or communication of some language material.

This would lead us back to a fundamental consideration in regard to the nation of human language: The twin-dimensions that characterize any language. We may for the time being label these as (i) the *aspects* of language, and (ii) the *skills* of language. Language is both in the human cognitive system as well as on the pages of a book. No one will dare say that the symbolic, orthographic representation on the pages of a printed or written book is not language. At the some time no one can deny that a sleeping man possesses language at the time he is asleep. The language as we have in our mind and on the pages of a book is certainly not what we have understood as the language skills. Instead, that language forms material for or the content of what we call the language skills.

What we have called the *aspects* of language include whatever is abstract, what we could call a system, a structured system, an organized or a set of *linguistic patterns*. It is like looking at a beautiful mosaic floor with sets of describable patterns running through and through. These *aspects* of human language are the systems of phonology (orthography), morphology ( both in speech and writing) syntax and semantics ( as relevant to spoken and written language), not to mention aspects such as morphonology which includes morphology and morpho-phonemics. A details listing of the aspects of language would include two sections, the first beginning with the *sound units* of language and ending with *spoken discourses*; and the second beginning with the *letters* of the alphabet of the language and ending with what we shall call *written discourses*. In the final analysis we obtain a listing of the components that ultimately go into the making of that structured, abstract system what we call language.

It is interesting to note that the system of aspects described above is somehow independent of the individual speaker. Even when an entire speaking population i.e. a linguistic community perishes, a language as a system of aspects will survive intact in that single individual just as the written form of that language will survive in a single book even if we may imagine all the rest of the written material in that language as perished. These aspects of the language seem to have some level of *objectivity* superseding the individuality of the speaker. It is this 'objective quality' of the human language that enable us to look at every language as some independent and *unified system* which the members of the linguistic community partake, although we know perfectly well that the particular language cannot survive except in the individual members of the speech community. Again it is this 'objective quality' of language that requires the individuals to learn or pick up the language as a system that needs years of practice before one can say that one has mastered a language.

Secondly there are the *skills* of language by contrast to the aspects which we have examined. While the aspects of the language as seen above make a *formal system*, the skills by their very nature form a *functional system* i.e. an order of operations and activities. The skills are behavioral, and the speaker of a language has no other choice but master them by way of intense practice. While the linguistic aspects as a formal system is the material of the mind, the skills are the off-shorts of the linguistic competence as its operational manifestation. Whatever is practical, behavioral operational, habit-oriented and functional that we can accord to language goes with the language skills, because it is through skills only that one way or other competence reveals itself.

What has it all to do with competence and performance. What demarcating are we able to draw among all these ? Skills, we are sure, have two dimensions: (i) the possession of the language ability i.e. ability to speak, and read and write; and (ii) the actual operation of these abilities. It is one thing to say that 'A' has mastery over spoken English, and it is quite another to say that A speaks English well at a given time. The former is the *ability* that we call skill, and the latter is the *operation* that we call skill. The actual use of language including the learning of it enables a speaker to acquire the former which in turn reveals itself in the latter. Consequently, we are in a position now to draw a parallel between *competence* and *performance* on the one hand, and the *language skills* on the other. The four basic skills of language (listening, speaking reading and writing) persons that linguistic property which corresponds to competence on the one hand, and performance on the other. That property of language skills which we call 'ability' (present in a speaker even when he sleeps) corresponds to linguistic competence, and that property of skills which we have called 'operation' ( actual use of the language) correspondence, in turn, to performance. Therefore the term language skills infact is a comprehensive term which takes care of both competence and performance.

It is the development and possession of the language skills rather than a knowledge of the aspects of language which results in the acquisition of linguistic competence. Intellectual or cognitive possession of the aspects of language should be the result of the individual's mastery of the language skills. In otherwords it is possible for an individual to have an intellectual possession of the knowledge of the aspects of a given language without the ability to speak, read or write the language. In this case the knowledge of the particular language has not gone any further than the knowledge of some equivalent information as a set of the concepts. Therefore the essence of performance consists in the actual use of the language in any of the four basic skills. The competence part of the language skills gets actualized in a set of operations in the performance part of the skills.

All the same we do discover an essential relation between the language *skills* and the *aspects* of language. The typical instance for us to examine would be a bilingual who can use more than one language at a given time. Let's examine his performance. Bilingual A *speaks* English, Hindi and French; he *reads* English, Hindi and French; and he *writes* all the three languages. Theoretically we are able to isolate bilingual A's ability to speak, read and write from his knowledge of English, Hindi and French. Apart from the three language proper, bilingual A's ability to speak, read and write is a void, namely, a capacity that has no *content* of realization. This would certainly lead us to the conclusion that the aspects of language which forms its content matter become the content matter of the four skills without which the skills cannot operate. The performance part of the language skills is therefore a *functional system* which operates on the material consisting of the aspects of language.

The competence of a language, therefore, consists of two things: (i) the possession of the aspects of the language which includes all the rules relating to the patterning at the levels of phonology, morphology, syntax and semantics; and (ii) the possession of the language skills as an operational system which employes all the former aspects and rules of patterning for the production of language. Linguistic performance, on the other hand, consists of the four basic language skills concretely oriented towards and involved in the actual *comprehension* or *production* of the sentences of the language according to the rules of patterning which the individual possesses as part of his competence. Competence is, so to say, the inner dynamic principle which sets forth performance to operation for the production of language. Yet both are so much part of each other that at the moment of sentence production i.e. the generation and transformation of sentence production i.e. the generation and transformation of sentences both competence and performance function as an integral system which we ultimately call language. Competence and performance are levels of the individual speaker's language exercise. One cannot be defined or described without somehow entailing the other; one is by its very essence related to the other as the co-principle of language production. Both are founded in the very human cognitive structure and require the kind of development that goes without human nature as such.

Man does not acquire any language in tauto; language acquisition, as we have seen earlier, is a process of development which involves the development of the co-linguistic principles of competence and performance.

## 3. Linguistic Competence: A Process of Development

Competence as a linguistic phenomenon is not acquired by the child in tauto at a given period of time. It doesn't at once take place within a day, week, month or year. Linguistic competence of the kind we have examined in the earlier sections is a matter of progressive *development*. In otherwords it will be synonymous to say that the child acquires the native language little by little or progressively, and that the child's competence of his native language gets built up progressively, namely, as the result of a process of development. In fact questions related to the development of competence in an individual person can be answered only by way of an adequate description of the entire range of the child's language acquisition.

Competence is a formative principle that begins taking shape at the earliest phase of the child's pre-verbal behaviour (see sec. 1). There are quite a number of observations made by the another in a longitudinal non-experimental investigation conducted with ten children between the age of five and fifteen months, with a view to studying their pre-verbal behaviour patterns. The following observations were recorded:

(1) It was found that the children made very rudimentary attempts to communicate with the adults even at the age of as early as five months. These attempts were so primitive and rudimentary that only very close observation could spot their communicative nature. Involuntary physiological responses to varying stimuli could be spotted even earlier than that; but the pattern of behaviour observed in this connection are expected to be voluntary.

(2) The children under observation not only made attempts to get their intention fulfilled by means of non-verbal behaviour, but also attempts were made to call the attention of the parents and others by means of articulations which belonged only to the random articulation category, from a psychological per-

spective, and to the stage of distinctive sound production from a linguistic viewpoint.

(3) From five months to fifteen months the behaviour patterns were observed to be varying so much that a definite progress in terms of (i) communicational ability, (ii) motor ability, (iii) explicitness of behaviour, (iv) clarity in articulation, (v) force of articulation and (iv) greater response to adult demands (result of greater comprehension) was observed.

(4) Between this age range observation was also made of definite progress in terms of (i) increase in the number of nonsense units with definite semantic content (as detected by the investigators), (ii) increase in the number of specific gesticulation which accompanied any type of utterance, (iii) increase of the consonant sounds including clusters and their clarity, (iv) increase of vowel sounds and their clarity and distinctiveness in articulation, and (v) a definite increase in the number of phrases, especially the noun phrases the children attempts to produce.

(5) The observers found the children progressively responding to the requests of the adults with a certain market increase both in the intensity of the intonation and in the intensity of the facial expressions that accompanied the utterance while the response were made.

A number of similar observations enabled tne experimenters to draw the following set of conclusions on the nature of the pre-verbal development that marked the earliest phase of the formation of linguistic competence:

(1) Linguistic competence is a progressively emerging factor in the sense that it is difficult or almost impossible to mark the beginning when the competence of an individual person begins its development onset.

(2) Linguistic competence goes deeper than and far beyond the earliest complete utterance in the structure of the language. Competence has its deep pre-verbal roots in comprehension.

(3) The pre-verbal behaviour of children reveal the presence of a developing competence in the form of a maturing cognitive structure which becomes the basis of the all later linguistic

behaviour. To differentiate this cognitive structure as related to the child's experiences with the world outside and the child's competence as the basis of his language experiences is extremely difficult because of the intricate relationship that exists between language and the child's other cognitive experience.

(4) Language acquisition essentially means the development of linguistic competence. The child progressively acquiring his language is developing the basic theory of his language ( in transformational terms), which will be the bulwark of all his language experiences, as well as the generator that helps him produce the infinite number of sentences using the lexicon of his language.

(5) Comprehension (recognition) and non-verbal responses are the earliest manifestation of the developing competence. Just as competence in the speaker effects the production language proper, competence in the rudimentary stage effects comprehension and non-verbal responses from the child.

*Competence* is a structural principle just as *performance* would be called a functional principle. As a structural principle, competence means the well-designed accumulation or orderly acquisition of two things: (i) the *lexicon* of the language, and (ii) the *rules* which decide the correct and acceptable ordering of the lexical items for the formation of the sentence of the language. Over and above these, competence is required to take care of what is generally known as the *constraints* in the formation of sentences. The same semantic unit will be expressed in different languages in a way which calls for a number of constraints when sentences are formed, just as there are also constraints in the philological component of a language which permits, for instance, the use of only a limited number of sound sequences. Competence as a developmental factor is governed by several such aspects of language acquisition. The constraints that are essentially part of the philological, morphological, syntactic and semantic components form a major aspect of linguistic competence. In otherwords, the child in the process of bearing what is permissible in the language in constructing the sentences as part of a discourse must develop an awareness of what is not permitted under the 'linguistic theory' of the particular language.

The principle of analogy empowers children to form sound sequences, morphological and syntactic constructions in a way diametrically opposed of times to the constraints which regulate the formation of sound sequences, morphological and syntactic construction. The child who forms phonological sequences such as *black*, *slack* and *glass* will have the tendency to produce an initial 'ml' cluster forming something like 'mlack' even though. It is not a permitted sound sequence in English. Or even in permitted clusters of sounds, substitution is often made because of analogy such as the production of 'shope' meaning *soap* following the sounds in *shirt*, *shoes*, or *shame*. In the morphological formations of language numerous analogous instances are often observed in the language of children. The most obvious example is the use of the plural and the past tense suffixes ( -s and -ed) in an analogous manner. The production of 'mans' or 'oxes' follows from the child's acquaintance with *boys*, *girls*, *toys* or *pups*. Similarly, the production of '*goed*' or '*n*' '*spitted*' follows from the child's acquaintance with formations such as walked, moved and wanted. In case of syntactic formations instances of analogy are limiters. Wrong analogous syntactic constructions are almost on everyday feature in the language of children. The following constructions observed by the another in a group of five three year old children, which are believed to be the produced of analogous learning :

1. Why don't you eat faster, son?
   I am *eating spoon* mummy. (*with* dropped).
2. Look he *climbing up* the tree. (*climb up* the table).
3. My hairs gone white (hair, has gone white)
4. She *spitted my* begs. (spat on).
5. Uncle *drinking* 'beedi'. (smoking).
6. That glass *broke*, dady. (is broken).
7. Please, be *sitted*, sir. (in place of seated)
8. She is *seeing* at me. (looking at).
9. I *ran him* ahead. (ahead of him).
10. Daddy rubbing the table. (cleaning).

In fact the formation of competence in the sense we have

understood it requires a bridging of the two factors of analogy, and constraints that are proper to the language. When the child acquiring the language is prone to say *My brother goed* or *He spitted on the floor*, it is the mastery of the syntactic constraints of the language that puts rein on such constructions and enable that child to produce the grammatical sentences of *My brother went* or *He spat on the floor*. Constraints of this kind are part of both the base structure and transformational sentences. From the beginning of language acquisition (especially when the child forms the first grammatical sentence of his language), to the time when he can be said to have acquired the basic constructions of the language, throughout it is a process of learning the permitted formations and the constraints of his language.

Competence in the speaker of a language comes as a result of the speaker's years of acquaintance with the language. It is the result of a continuous formation of the language habits that are characteristic to the sounds, grammar and meaning array specifically related to the particular language by contrast to the philological, grammatical and semantic specifications of other languages. Competence as a progressively developing factor becomes a very complex notion in the context of bilingualism, namely in an individual who uses more than one language. Base formation, transformational constructions, analogous formations, and the constraints that are deep at the core of all aspects of a language function certainly at different levels for different languages. Not much insights has yet been obtained in regard to the nature of the competence of a bilingual person. From a broader psycholinguistic perspective it may be said that linguistic competence takes, perhaps, a whole lifetime for its fullest formation; and in a narrower sense it is a process of formation that gets completed as the individual acquires command over all the basic structures of his language that enables him to function adequately in all communicative situations. It is this dynamic aspect of linguistic competence that renders it to be the worthy foundation of all the creative experiences the speaker is expected to have.

## 4. Relevance of Competence to the Classroom

Linguistic competence as a notion is usually used with reference to the native language learner, namely, the child who acquires the $L_1$ in the home atmosphere. But competence is a nation that is directly linked in all the ways with the acquisition of any language, for that matter, the first, the second or the third language. All the same, the formation of linguistic competence in the acquisition of different languages vary in terms of its intensity depending on the kind of environment where the language is learned. The learning of a language in the home atmosphere and the learning of a language in the classroom different considerably as we have dealt with it in detail in chapter. 2. What is most characteristic to the home atmosphere is the continuous presence language stimuli which the child finds it easy to acquire for himself; and what is most characteristic to the classroom is the scheduled and limited presentation of language stimuli which is insufficient for the acquisition of the language.

Just as all the language that the child listens to and uses at home leads to the formation of the native language competence, the $L_2$ teaching in the classroom should primarily be aimed at the formation of the kind of competence required for the satisfactory use of the foreign or second language. Here we are reminded of an important point discussed earlier: classroom practices an language can lead to two distinct things; (a) the skill-oriented knowledge of the language, and (b) pure information about the language. As we have already seen, the former alone leads to the formation of competence in the pupils while the latter provides pure information on say the structure of the particular language. This is how linguistic competence becomes very relevant to the classroom, and the teacher is required to have good grounding on the nature of competence and the manner in which it can be formed adequately in the pupils.

A comparative analysis of the two leading situations would give better insights into the nature of competence as related to the classroom. In *situation 1* priority is put on the learning of a given set of lessons in which certain amount of systematic language material is presented. The teacher's attention is focussed on the reading and writing of the material both by the teacher himself and by the pupils. In *situation 2* priority is put on the learning of the basic structures and vocabulary items of the language by means of listening and speaking (aural-oral skills), adding to it by certain amount of reading and writing. In situation 1 we hardly find the pupils actively engaged in the use of the language in the proper sense of the term as expected in the classroom; in situation 2 we find that pupils actively using the language in situational contexts. What is important here is not the stress on the skills of reading and writing or an listening and speaking. Our important consideration is the *pupils' involvement* with the language which would certainly keep on adding to the formation of competence. Situation 1, as we have seen it, would be parallel to the author's own experience in learning *Latin*, and situation 2 would be parallel to his learning of *Hindi*. The Latin class consisted entirely of the learning of formal Latin grammar in English translation of words, sentences and discourses to and from Latin, and reading and writing of some material or other. The learning of Latin and Hindi took place simultaneously and in fact almost double the time was dedicated to the learning of Latin. On the other hand the teacher of Hindi took upon himself the task of introducing the pupils to spoken Hindi with adequate time dedicated to the learning of reading and writing. The learning took place for a period of interesting to note, the group of 20 students who learned Latin and Hindi simultaneously was able to speak, read and write Hindi incomparably better than Latin. The pity was that while the students learned to read and write Latin just as a learner of English in of lower classes of an $L_1$-medium school would do, they were unable to use Latin for any functional or communicational purposes even as a group of students would do in case of English.

Of course, the parallel may be inadequate and the compassion illogical; but one thing is certain that in situation 1 what we learned was more *about* the language through the medium of another language (English) and in situation 2 we learned the *language proper* making use of the some language as the medium. While in situation 1 it was more like gathering some linguistic information, in situation 2 it was the learning of the skills of the language. Instead of common thing to memory certain sets of rules and definitions, the pupils who learned Hindi (for instance) picked up the basic forms of the language and used those forms at once for purposes of communication by way of situational practice in the classroom, and for actual communication outside the classroom.

An analysis of the outcome would lead us to a few conclusion:

1. The initial phase of the learning of Latin was an introduction to the *classical aspects* of the language. There was no oppor-

tunity for the pupils to more from the simplest possible elements of the language to it more complex structure. Consequently the learning was more of committing things to memory than understanding and *internalizing* the structural aspects of the language.

2. The learning of Hindi took place in such a way that the learners from the outset got acquainted with those elements of the language which (a) were the simplest structural and lexical aspects of the language, and (b) were the most necessary and relevant elements required by the pupils for purposes of communication.

3. The steady and progressively ordered learning of the structural aspects and vocabulary of Hindi language was gradually helping the learner internalize the basic as well as transformational rules of the language. It was a process of internalizing the systems of Hindi language.

4. The final outcome of this process of internalizing is the formation of the competence of Hindi in the learner. The learner in course of the three years of learning got so much accustomed with the structural aspects and vocabulary of Hindi that unlike the process of memorization, he came to *develop* (see Section 3) a basic system which consists primarily of (a) a theory of language (in the transformational generative context) which functions as the generative source of sentence, and (b) the language material which forms the content of the patterns that the learner internalizes.

(5) The chief reasons for the differences in the formation of competence lies in the learner's acquaintance with the language proper. In *situation 1* the learner got more acquainted with the language of the medium (English, in present case) than the target language (Latin). In situation 2 the learner is directly, and intensely in touch with the target language itself (Hindi, for instance).

(6) One wouldn't certainly say that no language learning and further the formation of competence takes place in the learning of a language through reading and writing. Reading and writing as the skills which involve two levels of symbolic

representation poses more problems in the formation of competence by the internalization of structures than would listening and speaking as direct symbolic activities. What is important is the proportion in which the learning activity takes place. We are concerned with the direct use of the language by the pupils. Latin, for instance, would have been learned much better if Latin had been used even if stress was put on reading and writing. Instead, there was more learning of English than of Latin in the classroom.

The formation of the competence the second language is the teacher's primary target in the $L_2$ classroom just as interpersonal communion in the native language enhances the active acquisition of the $L_1$ in the family atmosphere. Adherence to these ideas on the formation of competence by the process of internalization places language teaching in the classroom on a new footing. We would no longer like to consider the pupils in the classroom to be guinea-pigs waiting to undergo the traditional stimulus-response mode of operation. It is with a fresh outlook that the teacher now is required to enter the classroom. The pupils are human persons waiting to acquire a language which they think they like, with the help of another person (the teacher) in an atmosphere of concern and cordiality. The classroom is expected to have the kind of personal and cordial air required of any inter personal communion. The pupils are now intended to learn though this interpersonal communion which paves way for the kind of *creative outlet* that is the final outcome of the teaching-learning process.

Where infra-human type of 'learning' was expected, we have today 'personal' and involved learning, which is oriented to enhance the creative personality of the child. We no longer consider that it is the 'mind' of the child picking up certain language learning, habits; we would like rather to consider learning language as a matter of interpersonal communion among the teacher and the learners as persons with gaining of insights, proper understanding, voluntary initiatives, and with the creative side of the pupils' personality thriving for freedom of greater expression. The pupil instead of sitting beside a set of books and existing has brain with rules and formation of all kinds for disciplining the intellect, is given ample opportunity for *self-expression*. The formation of linguistic competence requires all this and more. Our aim is not to enable the pupils to say a few things from memory, but creatively form as part of his cognitive structure a *system* (competence) as the result of systematic but free exposure to language. It is here that we call for language exercises in which the pupils one expected to think creativity rather than provide a sheer answer that is contextually set. Language learning should thus result in the formation of that system which we call *linguistic competence*; all work in the classroom and outside need to be oriented towards this effect.

## 5. Language Performance and the Classroom

The second language teaching classroom poses characteristic problems for the teacher. The teacher has at his disposal a large group of pupils, limited resources and limited time. It is against this background of limitations that he is required to function effectively. Most of the teacher's problems in regard to language teaching can be solved by looking at the classroom as a place where intense atmosphere is created to give shape to systematic *performance* by children with a view to forming adequate linguistic competence.

What do we mean by this? There are quite a number of factors to consider. Let's try to understand the present-day situation in which the teacher works. He is bound by numerous expectations which may have nothing to do with the academic success of the pupils. The courses that are prescribed for the respective term or year need to be completed whatever be the quality of the work that goes on in class. The principal of the school, as well as the parents at home would certainly want the teacher to get a minimum amount of written work done almost everyday. This requirement to see that the pupils' books contain daily allotments of written exercises put the teacher in an awkward fix. He would ordinarily wish to satisfy these requirements than exert his energy for ample language practices in the classroom. Again, the pupils themselves would wish to sit quietly and read and write lessons rather than involve themselves in active use of language in the classroom. As for the teacher himself a time comes when he requires added motivation to remain an active classroom functionary instead of retiring to his chair leaving the pupils to take case of some or other writing work. It becomes either difficult or impossible for the teacher to use even those audio-visual aids which are available in the school. There are, thus, several important factor which render creative teaching of languages almost impossible unless the teacher of English takes it upon himself as a committed takes to do his work adequately in response to his professional call.

The classroom is the place where ordinarily the $L_2$ learner can have access to good language. In ordinary circumstances the learner transacts all his day to day affairs at home and in the community through his mother tongue. With all good intentions he may not so easily come across a situations where the $L_2$ can be put to use or listened to. The importance of the classroom can be realized only against this background. The $L_2$ learner is looking eagerly up to the teacher as his only model in the learning of the language. The teacher, in turn, should fix his attention on the formation of the competence of his language, and to this effect all that he should do is to organize his classroom resources to enable the pupils to *perform* in the language.

By performance use have meant the active use (operation) of the language in all the four basic language skills of listening, speaking, reading and writing. *Performance* leads to *internalization* and this in turn to *linguistic competence.* The teacher should see the classroom primarily as a place for creating the $L_2$ atmosphere in which the individual learners are given adequate opportunity to perform as a 'speaker' of the language. The classroom can be viewed as an ad hoc 'linguistic community' similar to the $L_1$ learner who is placed in the midst of the actual linguistic community. The child at home is involved in the performance of his language as a learner of the language with he adults constantly figuring in for the actual language performance. Of course this situation, as we have examined quite in detail in earlier chapters, is too ideal for the classroom. All the same the $L_2$ class is meant for this; the teacher is required to play the role of the members of the linguistic community amidst whom the $L_1$ learner grows up rather than being a supervisor, examiner or even guide in the sense we understand him.

If *performance* leading to competence is the teacher's central concern, much of the owe and air of silence expected of the classroom even today should disappear. Such things have no place where total involvement is the principal criterion. Again, this would mean that there should come a change in the traditional notion of the classroom, itself. the bounds of the classroom one required to be beyond the school itself since the linguistic community is the target. Where a community which speaks the $L_2$ is not available, the classroom must be extended to socio-communal experiences that are available outside the school. Leading the learner out of the classroom to the midst of the $L_2$ speaking community or a provision of the parallel experiences is what the leader should do.

As we have seen in the preceding section, the pupils should be highly motivated to acquire the basic structures of the language in such a way as to be of use to them as in the case of an $L_1$ learner. It is this high level motivation that is the most compelling factor in the case of $L_1$ learners. At the some time it is a visions circle: greater $L_2$ atmosphere in terms of language performance in class would lead to greater efforts on the part of the learners to pick up the language chiefly because they will, then, feel the need for it. The greater the need for the $L_2$ in class and in school, the better will be their efforts to master the language.

Language performance in the classroom can be initiated in terms of speech of the classroom has a homely atmosphere. This may sound rather odd. By homely atmosphere should no longer feel strangers to the work done in class. In fact even after eight to nine years of learning in school, perhaps as part of the same group, there are few pupils who feel adequately free to transact in class. It may be that our classrooms are still to formal for any kind of informal interpersonal communion that is an integral part of the pupils' family life of which language ($L_1$) forms the most essential part. Children should grow up and be formed in school in an atmosphere where inhibitions have no place. This is true of the learning of $L_1$ as would be recognized by all those who are familiar with child psychology. Free atmosphere, lack of emotional strains, and absence of undue inhibitions contribute significantly to the language performance of children.

In most cases what happens is that the pupils are kept under unwanted strains in class due to a set of class tasks which do not at all contribute to the formation of competence. In some cases the pupils are asked to write down every bit of the series of exercise given at the end of every lesson, while the teacher comfortably relaxes his table. Hardly any learning takes place even after months of this kind of learning as will be proved from the fact that the majority of such children will not be in a position to frame two correct sentences orally or construct a paragraph in feasible language.

A conscious, willing and wanted recourse to the $L_2$ in the classroom can be the only solution to proper language acquisition of we wish that our pupils should be in a position to employ his learning of the language for functional, communicative purposes. Even though language performance means the working of the four language skills of listening, speaking, reading and writing, a solid formation of the competence of the second or foreign language can be obtained only if proper stress is put on the listening-speaking skills. It is a myth of we still believes that language competence as a cognitive system can be formed through the exercise only of reading and writing with the learners never exposed to the spoken language in a natural, congenial atmosphere which boosts their language learning motivation. Any system which attempts to have compromises will certainly jeopardize the right formation of competence.

# 5
# Psychological Factors in Language Acquisition

## 1. Intelligence

Intelligence has been recognized as the primary factor which controls language behaviour. From time immemorial it was believed that man has an abstract mind which exerts control over and determines all his behaviour. But not two among those who studied the human mind did not agree as to its nature. Language the mind have always been seen as 'operation' and 'faculty of operation' and as such both have been found related in several ways. This is one way of looking at the relation between language and the mind. But in present day psychology not many feel at home with a word like 'mind' and at the same time for technical convenience a distinction is drawn between the mind and intelligence. In manuals of general psychology one chiefly comes across the word 'intelligence' rather than 'mind' while referring to the faculty that is the functional principle of abstract thinking.

It is possible to come across definitions and varied descriptions of intelligence. We may examine some of these before looking into the fundamental relation between language learning and intelligence.

(1) Intelligence is defined by many as ' the ability to learn'

Perhaps, this is the common man's definition too. Several activities schools adjusting, assimilating, integrating and organizing are considered components of learning process. Intelligence is found to be the general impetus as well as base for all learning activities. The level, intensity and the speed of learning are determined by intelligence.

(2) Intelligence is defined, secondly, as ' the ability to carry on abstract thinking'. The term intelligence, in this connection, is always related to abstractions, organizing concepts, and theorizing. The intelligent man organizes his thinking in logical manner and on the basis of rational principles. The intelligent man is capable of finding the rationale behind aspects of behaviour. His behaviour is always purposeful.

(3) A more behaviorist definition of intelligence reads as 'the adaptation or adjustment of the individual to his total environment'. The human individual lives in the social environment and he is in a state of constant interaction with society for varying purposes. The intelligent man knows what his problems are and how to tackle them; he develops ample 'social intelligence' to know the problems of others and feel one with them in trying to solve these problems. The intelligent man knows also when and how to take a decision and what to decide. An intelligent man, again, exercises his reasoning faculty in all his dealing with others.

Intelligence functions, also, in man as a custodian of emotions. Feelings, emotions and passions dominate over man is varying degrees. Intelligence functions as the controlling factor in this regard. Intelligence enables man to exploit the resource of his emotions and channel this resource to constructive behaviour. The intelligent man's passions do not misguide him; instead he guides his passions to purposeful, constructive behaviour.

(4) According to Spearman, 'general intelligence is the mental world. The man of intelligence is regarded as having tremendous mental potential with which to guide his personality.

(5) Thrustum believed that 'intelligence is not one factor, but a complex of abilities', Abilities such as number, verbal, reasoning and role-memory are primary factors of intelligence.

Intelligence cannot be thought of as a single factor which

guides all human activities. It is a matter of common experience that aptitudes and abilities differ greatly from individual to individual. No one can assert that only the mathematician is intelligent; nor can any one say that only a good administrator is intelligent. There is full agreement that intelligence manifests itself in varying degrees in all skills, abilities and aptitudes. This is the basis for considering intelligence as a complex of different factors.

(6) Guilford's definition of intelligence in his four-factor theory is not very different from the belief that intelligence is a complex of abilities. The sum-total of intelligence consists of 1. Concrete intelligence, 2. Symbolic intelligence, 3. Semantic intelligence, 4. Social intelligence.

(7) Piaget speaks of 'functional intelligence and structural intelligence'. Intelligence, here, determines the way we do things. Man's behaviour reveals his intelligence-determinant.

(8) For Flavell 'intellectual functioning is a specific manner of doing business with the environment'. Intellectual development takes place in four phases: 1. Sensory-motor development, 2. Pre-operational thought development, 3. Concrete operational period, 4. Formal operational period. In this context, intellectual development is process of development towards a psychologically mature personality.

All the definitions we have examined above somehow or other relates intelligence to the development of the mind, control over the environment, and manipulation of abstractions, skills, and aptitudes. It is doubtless, therefor, that intelligence controls all facts of human behaviour. But of all these, man's verbal behaviour, language, reveals the level of intelligence. Language is not an isolated factor; it is somehow related to all other behavioral facts of man.

(1) Intelligence is at once, related to language acquisition process: The predominant psychological factor which controls the acquisition of language is intelligence. Intelligence controls the speed of language acquisition. An intelligence child fully exploits the language learning opportunities. He is quick in comprehending the language of adults and in internalizing the linguistic systems. The manifold experiences of the child in the family and outside leave in him deep linguistic impressions. He is quick in relating experi-

ences with his language.

(2) Intelligence, as the *operational principle* of abstract symbols i.e. concepts, enables the child to hasten the acquisition and organization of concepts on the basis of his experiences with the world outside. This process is directly related to language. The acquisition and organization of concepts has one to one relation to language acquisition and organization. It is not possible to visualize conceptual development in man apart from the language which he uses in order to give expression to his inner world of experiences. Intelligence is the governing factor in man's inner world of experiences.

(3) Intelligence not only determines the speed of language acquisition, but also its intensity and depth. Intelligence cannot be separated from *memory*. An intelligent man with poor ability to preserve and recall symbols will certainly make a poor man. Memory may be considered the 'factor co-ordinate' of intelligence. Good language performance calls for good intelligence and good memory. As language is essentially a manipulation of symbols, it requires the ability to store and recall these symbols (words and expressions) at will.

(4) The organization of linguistic elements requires the Co-ordination principle, intelligence. A high level language production means the acquisition, the preservation and recall, and the organization of linguistic elements. We speak of a clever child when the child comes out with sentences that are apt to a situation; and there often come as a surprise to adults.

(5) Intelligence enables the individual to employ language as the principal means in interacting with his *social environment*. This is recognized by all psychologists. Language proficiently brings from general intelligence as well as from what Guilford calls, 'symbolic' as well as 'semantic' intelligence. The individual directs his linguistic ability to a successful handling of social situations. A person endowed with the necessary sociability and aptitude in language will easily float in social situations because as an intelligent man he knows what language to use, when to use it and how to use it.

Just as intelligence is a complex of abilities, language too is a complex of component abilities. Language involves a range of components beginning with abstractions down to manipulation of articulatory organs. All relations between intelligence and language boil down to the fact that intelligence is the determining principle right from language acquisition to employing language proper in all given situations.

## 2. Resourcefulness

Intelligence, creative ability, problem-solving ability and resourcefulness are all convergent principles of behaviour involving multiple factors or smaller abilities. When the component-ability of each of the above are broken down, we find that several of these component abilities overlap. Resourcefulness is defined and described in several ways. Resourcefulness is defined in terms of *adjustment* to the environment, relativeness, organizational and administrative ability. It is often seen as an all-pervading aptitude that has its say in all aspects of individual behaviour.

At the same time resourcefulness is always thought of as related to *verbal behaviour*. In this domain resourcefulness is distinguished from intelligence as such. All intelligent individuals need not be resourceful; there are very intelligent people with poor language ability. Resourcefulness functions as a verbal channel to intelligence; when intelligence manifests itself in verbal behaviour we may strictly call it resourcefulness. It is possible to diversify resourceful behaviour.

(1) An individual is said to be resourceful when he employs his language for successful, socially acceptable adjustment. We come across several persons with very good command over language. But either a-social or antisocial by nature. Intelligence is not only, as we have seen, the ability to engage in abstract thinking, but also it consists in social adjustment. A very high level of intelligence calls for a balanced attitude at all levels. Without this fundamental social adjustment, language proficiency does not lend itself to resourcefulness.

(2) Resourcefulness consists, secondly, not only in mere *social adjustment* in a passive sense of the term, but in the utilization of one's language ability to control and change the social environment for the better. A passive submission to the ways and norms of socially requires no high level of resourcefulness. A resourceful

person most creativity uses his language ability to control his environment and change it in the most constructive manner. He stands against injustice hypocrisy and social malpractices, and exerts his resources for constructive reforms.

(3) Resourcefulness consists, also, in making the best use of one's language in professional efficiency. A resourceful person excels in his professional career since in him there occurs a combination of intelligence and language proficiency. Many intelligent men and women who are otherwise well equipped, seem despairingly unsuccessful in their professional life just because they are handicapped in language proficiency. Mere verbosity without the guiding intelligence is certainly a worse melody which has no remedy. A successful professional life requires resourcefulness: The combination of intelligence and language proficiency.

(4) Resourcefulness means also an *organized utilization* of one's aptitudes, with language always making a headway. One comes across a great many individuals who, having had no educational background, take resort to several kinds of occupations and interests based on outstanding qualities in them. In such cases it is, again, a combination of intelligence with exceptional language proficiency that makes there men talented. These men are found in all walks of life; but they seldom rise above the ordinary due to the lack of adequate education and training.

(5) A resourceful child does not find it a problem to master several languages. Mastering languages satisfactorily and speedily is not every one's cup of tea. The resourceful child takes others by surprise when his intelligence captures one after another language to which he is exposed. While less resourceful children find it different to cope with the learning demands of even the mother-tongue, more resourceful children acquire several languages simultaneously with a high level of feasibility. For less resourceful children language acquisition is a slow, lingering process even though they reveal signs of high intelligence in certain other aspects of behaviour such as, probably, in handling mathematical symbols.

In resourcefulness language proficiency works, as though, the chief outward *vehicle of intelligence*. An intelligent man with language handicaps has all probability that his intelligence gets suffocated as language serves as its chief outlet and functioning channel. It is possible that in the greatest figures of World History, intelligence and language got combined, and a superior resourcefulness must have been the secret of their success. A resourceful individual reveals himself easily in course of his early language acquisition stage, during his education, and above all in his professional life. Greater success in store for a child who is really resourceful than for one who may reveal any other form of intellectual ability.

## 3. Creativity

Of all in intellectual activities the most complex are problem solving and creative production. But both these activities have so much in common that there is always something creative about any genuine problem solving, and all creative production is carried out with a view to solving some problem. We saw that resourcefulness is the combination of intelligence and language proficiency; resourcefulness is thus rooted in intelligence. Creativity or rather creative behaviour is the sum-total of high level intellectual operation. Creative behaviour, thus, direct, springs from intelligence. While resourcefulness is defined in terms of language, creative behaviour need not have its roots in language. It is possible to come across highly creative children and adults who are not very proficient in any language; their creativity doesn't behaviour. Verbal behaviour functions as a mere aid in the creative behaviour of such individuals.

Intelligence of any sort reveals itself in some form of creative behaviour. An intelligent man cannot afford to be not creative. It may thus be said that creative behaviour is the concretization of intelligence. The essence of creative behaviour, then, lies in thinking in a way different from traditional ways, doing things with a touch of novelty, and in bringing and things that are not of the ordinary. In the highest form of creative category we include scientists, inventors of various kinds, writers, mathematicians, artists, musicians and all those who in professional life one capable of controlling and organizing things, events, and people towards a creative end.

Just as intelligence is not a single factor but a complex of several component-abilities, creativity is a complex of several component-abilities.

(1) A creative child's mind remains ever active and usually comes out with some surprises for the parents. It is possible to observe him manipulating his play things and objects around him, and he has always something interesting to show the parents. His unquenchable enthusiasm leads him to ever new 'experiments' with the objects around him. He does not invent anything new; but be organizes things in a new way and finds something new in the old. All this new manner of organizing things is a reflections of his inner creative thinking of a rudimentary type.

(2) Creative behaviour consists in levels of ingenuity rooted in the individual's intelligence. We may not go around calling everyone a genius; but ingenious patterns of behaviour are not so uncommon around use in the usual walks of life. If on the one hand, creativity is thinking in a new way, it also entails that the new manner of thinking is productive. *Productive behaviour* follows from productive organization of concepts. It is only, that in children such productive organization of concepts is not so explicit and systematic. It functions at a more rudimentary level of conceptual orientation. A child playing with clay comes out with images which none has ever shown him; observing the keenness with which he manipulates the day, we are sure that there is a lot of conscious awareness in him of the form that takes shape in the clay.

(3) Creative behaviour consists in directing one's thinking and doing to a well-set *goal* aided by definite *incentive*. A haphazard outcome in a random activity cannot be called creative production. The scientist may come across an instance that is not a consciously directed effect; the scientists ingenuity in creativity lies in the flashing illumination that his mind entertains with regard to a new invention or discovery on the basis of the experience he has just had. Keeping before him this invention as his foremost goal, the scientist organizes his entire thinking, his material and his experiences, and ultimately, achieves the intended goal. It happens that several people stop helpless at half-way through at the illumination-phase. We may call it a creative experience, because the illumination the scientist receives is essentially creative. This illumination becomes a productive behaviour only when the scientist moves towards the new goal and thereby achieve the feat.

(4) Creative people are independent thinkers; they disagree with the existing systems and values. Independent thinking and

non-conformity with the existing social, political, economic and moral systems and characteristic traits of very creative people.

It is in *non-conformity* that creative thinkers base this ingenious attitudes. The inadequacies of the exi-ting systems-excite their creativity and set their minds thinking in new directions i.e. new possibilities and new solutions.

Finally we may examine the fact that language acquisition and production are creative behaviours of a characteristic kind. Even though creative behaviour does not necessarily involve language proficiency, when *intelligence, creativity* and *resourcefulness* function together we find that an individual excels in everything. Language proficiency crowns all other endowments on the individual's personality. Each aspect of creative behaviour which has been examined above receives excellent outlet in resourcefulness. For the resourceful person creativity is a boosting experience and in him creativity receives the fullest expression.

Above all, it becomes a great endowment when creativity is precisely in the use of language. The greatest of writers are produced by a combination of intelligence, resourcefulness and creativity. Again, in literature we find the most creative use of language. In writers, especially in literary figures such as a novelist or a playwright, over and above the ordinary linguistic creativity (an ability all the speakers of a language possess) there is an added creative dimension which we may call '*literary creativity*', a talent rooted in the combination of intelligence, resourcefulness and creativity. Here literary creativity language proficiency receivers, as mentioned above, the fullest possible expression. It is possible, thus, to establish a gradation in language proficiency between the ranges of basic *linguistic creativity* which everyone shares and the topmost form of literary creativity. Between these two extremes we may include people endowed with degrees of creative expression in language.

## 4. Motivation

It is no surprise of we say that motivation functions as the activating impetus behind the psychological factors which we have examined in the foregoing pages. Intelligence, creativity and resourcefulness are rendered inactive and unproductive if sufficient activating impetus is not provided by motivation. Motivation may be defined as the powerful pull towards a goal, which an individual experiences. The goal of the motivation may be simple or complex, proximate or remote, physiological, emotional, social or intellectual. The strength of motivation will depend on the nature of the goal in mind.

Every deliberate human activity requires the pushing strength of motivation or motivating factors. The higher the motivation, the greater going take the strength, enthusiasm, and the vigour with which to approach the goal. First language learning is a domain where simple motivational factor play a significant and observable role. The fact that motivation and language acquisition are highly related can be illustrated in the following manner. The $L_1$ learner is placed in a characteristic environment. The child at first is 'dumb and leaf' creature; the mind of the child is said to be a 'tabular rasa' with no impressions created on it. Among all living things, we are compelled to agree, that the human infant is the most non-specialized and helpless creature at birth. The puppy, or the kitten are so specialized at birth that it can survive by means of its own active role : the puppy can feed on its mother's milk, eat, more around, and little later it is even above to swim in water. At birth the infra-human offsprings are endowed with several specialized activities for survival. The human infant, on the other hand, is a helpless biological entity with magnificent and potentialities and no actualities. The greatest motivation of an infant or a child, therefore, is to achieve realization of its blooming potentialities and become more of a human being. This fundamental motivating impetus of man to become more and more of a perfect human being is what keeps us going through all vicissitudes of life, on the one hand, and on the other, it is the same fundamental motivation that has produced, age after age, great men who have succeeded in approximating maturity and perfection as human beings.

The fundamental motivation to become a perfect human is inherent in human nature, and mostly works at its subconscious level. An awareness of this perfection and an endeavour to reach the same already makes an individual great. Apart from this essential motivating factor, there is another impetus working in the child. The infant is born in society; it needs the basic physiological requirements : food, warmth and care. At this stage the infant is physically and physiologically motivated to develop in itself a device to meet these needs. The pre-linguistic cries, random articulation and other behavioural patterns of the child spring from the motivation to obtain the basic requirements for survival and comfort. In other words such early manifestations of language are motivated by the basic needs.

For the child, language is the chief device to meet further emotional and sociological requirements. There are not many alternatives left for the child except to develop the first language and succeeded establishing contact with the world outside or leave the very survival at stake. The child, unlike an adult trying to learn the $L_2$, has no other alternative but learn the language. The child has thus the maximum language-learning motivation. This motivation, again, functions at the subconscious level. The child is intrinsically compelled to master its nature language.

Another domain of power in motivation is *self-expression.* This too, so to say, is a basic need of the child's personality. Self-expression enables the child to master his language at the earliest. It is a pleasure for the resourceful and creative child to go around using his language at all instances at hand, thereby becoming proficient in its use. The creative child experiences much greater motivation both in the creative use of language and other forms of creative behaviour.

It is not only in childhood, but also as years go by the individual's language growth and proficiency are highly influenced by the strength of his motivation. As motivation is a deciding factor in achievement in psychology we speak of *achievement motivation*' Psychologists believe that there can be systematic boosting of achievement motivation and thereby increasing the expected output. Strong motivation leads to better utilization of one's faculties, and this ultimately yields greater output. This is very true of learning languages, both at home and in the classroom. It is not possible to provide the school going child with as powerful a motivation as is present at the time of learning the $L_1$. But it is within the control of educationists and teachers to provide the child in the classroom with stronger motivations, both proximate and remote. The fundamental thing to remember is that intelligence, resourcefulness and creativity are psychological bases of learning process, which continually require the activating impetus of powerful motivations. Where such motivation is absent, language learning certainly lends itself to drudgery.

# 6
# Sociological Implications of Language Acquisition

## 1. Language and Society

The treatment of language in relation to society is more or less reserved to the sociolinguist from a specialized view-point. The sociologist studies the behaviour of man in human society just as the psychologist is expected to study the behaviour of man as an individual person. Language as the most specific of all human behaviour, proper to man as man, becomes the object of study by all these disciplines because language is key to almost all his patterns of behaviour. All social sciences are concerned about language as human behaviour from one or other specific viewpoint. Psycholinguistics in its investigations of language as a process (by contrast to the study of language as structured system) calls for all sorts of considerations including its interactional implications on the individual in human society.

The human child is, on the one hand an organism, and on the other individual person bearing much sociological significance. He is born to and lives in a society. It is in this society, what we shall call the *linguistic community*, that the child takes the first 'community' that the child takes the first 'lessons' in language. Society is the arena where the individual child confronts language. This how a trichotomy arises between the child, society and the language. It is thus are encounter, ultimately, of society, language and the individual. There are quite a number of questions that props up in this context regarding the relation between society, language and the individual. What is the role of language in the survival and advancement of society ? Does a society exert greater influence on and determine its language: Or is it that the language of a society exerts greater influence on and determine the life and advancement of the society? Again, has the individual as such an upper hand on his language? Does the language of an individual exert greater influence in determining and moulding his personality? In later chapters we shall examine the mutual influence which language and thought exert on each other and two essential link between the two.

Our immediate concern, all the same, is about the sociological implications of language acquisition. The child as an individual is endowed with the basic potency and faculties to acquire languages which in turn function for him as the medium of all his interaction with or *interpersonal communion* in society. A society without a language of a unimaginable as the existence of a natural language without the corresponding society. Language and society are so inter-linked and so much a part each other that one cannot be thought of except in relation to the other. It is in this context that we place the child who is acquiring a language. In the purely behaviourist explanation of language acquisition this very important aspect of language learning is often overlooked. The communicational aspect of language and its teleological nature can be explained only in relation to the community where language is used. Language for the child is his tool for interaction with his community as well as the community's tool for interaction with the child.

Language is human society's most precious possession not only because of its communicative values, but also because language is the vehicle of culture. Culture is the embodiment of all that a society believes, produces, and does. In this general sense language becomes an integral part of culture. The child who is introduced to his language at infancy is in fact getting introduced or initiated to the culture of his community. For the maturing and developing child the parallelism between language and his experiences together function as a representative mode of culture. Whatever be nature of the attitudes, the beliefs and the pattern of his community's behaviour, they are all presented to the growing child through the verbal behaviour of the community. It is the this paramount, dominating pattern of influence on the growing child and his psychology by the verbal medium of language that makes us wonder how far the human individual is free from the specificities of the language through which he comes to know almost everything around him. By the time the individual becomes self conscious and is in a position to think for himself, the semantic specifications and categories of his community almost dominate him and as some would call it, determine much of his further behaviour.

Language, it may be said, records the cultural history of a community. New experiences and new realms of thought get embodied in every language as the particular community culturally advances. Every bit of experience such as discoveries, inventions or undertakings of the community further add to the language store of the respective community by means of new coinages and expressions and additional shades of meanings. This function of cultural recording by the language of a community is the chief way of perpetuating the community's experiences and thus passing than on to the later generations.

We have said that a language is the embodiment of a community's socio-cultural experiences. This has also great implications in the language behaviour of the members of the community. The belief in earlier times was that all languages were mere 'representative moulds' of one and the same set of concepts which received different denominations in different languages. Even the grammars of all languages were held to be one and the same until it was discovered that every language is in some way unique despite the fundamental linguistic universality of language. As we examine languages we find that not only the beneficial ordering of *sounds* for the production of morphemes and words and the ordering of the elements of sentences *differ* from language to language, but also there are significant differences in the meanings that every language tries to represent. This aspect is important in our consideration of the relation between language and society. What we have examined earlier under the labels *meaning units* and *conceptual elements* specify the socio-cultural experiences of a particular community which a language represents.

Meanings are nothing but the conceptual representations of the manifold experiences that a society has long been inheriting and accumulating in its language. These conceptual representations, in the last analysis, are a given set of conceptual elements which are organized and reorganized according to the factors of a particular community's experiences by contrast to the factors which characterize or specify those of other communities. In other words, of experiences in regard to the things it uses and the activities in which the individuals themselves and the community as a whole are involved. We would consider, for instance, activities such as dancing, marriage, or burial, the communities religions socials and cultural beliefs, and the things the community makes use of such as instruments, tools, furniture, food articles and things for day to day life. Just as milk, for instance, is a meaning unit which is analyzable into its essential *conceptual elements* of liquidity, whiteness, sweetness etc. it is also characterized in various communities in terms of the time it is taken (whether with meals or at other times only), or as vegetarian or non-vegetarian food, or in terms of the source of milk (a cow at home or dairy where milk is processed and distributed). No one can deny that a meaning unit such as milk is differently, specified except in its very essentials, in different communities. This is true of all features of a community's experiences. The child trying to acquire language is introduced to a symbolic system which presents a complex net-work of conceptual elements which he is expected to assimilate and internalize as part of the child's attempt to become an integral part of his community.

Language is a changing phenomenon, we know well that this is in consonance with the fast changing requirements of the community. Changes in the community's mode of thought and behaviour are part of its expected socio-cultural advancement. Despite this advancement to a great extent the language preserves much of the communities old ways of behaviour in its onward march. Language as a symbolic system does not get rid of the forms and expressions so easily and fast as the community would do with its attitudes and patterns of behaviour. For this reason it happens that the language becomes more loaded with the forms and expressions that are on the one hand newly received and on the other dated in use, especially, because of the perpetuated written material which are not got rid of because of the changes in the language.

An important consideration for us is the parallel status of the language and community. As a community advances, greater complexity is added to its language heavily burdening the syntactic and lexical systems. It is a process of evolution in which the individual speaker or a generation of speakers play the major role. It is interesting to role that the initiation to such an evolution by way of constant change comes from the generations of speakers, and the resultant burden of this evolution is borne by the subsequent generations of speakers. Even though language is the heritage of a specific community, and a deep parallelism is established between the language on the one hand and the community on the other, the *sole agent* in whom linguistic activity as a social behaviour rests and by whom the linguistic change is one way or other initiated is the individual speaker. Just as society is an abstraction and what really counts is the individual, language in the unified sense we understand it is only an abstraction of what is spoken and written by the individuals of a linguistic community to obtain both individual and common ends.

## 2. The Child as a Learner at Home

The process of learning in the child is so integral a part of his growth and maturation that it is difficult even to consider them separately. Learning is often seen from two perspectives: (a) in its very broad sense of learning to *adjust* himself to the environment by the formation of active *habits*; and (b) in its narrow sense of as a strictly cognitive process of acquiring his *language* as well as *knowledge* of the world around. The child at birth is considered to be well-oriented organism consisting of potentials and faculties supposed to grow and develop into an adult human person. It takes a few months before the infant 'learns' to recognize by comparing and contrasting with his own dim cognitive structure the figure of the mother (society) who in fact is the first representative of the society to which he is born. This dim recognition of the mother as an entity distinct from himself is the first most significant event in the infant's advance towards socialization and development of personality.

One of the controversial aspects of the infant's recognition of the external world is whether the infant at its earliest phase of cognitive development (to which no clear experimental cue can be obtained) first recognizes itself as an entity or it terms back upon self-awareness (whenever it takes place) from the awareness the infant obtains of the mother (who is a symbol for the external world). Most philosophers and psychologists one of the opinion, based chiefly on logical grounds, that the infant receives or develops an awareness of the *self* only *by contrast* to the awareness it receives of something extrinsic to its own consciousness. The mother is considered the first extrinsic object of the infant's conscious awareness. Socialization as a progressive factor is based on this early experience of the child.

It is also held that the infant receives the extrinsic awareness of its own physical body earlier than its awareness of the presence of the mother. The infant comes to understand that the 'physical things to which to cognitive experiences are related is a part of the self, that the recognition of the body is the beginning of the infant's recognition of things extrinsic to its consciousness. Whatever bodily pain or pleasure the infant experiences is throughout of as the starting point of the awareness of the body as something distinct from the cognition itself. Whether it is the body which the infant contrast itself with or it is the mother with whom the infant contrast itself, one thing is certain that *consciousness* of the infant requires something extrinsic to itself to come to know itself. For this reason we may say that the early awareness of the infant is definitely a relative factor in the sense that it is in relation to its extrinsic experiences that the infant knows itself.

Awareness of the mother comes as the most significant experience in the infant's early life. This as we have said is the beginning of an onward march of the human person's consciousness which continues to envelop a long series of experiences until the human person receives a vision of humanity itself and comes to know himself as an integral part of this humanity. It is a long development, which, perhaps, takes a whole life time for the person to consider the humanity as an extension of the self. But the beginning of this long development is set here when the infant relates the self to that image, which it will later recognize as the most intimate and the most essential for its own survival. As psychologists would agree it is this early recognition of the image of the mother as the most intimate and essential which the person later in life projects over to the humanity itself as the most intimate and most essential for the individual person's survival.

In the context of language acquisition (see Ch. 2 sec. 3) we have termed this earliest phase of language development as the stage of *random articulation*. Beginning with the first cry with which the infant opens its lungs there takes place a continuous and unbroken chain of articulation so much needed and so much the base of later language development. The infant as a learner acquires elementary habits and mostly it is in the realm of reflex behaviour in response to the stimuli from the external world. The first encounter with the world outside of its own demi-consciousness in the image of the mother is the beginning of a process of learning that later render's the individual's existence in society worthwhile or not. It means adjustment for the individual; it means happiness and joy; it would mean success in life; it would above all means survival in society. The individual is born to live with other members of society. This *learning to live with* and learning to adjust to human society is the biggest and most significant of all learning so far as the individual's socialization is concerned. All learning, psychologists would agree, is ultimately oriented to the individuals; successful co-existence in society.

The individual's socialization on the one hand, and the acquisition of language on the other are aspects of parallel process of development which would remain impeded in case any one of the two is seriously hindered. In fact it may be said that language acquisition in the child is oriented to adequate socialization. The semantic categories which the child is expected to acquire in his learning of the language and the efficiency with which the language acquisition takes place are directly related to the process of socialization. In case of the infant we have been examining, the earliest phase of language acquisition (what is called *pre-verbal stage* in earlier chapters) described here as *random articulation* is a self-stimulated activity. In articulating the sounds as heard the infant is neither responding to the stimuli from the mother (or other members of society) nor is the articulation imitations of any adult sounds. Researches into the nature of the content of this early articulation have shown that there are few sounds distinctive enough to be labelled as one or other sound in the respective language. This is why we have called it throughout a self stimulated activity (see ch. 2. sec. 3) or *vocal-ear reflexes*. The learning that takes place at this stage is the infant's acquaintance with the adults of the family and any level of interaction, non-verbal by nature, that takes place as a result of this rudimentary interaction. The infant 'learns' to smile, beat its arms and legs and show bodily signs of acceptance at the approach of the mother. This is the result of the kind of little familiarity that has grown between the two worlds: the infant's consciousness and the external world.

Learning in the true sense of the world as a result of direct interaction with the external world begins as further development takes place in the child's cognitive structure. The external world has now become familiar especially in the person of the mother, and the child's cognitive realm is ripe for interaction. This takes place in what we have called the *ear-vocal reflex* of the child, the second phases of early language development when the child *listens* to the voice of the mother, picks up the distinctive sounds which it consists of, and *responds* to the voice of the mother in terms of certain sets of articulation (see ch. 2. sec. 3). This is the beginning of actual interaction with society after the image of the mother having been recognized. The child is now in a position to give rudimentary response to the voice of the mother not only as earlier in terms of non-verbal movements but also by trying to respect, as through, the voice of the mother. It is the beginning of an inter-personal communion with the social world which determines in the person's life the success and happiness that he endeavours to attain as a human person.

As a result of further development we find more and more facilities of the child entering into the process of language accusation. First it was the conscious realm that solely functioned to give response to the random articulation which the articulatory organs produced without receiving any concrete stimuli from outside through the sources. Further development shows the active involvement of the auditory organs through which the infant listens to the voice of the mother. Now we find the *visual faculty* becoming an active aid in the acquisition of language. The child at about the age of 12 months recognizes there distinct aspects of his experience : *the self, the mother* (society) and *objects* around. Accordingly the interaction differs: the self is posed as the centre of all experiences, an experience centrifugal by nature; the mother is perceived as the most intimate and essential caretaker; and the objects around the handmade of the self in its endeavour to subsume everything. The child begins not only manipulating but learning the names of things relating to the mother's utterances to objects around. This infact, is a very significant stage which later unfolds into what is usually referred to as a 'naming explosion.'

The process of learning the verbal equivalents of things and actions within the preview of the child's experiences takes the child a long way in the parallel process of socialization. The language now becomes subservient to the wishes of the child in his interpersonal communion with the members of his family. Here is a learner at home for whom now language has become the principal and most effective tool for social interaction. The child grows up in the midst of a flood of language stimuli which provides intense motivation and congenial atmosphere for him to pick up the specifications of language so necessary for his effective interaction in society.

## 3. Language and the Child's Cognitive Development

The parallel development of language in the child and the child's cognitive ability in terms of abstract thinking is an area in which ample research has been undertaken. To say exactly who, at what given age abstract thinking, that is manipulation of abstract symbols begin in children, is still difficult. One of the basic questions in regard to this area is whether in the child *thinking* leads to language activity or vice versa. We are here specifically concerned about the language activity of the child is a sociological setting and the child's related cognitive developments.

We have seen that the infant at birth is incapable of language or cognitive behaviour which can be subject to our observation. It is not better than another infra-human animal in all its behaviour. It takes time before the infant begins manifesting signs of any pre-verbal thinking. The earliest recognition, we have said, of anything extrinsic to the infant is said to be the mother who stands for any member of the family who takes care of the infant. We have also said that it is in contrast to the mother that the infant recognizes itself as something unique. This earliest recognition of an element of the world external to the child is most significant in ways more than one. Up to this moment, perhaps as our observation goes, the infant possess a consciousness as part of its cognitive structure which his dormant and 'undeveloped', which should be incapable of any thinking the way we understand it. In other words as philosophers of all ages would call it, the infant's mind is in a potential state i.e.

as *faculty*which awaits development. The human being, we shall not hesitate to say, is born with a set of similar faculties which at birth begin their development towards maturity. Just as an apple seed or a mango seed necessarily grows into an apple tree or a mango tree respectively, and not a banyan tree or a people tree, the human infant is destined at birth to develop into a *thinking* and *speaking* animal.

The infant's *encounter* with the world outside in the person of the mother who constantly stoop over it creating in the infant the earliest feelings of affection and security. In fact, it is at this encounter that the formation of the first set of conceptual elements in the cognitive realm of the infant. There is absolutely no reason to believe that the mind of the infant entertains any concepts earlier than the first encounter with the world outside. We may call this encounter the first *objective experience* of the infant. What is most significant about this experience is that it is essentially a *social experience*, the first social encounter of the human being, in other words, this encounter is the first interpersonal communion of man with his society. Thus this first encounter of the infant with the external world, whenever it takes place, has a triple dimension : (a) it is a *linguistic* factor, laying the foundation of further language experience ; (b) it is a *sociological* factor, the first social experience of the infant; and (c) it is, above all a *cognitive* factor, namely, the first feeding ground for the acquisition on concepts that form the content of thinking.

It can be seen that the earliest roots of the cognitive function of thinking and of language lie in and the same fundamental human experience with the external world. Neither language nor thinking is triggered off except in and through this first encounter we have examined above. There is infact no sense at all in giving any precedence to one over the other except for the fact that the formation of concepts as the material for cognitive function in the infant can very well precede the first language activity. Again a distinction is to be drawn here between *comprehension* and *production* of language when we speak of language activity. If we mean production of language of any kind, certainly it occurs much later than the first sign of the child's recognition of the world around (a sign which categorically places in infant's behaviour above that of intra-human animals). In this case thinking of some rudimentary kind would certainly precede the production of language. But if by language activity we mean comprehension of some kind, we must have our own reservation in coming to any kind of conclusion in this regard.

What would be the kind of comprehension that takes place in the infant at the pre-verbal period? It is worthwhile to examine this. We have seen that the infant's first encounter with the external world in the person of mother due to the active attention. She bestows on the infant is a factor of triple dimension : *linguistic*, *sociological* and *cognitive*. The presence of the mother, for the infant, is behavioural, communicational, and factual. This encounter of the mother and the infant *arouses* the infant's sense and intellectual (cognitive) faculties. Here we find an external agent as though calling out the infant from its cognitive slumber. The mother is the embodiment not only of active, dynamic external world which is acting on the infant's cognition, but also of language and society. (see the triple dimension discussed above). Throughout her encounter with the infant the mother uses language that is befitting to the situation. In course of time the infant's sense of audition is aroused by the mother's voice. This stage we have earlier called 'echolalia' or *ear-vocal reflex*. Even before this so-called echolalia takes place the infant's encounter with the mother is active and the infant, as we may assert, is in a *stage of comprehension* (linguistic by nature) parallel to the cognitive function of the formation of concepts as a result of the infant's recognition of the mother as a person (active, dynamic and affectionate) distinct from the self. In other words we may say that language activity a production of language certainly comes much later than the first cognitive function of thinking in the infant, while language activity as comprehension of language as an accompaniment of the recognition of persons and things extrinsic to the self, more or less occurs simultaneous to the first cognitive activity of thinking in the infant. This distinction is in many ways important.

It is hardly possible, in other words, to draw a distinction between the beginning of intellectual activity and of language activity in the infant. It is a conspicuous fact, as we infant's preverbal behavior, that comprehension of adult language in some manner or other takes place much earlier than the first distinct production of language. For this reason we shall have to be cautions while talking about language activity in infants. All the same, as we proceed further in the analysis of the relation between language and cognition we are able to see things more clearly. As months go by the child extends his first encounter with the other over to other members of the family and things with which he comes in touch. Just as the initial experience was cognitive, linguistic and sociological in dimension, the subsequent experiences retain the same characteristics in a more intense manner. If these dimensions were vague in the infant's first encounter with the mother, we find that these are the outstanding features of the child's experiences with the external world.

The child now encounters experiences of a wider range : the feeding ground for *cognitive experiences* are now greater and varied. As he is able to more around he sees, hears, tastes and manipulate greater number of things. The language is not so developed to name these objects or to make them the content of his linguistic expression. But the mind of the child now invariably finds development. The child obtains deeper and greater comprehension of the linguistic and non-verbal behaviour of adults. It means greater and more intense non-verbal involvement on the part of the child. These experiences which take place initially at the level of the *senses* continue feeling conceptual units to functions as the content of the child's *intellectual* experience (both together as essentially unified experiences we have been calling *cognition* so far as the human child is concerned). The language of the adults carries out the essential function of initiating the child's mind into the manifold features of experience with the child's world around. This must take place must earlier than the first unified utterance the child will be able to produce in his language. It is quite groundless on our part to consider that the silent child is not a thinking child, contrary to what all his behaviour manifests.

The second dimension of the child's wider experience is linguistic. We have said that the child's cognitive family finds proper development along with a level of comprehension that he achieves. This comprehension is not only intellectual but also linguistic. The entire range of *linguistic competence* (ch. 4) and levels of *performance* is founded on the level of comprehension that the child achieves. A measurement of the child's non-verbal and verbal behaviour will tell us the extant of comprehension that takes place in him. As the child's verbal and non-verbal experiences (linguistic and cognitive experiences) develop we find that he obtains better mastery of his language.

The third and the last dimension, we are concerned with, of the child's wider experience is *sociological*. Both understanding of the world around, and comprehension and production of language tremendously contribute to the process of socialization in the child. The child's *interpersonal communion* with the members of his society gets intense as he obtains greater command over his language and deeper understanding of what goes on around him. Cognitive development, linguistic development and socialization in the form of social interaction are things that have thus parallel development in the child.

## 4. The Child and Socialization

Childhood is the period when the person is initiated into society; he is expected to learn certain patterns of behaviour which are in consonance with the welfare of the community where the child grows up. The early childhood experience of man, as is well known have far-reaching influence on his personality. Psychoanalysts are of one mind in this regard. The early experiences of the child, as well, not only somewhat determine the psychological behaviour of man, but also determine the course of language learning that will take place. We are in a position to observe a number of factors that can influence the child's language acquisition:

(1) The most important factor that would influence the early part of language acquisition is the care and attention of the parents. This parental care-taking has its influence more than anything else in language acquisition. Families where the parents, especially when both the parents, are working and the care of the child is left in some disinterested hands it happens that the child is totally left on his own to pick up the early lessons of his language. It is groundless to claim that the early language development is quite on independent thing which will achieve maximum efficiency without proper parental attention. What is important is not any formal guidance or teaching of language by the parents, but the *presence* of the parents. We have all the while been talking about the *$L_1$ environment*. The greater and better this environment, the better the learning that will take

place. Parents undoubtedly, or anyone who will function so close to the childlike the parents only can provide such intense $L_1$ environment. A child left lonely at home may be in the company of a few other children, can hardly be expected to get familiar fast with the basic structures and lexis of the language. The formation of *competence* is bound to be slow and lingering under such circumstances.

(2) Secondly, the kind of environment that is avoidable to the child determines the kind of language he acquires. It depends in whose company the child spends most of his time. It may be parents, nurses, brothers and sisters, peer group or neighbours. Everyone of such company has some unique contribution to make towards the child's language acquisition. A contrast may be drawn for present purposes between two extreme cases where (i) the child grows up in the company and day in and day out presence of the mother and other family members (ii) the child grows up in the company of a nurse, who spends all his time in the company of dolls. These contrastive situation provides two extreme instances in which child (i) is favoured by the instance language atmosphere created by the mother, brothers and sisters, the kind of language that is ideal for the growing child for all his interpersonal communion; and child (ii) faces an unfavorable atmosphere where the language stimuli for his learning is the minimum alongwith the kind of neglect that is most unfitting for the child's overall development.

(3) Again, the socio-economic background of the family where the child grows up has significant influence on his language development. A child in a rich or socially upper-class family by contrast to one in a poor or lower-class family learns the language with considerable difference. This difference may be in terms of the content of the language, closeness of deviation from the standard dialect of the language, the basic vocabulary that form part of the standard usage, and in terms of accentuation and intonation that may differ according to social levels.

Language acquisition is a part of the child's overall growth, *maturation* and *development*. As such differences in the family environment and factors that affect the child's development are bound to influence his language development. Examining the two cases mentioned under item (2) we find that child (i) is a favoured one socially and linguistically. A better social atmosphere with greater interaction guarantee effective language learning, provided that the child is in no way deficient. The child's life in the family guarantee ample social transaction in terms of give and take, occasions to sacrifice and give way to others, feed-back from the rest of the family, care concern, and security from a wider circle of near and dear ones, and above all a wider range of personal communion that is most rewarding. The child learns to think, learns to speak and learns to live in society in a way that is expected of him. This childhood foundation in the development of his personality will have far-reaching influence on his later socio-communal adjustment. Language both contributes to and benefits considerably from the child's endeavour to achieve harmonious social adjustment.

In case of child (ii) we find quite an unwarranted situation for language development and overall personality development. The company that is made available to the child consists of toys and play things. It is a very peculiar situation that provides the minimum background for the learning of language. But as a human person he too is expected to learn language. The situation that the child (ii) faces may be called 'a social' as opposed to the thoroughly social situation which was available to child (i). The child, except when the nurse is present, has no one to talk to, nor has he any one to listen to . His language acquisition is greatly impeded by the fact that his social contacts are very limited. Such a child, it may be found, will have to depend on whatever he listens to, the very limited quantum of language that is available to him. For child (ii) the situation is characteristic in several ways: (a) linguistically deficient, (b) sociologically deficient, and (c) achieves very limited cognitive experiences for his personality development.

In fact, in the early phase of language acquisition language production is less important than *listening*. Listening to the native language is the principal activity which goes as the background for the formation of linguistic competence. There are several aspects to this listening activity which need to be considered here. The most essential condition for this listening experience is the sociological background which determines the child's contacts. The family, the peer groups in the neighborhood, and the visitors to the family etc. form the social units which contribute to the child's language environment. The greater the particular family's social contacts the better going to be the language environment available to the child.

The intensity of this environment, in turn will specify the amount of listening the child is able to have.

The sociological dimension of early language acquisition is also specified by the type of linguistic strata that the family belongs to. The language that forms the child's linguistic environment will determine the dialectic features of the child's language. This aspect is significant. This is what we have called earlier as the socio-economic background of the learner, on the one hand, and on the other the linguistic strata which the family belongs to in terms of the dialect which forms part of the language that the child acquires. If the child belongs to lower socio-economic level, it will invariably be that the child's language environment will contain, say, predominant slang usages. No doubt, the child's language environment is bound to be intense as he will a bound to be in the company of those of his social class, but the language that the child acquires will greatly deviate from the standard usage even, if it does not consist fully of any dialectical stratum.

By the age of four or five the child more or less frees himself from the intense and close parental care that he used to enjoy up to that age. This period, again, plays a significant role in the language development of the child. Up to this period, as we have seen, the child has been endowed with an environment that is cognitively, socially and linguistically favourable to the child's development. Now comes a time which would course considerable anxiety to the parents as the child is no longer confined to the exclusive care of the parents. He has now partially broken away from the parents supervision and moves in the company of the children of either his own age or of elderly ones in the neighbourhood. This course, infact, a change in all the three aspects of the child's environment mentioned above. The child now enjoys greater freedom outside home : freedom of speech, freedom of action and of observation. It means that there occurs a partial break with the past so far as his cognitive, sociological and linguistic experiences are concerned. He listens to the language of his own company much more than that of the member of his family. This brings a new linguistic dimension, along with it comes new words including slangs, dialectical words and new expression that he has had no occasion so far to listen to at home.

The shift of focus from the family to the neighborhood,

before it moves to the domain of the school, brings with it new problems of social adjustment. It is the time when the child experiences new needs and develops new attitudes and aptitudes in terms of life outside home. All this adds to the language development in terms of new words and new expressions expanding further the domain of the child's competence of language. This is the second phase in the child's encounter with the external world which formed the content of our discussion in the early sections of the present chapter. The encounter which begin with the image of the mother has now extended to the image of a portion of humanity which forms the child's neighbourhood. It is the same march of the individual from the self towards the vision of humanity.

## 5. Socialization and the Classroom

Family constitutes the first phase of the child's encounter with the external world, something which began with the infant's first encounter with the mother. The second phases of this encounter, we said, is the child's neighbourhood where there occurs a partial, but significant break with the child's past mode of social interaction and language acquisition. The third phase of the child's encounter with the world outside begins as he moves out to the world of *school*.

The there-fold experiences: *cognitive, linguistic* and *sociological* attain a new dimension in the classroom. The family is the symbol of parental attention, where the child is supposed to have most congenial atmosphere for his overall development. Home, for the child, is the citadel of security and affection where he had use first lessons in language acquisition. Home provided the necessary, free and intense atmosphere for the learning of a language which for him meant behaviour, communication, need-satisfying and adjustment. It was into a different and wider world that the child entered when he moved out to the neighborhood and obtained, as we have seen wider cognitive, linguistic and sociological experiences.

Home meant for the child the *least* of adjustment as he formed almost its centre all attention was directed to him. Home posed least challenges and problems for the growing child. The neighborhood, on the other hand, meant for the child *more* adjustment as it posed greater challenges and problems. In both the phases of development his language was fully at his disposed to transact with the people around. The expectations are limited; his achievements are not so much observed and measured as they would be done later. His behaviour both of home and in the neighbourhood did not have so much consequences at it would have later. No one measured his cognitive achievements and increase in knowledge; no one observed the pitfalls and drawbacks of his linguistic attainments; and no one noticed the implications of his social behaviour as much as all this would be done later.

Once the child joins school the encounters, the expectations, the achievements and their measurement, the significance of his behaviour, all this attain a new dimension. If family meant the *least*, and the neighborhood *more* adjustment, the classroom now means *most* adjustment of all kinds. For the first time the child has fully broken away from home and placed in a very new atmosphere. The classroom now poses new challenges and problems. Unlike the family the child does not have the near and dear ones near by to run to in times of problems and difficulties. It is a painful training towards independence and self-reliance as he is expected to more and more out of home and parental care.

What is more significant are the new expectations of the classroom which the child cannot afford to neglect. He is expected to behave in a set manner. The freedom of home and the neighborhood is expected now to have prepared the child for the restrictions that are part of this life in school. The classroom now means scheduled work, new cognitive experiences, increase in knowledge, obedience, attention, measurement of the child's performance and all that he has not experienced so much earlier. Above all, the classroom poses the new problem of adjustment. The child is no longer the centre of the new world, nor is he the centre of attractions. He has those around whom he does not like, and those whom he does not like, and those who does not like him; there are those who are more liked and appreciated; and there are those who command greater attention from the teacher and others. To the child it would all mean adjustment. He has now to learn how to get along better with others, to bear with the undesirable behaviour of his peer-group and to attach to his behaviour the kind of discipline and responsibility that have never been, perhaps, the case at home.

The ever wider social interaction and interpersonal communion that the classroom calls for, and the cognitive experiences that keep on adding to his mental development, adds a new dimension to what we have called the child's linguistic development. By the time the child is in school he has gone through two earlier language learning stages of home and the neighbourhood which have functioned as the citadels of $L_1$ learning. New once in school the language he has acquired forms the basis of all this adjustment. The language becomes his chief vehicle of expression and social interaction. His social adjustment to a great extent is directly proportionate to the command he has attained of his language.

Life in school adds a new dimension to his language learning. So far for his language meant exclusively behaviour, a communication and adjustment. His language could be hardly distinguished from these essential existential functions. But once in school language learning assumes a new role. Learning takes a new turn. The child is introduced into the more creative, artistic, aesthetic and intellectual aspects of language which hither to remained unknown to him. So far language was speech and communication for him; he was conversant only with the sonorous beauty of his language without being conscious of even that. Once in school he is introduced to the orthographic aspects with all its demands for specification, accuracy and control of muscles. So far, language offered for him no restrictions and constants other than what had naturally been part of the selective process he mastered as a learner of language. Now he is constantly corrected for his mistakes, and formally introduced to ever new aspects which are not always so interesting to him as those aspects of the language which he was highly motivated to learn at home.

Unlike the child's language learning experiences of home as part of his natural drive to equip himself in the process of development, he comes to experience a level of estrangement, inadequacy, artificiality and compulsion depending on the particular child's ability both to overall adjustment and in learning. This feeling of estrangement and inadequacy gets reflected in different stratum of pupils in different ways. The bright set of pupils who has not only a higher I.Q. but sufficient motivation and interest to learn overcomes the inadequacy caused by this shift from home to school with greater case and no conspicuous maladjustment as a result becomes observable in this sub-group. This set of pupils gets better adjusted than others of the lower strata of the class and the performance of this sub-group will mark significant achievement in terms of language learning.

Those who form part of the average set or sub-group of the class will have considerable problems, of adjustment and learning. The three fold requirements of cognitive, linguistic and sociological attainments as part of the child's overall classroom performance become tough on the average child. Again just as we should distinguish at least two groups among the bright learners (academically motivated and unmotivated), we shall distinguish two sections among the average learners : *motivated* and *unmotivated*. In other words, the motivated set of pupils (whatever be the motivating forces) from among the average learners, again find it easier than the latter set to find adjustment and respond to the classroom requirements. Just as the unmotivated lot among the bright learners, the unmotivated lot among the average learners do not exploit their natural talents and resources to find adjustment in the shift from home to school.

Lastly, we have the slow learner group which have peculiar problems of learning and adjustment. This group, again, can be distinguished under motivated and unmotivated learners. When slow learning is coupled with unmotivated attitude, the case becomes incorrigibility hopeless, especially the slow-learning is due to low I.Q. The performance of the motivated slow learner group can be considerably improved by means of remedial work. In other words, from the cognitive, linguistic and sociological viewpoints the learners that move out of the family atmosphere to the classroom can be divided into (i) motivated bright learners, (ii) unmotivated bright learners, (iii) motivated average learners, (iv) unmotivated average learners, (v) motivated show learners, and (vi) unmotivated slow learners. The achievement of every one of these sub-groups is characterised by the adjustment the members are able to make.

Language acquisition is a process that can not be isolated from the sociological development of the child. The child grows and matures; be learns how to achieve successful interpersonal communion in society; and parallel to all this he learns to employ his language most effectively in socio-communal situations. The acquisition of language that begins at *home* in the care of the parents in all freedom for self-expression takes a sharp turn as he moves out into the *neighbourhood* when the need for the self-expression of many of his kind collides wit his own need and the child is called on to greater adjustment. It is into a still different realm of language learning that the child moves out as he joins *school*. From the limited questions of adjustment in the neighborhood child is called on to greater adjustment against the needs of a large number of individuals like him. The individual learner is now in the third phase of his encounter with the external world with greater efficiency of language demanded of him for greater success in this encounter and in the subsequent process of adjustment.

# 7
# Bilingualism and Its Implications

## 1. The Bilingual Competence

Language learning and its production are so complex a phenomenon that a study of the same requires treatment of its various aspects. A broad distinction has been drawn between $L_1$ and $L_2$, in which $L_1$ represents one or more languages picked up by the child at the home environment, whereas $L_2$ stands for any language, foreign or regional, which the child is taught in the classroom. Again, clarifications are necessary in this regard. All variations of language are taught in schools: classical languages are taught in schools: classical languages, modern foreign languages and modern native regional languages; and the mother-tongue of the pupils. Of all these the present work includes under $L_2$, only those modern languages (not classical languages) which are taught in the classroom as foreign languages and as second or third language employing and foreign language teaching methodology. The distinction given above are necessary to have a proper understanding of bilingual situations.

*Bilingualism* is used in the present work as a state of having proficiency over more than one languages. Even though the prefix 'bi-' designates 'two', bilingualism as a technical term in linguistics is used in designating the ability to handle more than language. Whether the individual knows two languages or ten languages the fundamental bilingual phenomenon is the same. In India, especially, one often overhears a confusion between bilingualism and what is known as '*bilingual method*'. These two concepts may not be mixed up. Bilingualism, as we have examined, is knowing more than one language, and theoretically it consists in the study of the linguistic and psychological implications involved in knowing several languages. Bilingual method, as such, on the other hand, is a foreign language teaching methodology (which has not much to do with Bilingualism as a phenomenon); and it recommends the judicial use of the mother-tongue of pupils, and the most resourceful teaching device. This clarification is required as one tends to confuse both.

Bilingualism, theoretically, is an investigation into the linguistic and *psychological implications* of knowing many languages. We are here concerned with quite a few aspects of bilingualism:

(1) Bilingual competence has been a curious phenomenon for linguists and psychologists. Investigations have been undertaken as to what happens when a child learns several languages, and what the nature of the child's linguistic competence is.

(2) Bilingualism enquires into the bilingual *swapping process* in which an individual can without any hazards switch over from language to another amidst a conversation.

(3) What is the structure of the *bilingual skill* ? Language is not a set of abstract information; it is a set of skills with several practical implications. The bilingual skill consists of several bilingual compounds. A bilingual speaker manipulates language as he desires.

(4) Bilingualism has great *sociological implications*. It means all sorts conflicts in terms of social adjustment. To have mastery over a language means that individual somehow belongs to the community. Bilingualism, in other words, results in self-identity problems.

(5) It has been a very controversial point whether or not $L_1$ characteristics and habits *interfere* with the proper and efficient learning of $L_2$, and if there is such an interference to what extent can it be true?

(6) It is possible that a command over several language may mean

that one does not become as one's attention is scattered. It is investigated in bilingualism as to how far this may be true.

Investigations into problems such as above will highlight the features of bilingualism that make it different from being conversant with the $L_1$ only. Bilingual competence, above all, is a phenomenon curious enough for the psycholinguist to investigate. Linguistic competence is defined in terms of the linguistic systems, the syntactic structures, which the native speaker has internalized. (Ch.4) It is the particular language ability which a speakers intrinsically shares with other members of the linguistic community. The actual use of the language either in speech or in writing is designated by the term 'performance'. Performance springs from, and it is the expression of competence. Competence enables a speaker to produce the correct sentences, and only the correct sentences, of the language.

The fundamental question regarding bilingualism lies with *bilingual competence*. What is the nature of bilingual competence? There are several possibilities lying within the reach of our linguistic description. It is possible that a bilingual speaker internalizes and builds up the 'syntactic system of every separate language he masters. The ingenuity of his mind and neuromuscular system enables him to pick and choose among the systems of each language in times of need. It is also possible that the bilingual speaker's internalization process is based on a principle of differentiation wherein only the new elements, new aspects and specific structures alone will be acquired. In such a case the bilingual competence will consist of a bifurcated and branched structure. Elements that are common will form the trunk of the tree; elements which are specific to the particular languages will form the branches which are complex, manifold and varied. An understanding of the distinction between the *grammar*, *usage* and *use* of a language as explicated to Ch.12 will highlight the structure of bilingual competence as discussed in the present chapter.

## 2. Bilingual Swapping Process

Just as bilingual competence and its exact nature remains an open question bilingual swapping process is a phenomenon into which sufficient investigations have not been carried out. It is a characteristic thing that the bilingual speaker can at will shift from one language to another without any *repercussions.* The speaker who is conversant with only one language constructs correct sentences of the language at will. This process of *creative sentence production* by the speaker has already been described as performance. In transformational generation linguistic 'performance' is considered the result of a series of linguistic process is beginning with the semantic organization at the deep structure level, going through a number of mid-level transformations and ending at the surface-structure level, with the phonological component enabling the speaker to utter the sentences (Ch. 12).

If such may be the process underlying the production of the sentences underlying the production of the sentences of one language, are we to conclude that one and the same fundamental process can yield sentences belonging to different languages ? Or is it that there is always a deep structure surface structure relation through transformation behind the sentences of every language that the speaker employs ? Within the traditional universal theory of language, there is no such complexity arising out of language production because ultimately the switch over process happens only at a surface level and that too is through mere *translation.* Translation from one language to another enables the speaker to use several languages amidst a conversion. This explanation does away with several complexities arising from the bilingual swapping process.

At the same time, present day linguists do not believe in the universality of languages in the sense that all language possess one and the some set of basic structures. Languages reveal certain uniqueness with regard to their structural organization. The phonological, morphological and the syntactic components of languages are unique so much that each language has to be learned as a separate linguistic system except for a very basic set of elements (Ch. 12 for details). In this context, an explanation of *bilingual switch-over process* by means of translation is not satisfactory. If any one language requires a competence to enable the speaker to generate the sentences of the language, it logically follows that each unique language requires a competence of its own on the basis of which sentences in various language can be generated.

It is feasible, then, to believe that the bilingual speaker, on the one hand, builds up a *basic competence* which shares in linguistic aspects identical in all the languages he knows. A basic competence of this kind is rooted in a semantic system which, again, shares in the socio-cultural elements common to all his language. Here we hare undoubtedly greater *universality* than in any other component of languages. The basic competence, again, is bifurcated and branched into a specialized systems pertinent to each language at the speaker's disposal. By an act of the will, the speaker manipulates these specialized linguistic systems as part of his general linguistic competence, and due to the masterly hand he possess over the languages, it is possible for him to switch over from one language to another at the surface level of performance.

Bilingual swapping takes place at various levels. A bilingual speaker can involve in a conversation with several different monolinguals, meeting every one in his own grounds using his own language. The bilingual in such cases functions like a complex computer. Apart from speaking of different times in different languages, the bilingual can speak to another bilingual of his own kind and consecutively switch over to different languages. It is also possible for the bilingual speaker to switch over to different languages even in the midst of a sentence. Structurally, this process is the most complex wherein, despite the uniqueness of structures of different languages, the speaker not only employs different structural compounds, but also combines these components and make the sentence correct in accordance to the structural rules of the different languages employed for the purpose. In this manner the bilingual speaker possesses an illimited capacity to switch over among the languages he knows as the situation demands. The basic linguistic competence as well as the specialized competence of the language come into a variety of structural interplay in course of the bilingual swapping process.

## 3. The Structure of Bilingual Skills

The bilingual switch-over process is an indigenous factor which involves the bilingual skills. The monolingual listens, speaks, writes and reads. The psychological implications of these skills have already been examined under the structure of *communication*. Language as communication involves complex elements and processes. Communication has been seen as an *event*. The speaker with all his psycho-sociological background initiates communication;

the *message* bearing the *information-content* is the result of the process of encoding. The encoded message travels through the *channel* and is received by the listener. The listener is involved in a process of acceptance and rejection.

If such is the essential structure of communication, what happens when communication takes place in a bilingual setting? There is the speaker, on the one hand, equipped with the bilingual competence, i.e. knowing several languages, communicating to a listener or a group of listeners. It is possible that the listener or the listeners are bilinguals; or it may be that the listeners one monolinguals belonging to different linguistic groups. In all these contexts what happens essentially is a communication between two bilingual competencies; an exchange of information in different message-moulds. First of all there is the *bilingual encoding*; secondly, the *bilingual decoding* with which we are concerned directly, in psycholinguistics.

As we have examined earlier, an act of communication takes place in the direction of the listener. But a conversation is a communication-chain in which there is a constant shift in the speaker-listener roles. When the same thing is examined in the bilingual context, the process becomes all the more complex. Several bilingual possibilities are at hand: The bilingual speaker (x) initials the act of communication in language A; the listener (y) understands the language A, but cannot express himself in the same. Y therefore speaks (responds) in his own language B. X does understand but has no communication ability in language B. Consequently the particular conversation takes place between X and Y in two different language, A and B. Both the speakers are bilinguals, in a limited sense, so far as the two languages are concerned.

In another situation, we have at hand a bilingual speaker (A) who is conversant with four languages, speaking to a group of listeners among whom there is one 'lingua franca', the common language in which only comprehension is possible; each one has to take resort to his mother tongue to communicate. What happens here? The speaker (A), a bilingual speaks in the common language which is intelligible to all the listeners, while each one of the listeners respond and talk to the speaker (A) in his own tongue. On the one hand, there takes place a very complex decoding process in the speaker (A) since his organs of audition receive impressions of four languages, and on the other hand, the verbal stimuli which he as the listener receives do not form the linguistic grounds for his response. Instead of using the language of the speakers for his response, the speaker (A) has at once, to switch-over to the 'common language' for communicating to the listeners. In the listeners too there is no linguistic correspondence between the decoding and the encoding.

There is, again, a quite different situation in which two bilinguals are involved in a dialogue. Both are conversional with equal number of language and make use of quite a few of them, as it happens, when talking to each other. The speaker (A) uses a languages for the first few sentences to which the listener (B) responds in the same language. The speaker's next series of sentences, due to a variety of reasons, are made in another language. There occurs a bilingual shift and alongwith it a set of structural differentiations. The listener (B) replies, perhaps not in the same language, but in the one with which they started the dialogue. Again there is no correspondence between the audio-lingual stimuli and the verbal response by the listener, as both are in different languages, and consequently in different structural setting.

*Bilingual skill*, thus, is a complex phenomenon in which linguistic correspondence is often missing. The complexity of the speaking-listening behaviour and the processes of encoding and decoding involved therein are governed by the number of languages employed by the speakers. The entire thing could be compared to a mini-telephone exchange where a large number of connections need to made. The complexity in the brain is multiplied by the switch-over from encoding to decoding and vice-versa. Having listened to in one language the speaker chooses another language to speak in and having spoken in one language, at the next instance, the speaker has to listen to in another language. One may think of a situation when the same person, a bilingual, listens to a number of languages in which is friends speak to him. Against the background of a highly 'computerized' switch-over process, the individual listens and understands all that is spoken to him by several people in several languages all of which are known to him.

Bilingual skill is certainly a great linguistic gift to man. The monolingual communication process and its structure made complex many times more in bilingual communication. Information, in the present case, is transmitted not in a single message-mould, the language, but in several message-moulds. The question arise, then: is information which is the essence of an act of communication, affected in any significant manner? The most probable answer could be that the clarity and objectivity of information are governed by the speaker's and the listener's command over the languages used by them as bilinguals.

## 4. Sociological Implications of Bilingualism

More than anything else, bilingualism is a sociological factor with a number of psycholinguistic implications which reveal the personality structure of the bilingual. The linguistic aspects discussed above mostly concern the structure of the bilingual competence and skills. Under the sociological implications, we shall be considering several aspects of the bilingual's relation to and his interaction with society. The bilingual is placed in a characteristic social situation. The monolingual individual is very much a part of his society; he finds no difficulty in identifying himself with his community in normal circumstances. Language, as examined, is the principal factor which conjoins and keeps united the members of a community. Language for the monolingual means the only device to achieve maximum control over and benefit from his community. It is the chief medium to achieve satisfactory transaction with the community. It all simply means that the individual person's self identity, personality development and fulfillment, and a satisfactory career are chiefly governed by the language which connects him with his native community.

If language for the monolingual means social adjustment with the community, the bilingual finds himself in a peculiar linguistic predicament. His bilingual background poses several problems of adjustment. The most acute of all is the problem of self identity. Since language is almost identified with the speech-community, one who has the mastery of a language which is not native tongue, happens to be somehow identified with the community whose native language it is. The problem of identy crisis on the basis of language-community relationship is a phenomenon found today in all parts of the world as shifting communities one not uncommon anywhere today. In countries like India or the United Status of

America, where shifting communities are several, we find enough scope for investigations in regard to the problem of identity-arises. An American youth born to parents of German origin faces the problem of self-identify. There one three possibilities for communal identity: on the one hand, the young man may full at home with the German speaking English community or it is possible for him to feel at home with any English speaking community on the basis that he is an English speaking American. The third possibility is that he feels at home at both the levels. Both investigations have shown that it is quite unlikely that the individual feels himself to be part of both he communities definite preferences are likely.

Similar situations arise in India too. People move from state to another influenced by factors such as unemployment, and settle down in status other than their own. As a result a great number. of Indians suffer from the definite loss of self-identity. A Bengali gets settled in Gujarat; his son goes to school. The Bengali is married to a Marathi. The boy has picked up Bengali and Marathi from the parents; he has also learned Hindi partly from the family atmosphere and partly from the school. The has learned Gujarati from the neighborhood as well as from the friend-circle. Since the parents are well-versed in English, the boy picked up English even before going to school, and once in school his proficiency in English has improved. The boy mentioned above, now, is proficient in the use of five languages. It is a phenomenon not uncommon in India.

As a grown up man he begins facing certain problems which existed earlier but not so much haunted him. What is his native language: What is his $L_1$ ? Which speech community does he belong to ? All the languages mentioned above are learned by the boy before he joined school. As he is conversant with all the languages mentioned, he can possibly be a part of each community which predominantly uses the language. It is possible for him to feel one with each of these speech-communities. But, at the same time, as he is out of the regions where his parents' languages are spoken. To a great extent, consequently, the particular individual has a rootless existence, not really possible to identify himself fully with any community in terms of satisfactory adjustment.

So far as everything goes well, and no inter-communal problems arise, bilingual individuals do not feel the identity-problem severally. But, the moment things go wrong, and when any inter-communal problems arise, the bilingual's identity-crises will be the first outcome. In normal circumstances the bilingual presumably got along with the respective communities; now, in times of trouble he finds himself in difficulty at both the ends. He becomes the target of considerable suspicion; the respective communities find it deficient to put trust in the bilingual as he, on linguistic ground, belongs to each community. The identity of his trouble will depend on the depth of his involvement in the affairs of the respective communities. The greater the involvement in the life of one community, the greater the suspicion by the members of the opposite community.

At the same time, intelligent, creative and resourceful bilinguals will turn out to be the gems of society. Having been equipped with the bilingual ability, it is possible for these persons to top the resources of social situations and float in society. They will rise above communal and provincialistic attitudes and factions and feel one with the people whose language they have mastered. Having acquired the language of the community, such persons share a high level of intimacy with the people, which will not easily be destroyed by petty communal problems or prejudices. Thus the trust and confidence, and the intimacy the bilingual achieves through the command over several languages can very well be tapped for communal interactions and betterment of communal relations.

## 5. Bilingual Development in Children

It is possible for us to distinguish the development of the first language as well as that of the second language as separate phenomena. There are several characteristics which differentiate both the language acquisition process. But it is not an unusual thing for us to find, in a country such as India, children who grow up from the beginning as bilinguals. In the preceding pages we examined the case of an individual who had to pick up about five languages before the school-going age. Such cases are very usual in the present day shifting communities of India and other countries. Children of metropolitan as well as cosmopolitan cities find themselves in complex bilingual situations. A bilingual child of this kind is compelled to pick up two or three languages as $L_1$, and later in school he is required to learn an additional number of languages as $L_2$ (which the child learns through a foreign language teaching method).

The bilingual growth of the child is a complex process as the $L_1$ languages are acquired simultaneously. Let us examine such a complex case: Tom is child of five years of age; his father is from the Punjab, and his mother is Gujarati. Tom has a family in the neighborhood which speaks Bengali; he is constant visitor of the family and is a good friend of his father, Gujarati from the mother, and Bengali from the neighbours. In addition to these languages, Tom has had certain grounding in English and Hindi as the family used these languages for all their transaction with people outside and in entertaining their visitors at home. Now, the child knows English and Hindi in addition to Begali, Gujarati and Punjabi. As a child, Tom grew up in an atmosphere of five different languages, each for him functioned just as his mother-tongue. In the case of Tom, it is not one mother-tongue, but two: Punjabi and Gujarati. But the characteristic thing about Tom's Language learning process is that for him all the five language mentioned above functioned like the mother-tongue.

As a bilingual child, Tom learned all the languages in natural, informal, family atmosphere where he did not experience the persuasive, artificial and formal features of the classroom. It is under the constant care of several members of the community, not under any one teacher, that Tom learned his languages. He experienced no restrictions of time as is the case in the classroom; and no anxiety in regards to the learning devices. Tom did not have to pick up his languages from the highly restricted, graded and mostly inadequate language of the teacher; his material was the non-graded, usual and natural language store of the people around, which Tom listened and understood and attempted to speak. It was not the people who graded and controlled their language; it was Tom who received in a fully graded manner from all the language material he listened to, things which each phase of his language development required. The entire bilingual acquisition was governed by the principles of proximity, particularity, simplicity, concreteness and utility of the language material. It is governed by a process of self-selection and self-gradation, and 'listening' to only the selected features which are relevant to the child's needs, from all that he 'hears' all the while. The child's ears are open to the entire language of the adult; but his mind picks and chooses only what he is in need of.

The bilingual child, on the one hand is blessed with the feasibility to learn several languages at the same time; but he is faced with several problems which at times have jeopardizing effects. Faced with the need to pick up several languages at a time, the bilingual child is required to tap his entire intellectual, and creative resources. The early sentences of the bilingual child sound absolutely clumsy and confused. We find a sentence structured with words and word-elements from all the languages. It is interesting to examine some sentence of this kind:

1. Cow pullu Khaave Chhe. [1. Eng., 2. Malayalam, 3. and 4. Gujarati]
   1 2 3 4

   The cow is eating grass

2. Mama cooking khaana [1. Eng., 2. Eng., 3. Hindi/ Gujarati]
   1 2 3

   Mama is cooking the meal.

3. Kutro mesa ooper sleeping [1. Gujarati, 2. Malayalam, 3. Hindi, 4. English]
   1 2 3 4

   The dog is sleeping on the table.

4. Mari puppy eating bahu choru [1. Guj., 2. Eng., 3. Eng., 4. Guj., 5. Malayalam]
   1 2 3 4 5

5. Khana venda; chaaya bus [1. Hindi, 2. Malayalam, 3. Malayalam, 4. Gujarati]
   1 2 3 4

   I don't need food; I need only tea.

All the instances given above reveal several bilingual facts.

(1) The early sentences of the bilingual child are structured on the basic patterns of the language child knows best. Among the three or four languages, the child knows any one language better than others. It is this language which the child comes in touch with during the major part of the day. It is highly improbable to say that he knows all the languages to the same extent. One may pose a hierarchical structure for the systematics organization of the bilingual competence, which will be in harmony with the base and branching competencies we spoke of in earlier sections.

(2) Even though the structural patterns of the early period are based one or the other language, we find the child freely employing words from all the languages he is learning. Although the basic pattern belongs to one language or other, the child intermingles phrases and usages which belong to the other languages. This is perhaps the most interesting aspect of bilingual development, as well as the most apparent and interesting to observe. Such sentences look like a chain of intermingled beads of different colours. It takes time before he begins bifurcating and differentiating sentences according to the syntactic rules of the languages.

(3) At this stage, although the utterance consist of words from all the language, the phonological aspects i.e. the structural elements specific to the language are unique, as well as the words are structural mostly as per the morphological rules of the particular languages. Words with which the child is most familiar, which ever language they may belong to are used for purposes of communication until the child is able to distinguish the languages as they are.

(4) The bilingual child experiences all the languages which be learns as if part of one and the same language. The child thereby creates a language of his own for the purpose of meeting his linguistic needs. This is same phenomenon which occurs when linguistic communities get so much mingled up, with the result that a new language with elements from all the component languages gets structured in course of time. but in the bilingual child this 'eclectic mode' does not last longer than two or three years by the time he recognizes the languages as separate systems.

The requirement to cope with the demands of learning several languages somehow delays the acquisition process in comparison to a monolingual child who acquires greater mastery over his only language. But the bilingual child is soon in a position to make up for the delay caused by the presence of many languages. Depending on the intensity of acquaintance with the particular languages, the bilingual child boosts up in the language acquisition process. It may be that the bilingual acquires an unusual acuteness and sharpness of learning as a result of his acquaintance with several languages. In the long run bilingualism seems to turn out to be a blessing than otherwise.

# 8
# Language and the Brain

## 1. Language and Biolinguistics

It is a question asked from very ancient times whether the human brain is the ultimate source of language. What is the fundamental relation between language and the brain? Is the brain an end itself in terms of cognitive function, or is it only the substratum of a unified cognitive function in man? Is language activity 'localized' in the brain in terms of specific areas of the brain? What is the nature of the biological dependence of language? There are fundamental questions of this kind which have lead to several controversies in regard to the relation between language and the human brain.

Man is a biological entity; he forms part of the animal kingdom but be virtue of a set of very definable qualities he is considered different from all other species that form part of the infra-human animal kingdom. Man has inherited as part of the genealogical tree of evolution a neurological structure, the *nervous system*, of which the *brain* forms the apex. The brain, as we know, is the most complex single structure in the human body. From very ancient times men knew that the brain has been the seat of or the control station of all activities in man. This knowledge dawned on them chiefly because a damage which any other part of the body was subject to caused partial harm to the functioning of the body while a damage which the brain was subject to was fatal to the body. A damage to the brain would leave man unconscious or drive him insame: a minor damage of any kind would have detrimental effects on the functioning of the body.

For these reasons, the brain was always held to be the centre of the physiological functioning of the body. All the same, something more significant was observed: a damage to the brain would mean, immediate effects on the functioning of the mind, as of the human *mind* is at once related to, subject to, or dependent on the human *brain*. A man with a damage brain would invariably produce disconnected, broken and perhaps illogical language depending on the extent of the damage; an insane man would produce language that has no immediate relevance to the concrete circumstances around, however connected and grammatically, correct sentences he may make. In other words, the *brain*, the *mind* and *language* activity were at once connected and cause-effect relation and established among the three factors.

Despite the above insights from conventional observation, great controversies arose as to the relation between the brain and the mind and the brain and language. We find three distinct schools of thought prevalent from ancient times in regard to the relation between the brain, the mind and language, each posing a view that has relative basis on human experience, hence their relevances even in present-day thinking. These schools of thought are *rationalism* which exclusively stressed the role of the mind, *Materialism* which exclusively stressed the role of the brain, and *Realism* which held the common and moderate position that the Brian and only the 'functional substratum of the human mind which in its activity was capable of rising far above the realm of the physical brian.

In present-day sciences we find the counterparts of the ancient schools of thought in a variety of ways, but these may be classed together *behaviourism* which more or less follows the paths of early materialism in exclusively stressing the role of the brain as the source of the psyche, the 'mind', and mentalism which stresses the active role of the human mind as the substantial principle of all human behaviour. Both *cognitivism* in psychology, and *Transformationalism* in linguistics have adhered to the mentalist principles in stressing the active, substantial role of the human mind, and its priority over the physical brain. But the second half of twentieth century has witnessed the development of a whole school of thought in linguistic, more or less confined to a widely distributed group of physiologists and brain specialists who believe that the human neurological structure, the nervous system with the brain as its centre is the exclusive seat of all language activity in man. This school of thought is known as *biolinguistics*.

Biolinguistics, developing quite independent of other areas in the linguistic science considers language a purely biological activity depriving language of all its noble and artistic values which have been traditionally attached to the functioning of the mind. Biolinguists do not deny that there is a mind as the principle of human activity, just as the behaviorists do not deny the role of the mind. But for both the mind is not as substantial principle as traditionally held by realists, but a mere product of the biological brain as the ultimate principle of all human activity. Biolinguistics lays stress on the neurological structure of man. Man is a product of the evolutionary neurological phenomenon. Neurological evolution had been heading towards man who was endowed with a magnificently complex neural structure with the brain as its centre. What the biolinguists do now is to go back to the brain to find answers to every question related to language.

In biolinguistics are find a fresh interest in the biological substratum of language. This interest chiefly sprang from the neuro-surgeons preoccupation with the structure of the brain in order to discover especially the localized centres of languages activity. Research into cases of Brian damage seems to point out that language is a neurally localized activity. Experimentation with the brain centres of chimpanzees and other animals have shown that certain specific areas of the brain are one way or other at once related to the comprehension and production of some level of symbolic activity. Most of the neurologists' conclusions on the functioning of language and its nature are based exclusively on their research into the brain structures of animals and abnormal or damaged human brains.

*Apparently* the brain alone seems to satisfy all the queries on human behaviour, especially on language proper. For biolinguistics everything is a process of manufacturing. The human language is manufactured at a variety of levels. The most fundamental activity is the process of *cerebration*, a cerebral activity by means of which the content of communication, namely, the semantic component of language is organized. The cerebration is further capable of ordering the semantic units into patterns that are required by the syntax of the language. The final stage of language production takes place through what the biolinguists call *phonation*. Phonation as a surface process conjoin the semantic content to the phenological units of language, this, producing what the listener hears, namely, the utterance. What is central to biolinguistics, thus, is the process of cerebration. The traditional mental and conceptual dimension of language is substituted by the cerebral and sign of dimensions.

## 2. Neurological Substratum of Language

What has so far been happening is a malady basic to human nature. An exclusive preoccupation with and a full-fledged specialization in any aspect of human knowledge ends up usually in prejudices and one-sided judgements on many vital issues on human life. It is such exclusive diametrically opposed to the fundamental and key beliefs and convictions of common man, the find of convictions which have sound theoretical bases.

The development of biolinguistics, especially in regard to its exclusive preoccupation with the neurological structure of man as the only substratum of language is an instance of this kind. Certainly, theoreticians have every freedom to follow their own course of thinking and research; all the same, their conclusions, should not as much as possible contradict the sound convictions of the common man. Language, as we have been pursuing the matter, is a very complex phenomenon to make inquiries into; this complexity has greatly contributed to divergence of conclusions reached in regard to the nature of language.

No doubt that the brain is apparently the centre and the source of all human behaviour, consequently of language as such. It is the control station of all activities that take place in the human body as well as all that man does as part of his extrinsic behaviour. The human body, itself a profoundly organized structure, is governed by its apex portion, the brain in a manner that more or less remains a puzzle even to present-day neurologists in terms of its unified activity. No wonder that neural specialists and a portion of the humanity are led to the belief that the brain, the neural structure, is all that there is ! A drunkard shows signs of a fully disorganized psychic system just because the linger he took has affected the working of the brain. A serious damage caused to the brain drives a man insigne showing signs to disorganized psychic system. A damage to the brain, as we have seen, leaves a man unconscious that equals the state of death when the total *absence* of the mind as the principle of activity is felt. More than anything else is important the fact that any serious damage to the brain causes serious *language deficiency* leaving the individual mute or partially devoid of his language ability.

These are facts that have down the centuries led even theoretician to conclude that the brain with its neurological structure is all that is there is man: the brain makes man what he is, and a damage to it renders man infra-human. These conclusions on the biologic grounds are certainly baseless. We have absolutely no reason to deny on the grounds of what we have seen, that there is in man no principle (faculty) that supersedes the biological Brian. One cannot go very far to agree with the sound convictions of the common man if one is not ready to believe what we do not perceive with the naked eye. It is not relevant at all for present purposes to enquire into this aspect of human attitudes. But one thing is certain that I walk straight into any habit and order a meal without even the least doubt that the food which will be saved may be poisoned. This is the simple faith of the common man based on his ordinary experience. It is not required to evoke the laws of logic to prove this single faith of the commonman. The most orthodox of empiricists doesn't care to sit down and test of his food in front is poisoned or not. Man's sheer common sense often contributes infinitely more than what the best of experiments cannot. This doesn't mean that we shall not move by empirical tests and experiments. What is important is that there *can be* a domain beyond the exclusive preoccupations we may have, a domain which we are either afraid or haven't cared to explore.

The brain and the nervous system are at best the *biological substratum* of man's language activity just as it is the biological substratum of all of man's cognitive behaviour. It is true that all we know of the world around (our cognitive experiences) and about our own body is the result of, say, the decoding function of the brain of messages carried to it from what are called *receptors* by sense impulses traveling through *nerve fibres.* Sensory stimuli one the starting point i.e. the messages which the brain receives are initiated by sensory stimuli such as light waves, vibrations of air, mechanical pleasure of varying type on the skin and other influences of the environment. The nerve fibres convert the externally affected stimuli into the kind of *energy* which can be borne to the brain centres. An impulse from a visual receptor is said always to be conveyed to a particular point in the *cerebral cortex* which is the enter surface of the cerebrum. The cerebral cortex *receives* messages from the sensory, brain centres related to the receptors, *sends* messages to the effectors under its control, *retains* the remnants of the past activity, and *integrates* incoming and outgoing impulses. These are the *associative* functions of the cerebral cortex.

Similarly an impulse from an auditory receptor is received by a different point in the cerebral context. The brain, considered as a whole, decodes the message in terms of the point activated by the stimuli. It would mean that impulses originating in the eyes as visual receptors will be decoded as *sensory information* about the visual qualities of an object, and impulses originating in the ears will be decoded as *auditory information* related to sound qualities. The combination of a. variety of these bring parallel sensory-auditory information of a detailed kind.

The enclosing of sensory, stimulation takes place in terms of the *frequency* and *number* of nerve impulses aroused by the extrinsic agent acting on these receptors. As a result of the responses of the brain as the central decoding-encoding mechanism, we become aware of factors such as brightness, colour, loudness noise, pressure and softness of touch. Messages from rectors are carried to the brain, as well as impulses from the brain are brought to the muscles and glands for bodily reaction and movement, by *nerve fibres*. The vehicles which in fact bear the messages are the *neurons* which are the key functionaries of the nervous system. A nerve, as we call it is a bundle of nerve fibres which bear the neurons up and down.

The central nervous system, as we know consists of the spinal cord and the brain. Although both one conducting and integrating mechanisms, most complex activities take place in the brain. The major divisions of the brain one the *brain stem*, the *cerebellum* and the cerebrum. The outer surface of the *cerebrum* is the *cerebral cortex*. All impulses travelling between the spinal cord and the cerebral cortex run through the brain stem. The cerebellum is the co-ordinating mechanism of the brain. It co-ordinates all reflex activities in the human body. Each of the cerebral hemispheres contain four lobs which one particularly meant to decode messages from receptors.

What we have seen above, in short, is the biological brain, and its functions and sketched in gist. It is true that the brain carries out a magnificently complex function of co-ordinating and integrating all activities in man. The brain receives stimuli from the external world, and from the parts of the body, processes the messages carried to it and responds adequately. In other words the brain is at once related to the world of the senses. The sense of sight, hearing, taste, smell and tough one supposed to be the doors of man's *cognitive faculty* to the world outside. Impulses of all kinds affects these sense, they are (as we have seen above) carried to the brain and two distinct things happen as a result: (a) man *knows* and gathers information in adding to his knowledge, and (b) man *acts*, namely, he reacts to the impulses that he receives in the brain. Human language functions chiefly as a vehicle for communication, thus, of two kinds : *intentional* and *informational*. Man speaks to let others know something, to want others to do something. Language activity in its normal functioning terminates either in terms of some intention or some information.

The senses, thus, are the doors of human knowledge, of which the brain is the *co-ordinating substratum*. This does not in any way lead us to the statement that there is no other ultimate principle at work in man. What keeps this brain itself alive and makes it worthwhile in all its activity? This would lead us to things that be outside the scope of the present work; but one cannot be blind to such problems as these just because we cannot answer them on the basis of our knowledge of the brain of the kind of human behavior that the empiricist psychologist studies.

Human activities are not limited to the activities of the sense of the man. The senses, namely, man's sense experiences are certainly the *starting point* of all human knowledge nothing enters into the human mind, which has not in some way passed through the sense. The sense are our liaison agents with the rest of the world. The human being's first contact with the world outside we have explained in terms of the infant's *first encounter* with his mother (See ch. 2 sec. 3.). Perhaps, the first imagination is the mother's and the first concept to pass on to the infant's mind is related to man.

If sense experiences are only the starting point of all human knowledge, it would mean that the brain which is the central co-ordinating mechanism of sense experiences is a mere *foundation* (substratum) of human activity. Just as a building would not stand without its foundation, all human experiences, however abstract, would require this foundation, the brain. The building, however high would collapse if the foundation is damaged; human experiences, however sublime they may be, would not stand without the brain. No sensible man, however, building is nothing other than the foundation on which it stands. There is the human mind, whatever it may be, of which the brain in all its super complexity is the biological foundation.

## 3. Biological Independence of language

The senses, as we have been examining, is the inlets of all impulses from the outer world entering human body. The senses, in other words, are the liaison agents between man's world of cognition and the material world outside. The brain is the *central co-ordinating mechanism* of human sense experiences. We have also said that there is nothing in the cognitive faculty of man which has not initially gone in through one or other senses. What would this mean?

This would mean many things which will highlight the nature of man's cognitive functions. In man cognitive activity does not delimit itself to sense experiences as in infra-human animals. Man's cognition has a realm that is higher than sense experiences. We call it human *thought*. As we shall examine in detail in Chapter 10, there is an intricate relation between human thinking and sense experiences. What demarcation shall we draw between sense experience and abstract thinking ? At what level of experience do we enter into abstract thinking? There are very delicate issues for which answers have often been attempted.

Man's concrete experiences with the material world of *touch*, *colour*, *sound* and *taste* and *smell* are the feeding ground of all basic *conceptual units* form the content of his thinking. This experience with the world of matter around begins very early in the child's life, namely, when the child is in a position to recognize things around, interact with them in same manner, and make them objects of his cognitive experience. With this interaction of same kind with the material world begins the human person's thinking process depending on the extent of concepts that the person acquires.

In other words, man's sense experiences are only one level of human cognition. Cognition in man is an inter-wound phenomenon of sense and intellectual activities. Sense experiences form the bases of this cognitive experience, and the experiences of thought which man perceives as something abstract are built on sense experiences. This would mean that the abstract intellection or thought which none of us can possibly deny, forms the major bulk of human cognition. Man *sees* a new object which he has not hitherto seen; the sense provide for his intellection material for *knowing* the object in terms of colour, sound smell or whatever might reveal the nature of the object. An interplay of all these aspects of his sense experience with the object helps him *know* the nature of the object. This knowledge of the nature of the object puts the individual's cognition already at the level of intellection. Now the man *knows* what the object is. No more new sense impulses the man receives, suppose, after this knowledge. The man's experience with the object has now added a concept to the content of his mind In terms of a set of conceptual elements with which the has been familiar, yet reorganized to form the new concept which we may call a *meaning*. While the concept is related to the essential nature of the thing, the conceptual elements are provided by the qualitative and quantitative components of the object such as, say, the object is white, heavy, large, rough, moving etc.

What is significant is that the man's senses, suppose, no longer contribute to a better understanding of the object under consideration. The man now stands and *thinks*. His new knowledge mores his thought; with his eyes shut he is now able to understand the object, relating it to his similar experiences of the past, or by tallying the new knowledge with what he already know as an experienced man. In other words, the man now has entered with which the senses at once has nothing to do. He walks home; he is, say, absent-minded,; his *mind is occupied* with the thoughts related to the object he has just seen.

Then, there is the *imagination* and its content, the images. In the instance we examined above, the new object the man sees with all the detailed visual and auditory aspects at once feeds into his imagination an image of the object. This image, depending on the nature of the impulses, may be visual, auditory, lactile and so on. It is after the formation of this image of the new object that the man's intellect receives the new concept as a result of the intellectual perception. While walking back home, the man's mind has a parallel preoccupation in regard to the understanding of the object : on the one hand, his intellect is busy interacting with and integrating the concepts related to the object, and on the other, as an accompanying process, the imagination as part of the human mind, is busy co-ordinating the images and helping the intellect in its attempts to understand the object better.

For biolinguists all these and other activities of the human 'mind' are nothing more than a 'higher level' of activity by the brain. But the grounds on which this can be verified are practically none. The brain provides enough explanation for the lower sense experiences of man which are the starting point and feeding ground of the activities of the mind. If we assign to this biological mechanism a role which is too scoring, abstract, aesthetic, philosophical, scientific, poetic and mystical, well it is stretching the capacities of the brain too far and devastating the dignity of man as man.

If the relation between the brain and the mind is such, what is the role of language in this context? The links are already clear. We have now been above to assign the roles of (a) *the sense receptors*, (b) *the brain*, (c) the *intellect*, (d) the *imagination*, (e) *concepts*, and (f) *images*. The sense experiences and intellection together we have called (g) *cognition*. Concepts feed the intellect and images feed the imagination, both posed here as the twin-faculties of (h) the *mind*. The demarcation between sense experience and intellection too delicate to receive treatment in a work as this.

This exactly is the process that takes place in the infant's very first cognitive experience (Ch. 7, Sec. 3) which we noted as the human person's first *encounter* with the external world. There occurs an initial development in the infant's cognitive experiences in terms of the infants interpersonal communion and interaction with the people and things around respectively. We have noted in Chapter 7 that comprehension of language precedes any production at whatever stage it takes place. The infant's sense experience with the mother and things around is the starting point. The infant on the basis of this sense experience begins at a given stage a level of intellectual perception of the mother and things around. After these initial cognitive experiences the child comes to a stage, say by the age of five months, when he understands the languages of the mother (however rudimentary this understanding may be). It is around the age of five months that the child begins showing some signs of actual intellectual perception. (The author has recorded quite a number of systematic observations which are too elaborate to be included here).

The very first utterance of the child which can truly be called linguistic marks a significant shift in the child's cognition. This first utterance, say mama, a verbal act which should be the product of the child's intellectual perception of the mother, marks the child's entry into the world of *symbolic behaviour*. What is this first utterance ? What is its significance ? It points out a level of cerebral, sense, intellectual and imaginative *maturity*, apart from the maturity that the vocal and auditory organs of the child have reached. The first utterance is the product of, thus, an all-round maturity and development. The child has *obtained* a verbal (linguistic) counterpart (or symbol) for the content of his cognition. The content of the child's cognition is the concept or set of concepts related to his experience with the *mother*. The child due to his past seven or eight months of acquaintance with the language of the adults has now come out with a verbal symbol for the set of the concepts that has become content of his cognition related the mother.

This verbal symbol which the child is using to designate the mother (and representing the concept we have talked about) is a *linguistic unit*. Thus 'mama' has become the first unit of the child's language experience. It is the first symbol, for instance, that the child in fact makes use of to designate his mental content. Thus we have three related and significant units : the *mother*, the set of *concepts*, and the *linguistic unit* of 'mama'. It must be remembered that human language is essentially an interplay, the product of these triple aspects of reality: the *object*, the *concept*, and the *word*.

The neurological mechanism with the brain as its centre functions exclusively as the *biological substratum* of language. Language, thus, has a level of *biological dependence*. But this dependence is not the whole of language. Just as human cognitive experiences have the brain as the foundation, human language experiences (i.e. has verbal behaviour) the brain as its foundation without which no man will ever speak a language. The vocal mechanisms the associative components of this biological foundation, language, thus has this essential biological foundation, but language like cognition sores infinitely higher than this foundation.

## 4. The Brain and Sense Experiences

Reality has always been seen dawn the ages as hierarchical and as consisting of levels of existence and experience. This consideration is not based on mere logical propositions, but on what reality at different levels *reveals* to be and observed by man as relatively *objective*, despite occasional illusions be experiences. (The earth and the sun one objective realities, but the human experience of the sun moving from east to west, thought perceived by the sense, is an illusion.)

At the lowest level at reality, as we experience it, and at the base of this hierarchical order is the *physical world* which is inanimate. In the biological sense of the term, we say, the inanimate world has no life (we are not concerned here about the philosophical problem of a level of 'consciousness' in the material things). Inanimate objects do not show any signs of life such as auto-motion, the need for food, reproduction and growth. This lowest level of reality which includes everything inanimate in this universe does not possess the ability to communicate in same manner or other. In other words the inanimate world entertains neither vegetation nor any form of cogitation. Except its existence and tailored motion and interaction the inanimate reality shows no sign of cognition at all.

The second level of reality consists of those things around us which manifest a higher form of existence. We call this level of reality *vegetation*. Vegetation would include things from, the tallest trees and the so-called 'sensitive plants' down to the infinitesimally small bacteria all of which manifest more or less identical characteristics of existence. Vegetation shares all the characteristics of the physical reality and on their foundation are built all that is specific to itself. It would be very significant to say that vegetation is not 'different from' but 'more than' the physical world which is inanimate. We call vegetation *animate* rather than inanimate. Plants grow, take food, reproduce you ones, and they have their own circulatory, respiratory and excretory functions. The cognitive functions of vegetation (plants) are rather controversial as this level forms the mediation between the inanimate world and the higher level of animals. Except the proofs for which 'sensitive plants' (e.g. carnivorous) plants are often cited, there are absolutely no signs which tell us that plants have any sense experience. Lastly, plans show no signs of possessing any communicative ability which is the product of some level of cognition. Plants, thus, form the second higher level in the order of reality.

The third level consists of *infra-human animals* which are endowed with *sensitivity*. Again just as plants shared the existential qualities of its lowed level, animals shares the qualities of plants as same kind of an 'existential continuum' and on its basis are built the characteristics which are specific to the animal world. Unlike the plants which do not entertain auto-motion, animals do possess the ability to move around. We say the movement of animals is auto-motion or *self-propelled*. Animals have digestive, respiratory, circulatory, excretory nervous and reproductive functions in a way analogous to those possessed by plants and befitting a higher order of existence and life.

The most significant quality which animals possess is their *sensitivity*, namely, the *sense experiences* which they are capable of. It is perhaps the most significant endowment in the rung of evolution. Animals show very clear signs for their ability to feel and sense things. What is characteristic to sensitivity is that sensitivity is directly proportionate to the quality of the *brain*. Sensitivity is at once related to the presence of a brain and a corresponding nervous systems. The entire animal kingdom with its unicellular (protozoa) and multicellular (metazoa) animals, ranging from the minutest amoeba to the largest animals, possesses what we may call an analogous ability to *sense* things around. This sensitive ability increases in animals, except for the fact that certain lower animals do possess what is known as 'specialized sensitivity' of same organs or other such as the special capacity of dogs to smell things out.

The unicellular animals like the amoeba has no specialized sense *receptor*, but, they are sensitive to a variety of stimuli. It can distinguish between food material and any other matter in water. We may say that the amoeba senses food from some distance. Although in such unicellular animals the function of 'sensing' forms part of the general 'metabolism' of the animals, as we go higher up we find that animals so still higher grade such as flat worms (phylum platyhelminths) and round worms (phylum nematode) do possess some rudimentary *brain* structure and corresponding nervous system.

In the animals, thus, the brain controls the activities of the various parts of the body on the one hand, and on the other the interaction of the animal with its environment are controlled and co-ordinated by the *nervous systems.* This system as we have seen in earliest sections consists of numerous specialized calls called the nerve cells or neurons. This nervous system consists of (b) the peripheral nervous system and (c) automatic nervous, system. The *brain* and the *spinal cord* form the central nervous system. The *sense organs* are receptor organs of the body which backed by the nervous system receives impulses from the outside world. Each receptor is specialized for the reception of a particular kind of stimulus. Animals have *organic sensitivity* which is associated with the functioning of the internal organs, paints, tensions, sex etc. What is interesting to not that cognition in infra-human animals is restrict to and solely controlled by the structure of the nervous system as we have in short examined above. Right from the lowest of animals up to the chimpanzees (in which we find the most advanced kind of behaviour) the sense are co-ordinated by the brain, and the senses function as the liaison agents with the world outside. Attempts are made to know the limits of animals cognition; animals like the chimpanzee are made to learn and develop certain habits that are specific to man (say, 'riding' a motorcycle). Apart from such attempts to develop a given habit in them, we know that left themselves animals do not at all manifest any behaviour more advanced than this stereotyped and biologically set patterns of behavior which are determined by their species. If ants or honey-bees are said to reveal a level of 'social life', what interests us is the fact that they have retained this 'social behavior, in a given, stereotyped manner so long as man has been observing them. No one has ever reported same level of *progress* or advancement in the behaviour of these creatures for this reason chiefly we say that any forms of such ' advanced' behaviour in infra-human animals is merely a specific type, namely, *determined* so by the species itself.

It is within the strict domain of sensitivity or rather *sensitive cognition* that any animals shows the kind of behaviour which may seem to be the result of personal understanding or personal involvement. One may not be misled by this superficial aspects of animal behaviour such as the affection a dog shows for the master. We saw that the physical reality and vegetation do not entertain any form of communication whatever. As we examine animals we fund that *communication* of some kind and expression of feelings are essentially related to sensitive cognition. Communication ability in its formal sense in fact begins with animals. Again, we find that as the structure of the brain becomes more complex, the nature of communication differs and the ability for it increases.

By communication we mean, in this context, any self-stimulated interaction between organisms. It takes place whenever the behaviour of an organism acts as stimulus for and affects the behaviour of another. The very essence of communication would mean that the behaviour of one organism acts as a stimulus for the behaviour of another. In lowed animals communication involves nothing more than the stimulation of one animal by another in such a way as to enables the second to produce some similar response. However elementary or rudimentary such behaviour may be, we do find animals interacting in large scale in terms of mutual stimulation for a variety of purposes. When such stimulation involves some sounds, it is normally called 'animal language'. But as we shall take note of in our further discussion or even as earlier sections do make it clear, the term 'language' cannot be applied to any verbal form of animal communication.

Animal communication, as we shall rightly call it, involves purely the activity of the five senses with which the animals we endowed. It is a sense-level behaviour which arouses similar sense-level behaviour in the recipient. The mewing of a cat, the roar of a lion, the crocking of a frog, chirping of sparrows, and the chattering of monkeys do arouse similar response in the members of their own species either in terms of approval or disapproval of some behaviour or incident in which they are involved. At higher levels animal sounds have a signalling function, say, as warnings of dangers, or cry for help etc. We shall mainly speak of 'animal cries' rather than 'animal language' as language is purely the accomplishment of man.

The neurological structure i.e. the brain and the nervous

system enables animals to have *sensitive-cognition* or what we have called sense experiences. But it stops with that. The associative, integrative, and communicational functions of animal sensitivity (of animal cognition) are very limited except whatever is required for the biological functions and survival of animals. No aesthetic, artistic, or any higher manifestations are observed as the product of animal cognition. Animals possess consciousness; they emit behavior; they are able to imitate man and learn things. But they are endowed with no power to *think* and *make decisions*.

## 5. The Senses and Symbolic Behaviour

The first level of reality consists, we said, of the *inanimate* world with no sensitivity; the second consists of *vegetation*, a higher form endowed with life but again so sensitivity; and the third level consists of infra-human animals endowed with life and *sensitivity*. As we come to man there is still the fundamental existential continuity, but we find a great departure from what has been seen up to the level of animals. In man we have the fourth and the highest level of reality susceptible to human experience in this universe. In man we have, in other words the highest form of life in the universe endowed with not only life and sensitivity but also a very superior form of cognition, the *mind*. Man as a part of the universe is rooted in its very lecture. He shares as the very foundation the characteristics of the inanimate world (his body is a complex built-up of manifold elements); he shares the characteristics of vegetative life (say, growth, reproduction etc.); and he further shares the properties of the world of animals in terms of sensitivity life.

As part of the what man shares with the rest of the animal world he possesses a *nervous system* and the *brain*. Now the question is whether man is to be considered just another sensitive animal because he too possesses a brain. Following the same argument, if rightly so, the animal must be considered as merely anther plant because animals possess vegetative functions just as plants do; or plants must be thought of as another form of stones because plants are composed of the same properties as stones. The question whether man is different from any other animal is not even worth considering for reasons that man clearly reveals the kind of behaviour that makes his nature stand out clearly.

There are all sorts of clues to the characteristic nature of human cognition and to the mind which is the seat of these cognitive experiences. Even though all of man activities reveal his capacity to think, imagine and make decisions, the biggest clue lies in human language. What is man's language? The answer to this we have been examining throughout, and it remains our concern throughout. What is most characteristic to language is its *symbolic nature*. Language is essentially symbolic. Symbolic behaviour is something remotely bound with sensitivity and it reaches its perfection in the rational behaviour of man. We have already noted in the preceding section that animals with their sensitive endowment are capable of some level of symbolic behaviour. Animals do communication among themselves; this communication is often attained by means of rudimentary symbolic behaviour. Certain animal postures and animal cries (observed clearly in birds) function as the media to communicate certain information related to the presence of food danger etc. These are rudimentary in the sense that such behaviour is absolutely limited to that particular species; the patterns of such behaviour are stereotyped with no change ever observed; never has any 'progress' been noted in such behaviour of animals and birds. Yet the symbolic nature of any such behaviour stands, and we are able to say that animals to involve in some symbolic behaviour with its deep roots in the species.

If sensitive life and symbolic behaviour are so related, and as a result in sensitive behaviour something corresponding to 'language' is present, then symbolic behaviour assumes perfection in human behaviour. Man is capable of involving himself in very complex form of symbolic behaviour. Such complex symbolic behaviour is the principal key to the fact that man possesses a form of life which is incomparably higher than the sheer sensitive life of animals. Man is able to produce two forms of symbolic behaviour: (1) *non verbal behaviour* and (2) *verbal behaviour*. We are capable of producing a large variety of non verbal patterns of behaviour. In all these patterns the fundamental factor is that same *meaning is conveyed* by means of some conventionally understood from of behaviour such as gesticulation. These non verbal forms of communication we culturally significant. For this reason we call it conventional i.e. agreed upon and recognized by the relevant community. In non-verbal communication (behaviour with a mind to communicate certain ideas) no words are used; or it may be that minimum words are employed which accompany non-verbal behavior. Non-verbal communication is often subtle, informationally effective and prevalent in many communities either formally as part of the community's used by individuals in times of a specific need.

The conventional *gestures* which form part of every society's behaviour are an important form of Non-verbal communicative behaviour. Gestures are easy, quick and efficient manner of conveying some important information which, as it happens, one wants to hide from the rest. Gestures which are so often used consist of head-nodding, head-shaking, the use of figures for a variety of semantic purposes, and facial expressions such as the use of the eyes and the lips, again, for a variety of communicative purposes. Gestures, thus can convey meanings which a series of utterances only will otherwise convey.

Non-verbal communication includes also a variety of signalling systems used especially as part of the training, say, for the scouts. These are very systematic ways of conveying messages across distant places, especially by means of *flags*. Those who are trained in the signalling system, understands the message at once even at a great visible distance. Again there is the use of smoke which the Red Indians are known for. This is also use of by scouts. A particular way smoke columns are sent up convey some specific meaning. All these are varieties of non-verbal communicative behaviour which man is capable of. All the non-verbal behaviour which we have considered above have one specific feature, namely, all of them function in one way or other as a *signal*. The word signal has a more elementary meaning than the word *symbol*. A red light at the railway station is just a signal which represents the concept of 'danger', 'stop', 'do not proceed further'. All elementary signals have similar simple things to convey, which one easily understood by people. But symbols are complex and have deeper semantic representation to make. While the red light at the railway station is just a signal, the National Flag of the country with its uni-, tri- or multi-colour is a *symbol*. This is because the National Flag of every country represents or symbolizes the philosophy and the ideals of the nation.

All the same we apply both the notions (signal, symbol) to forms of communication by man because it involves at times simple and other times complex notions. When we earlier spoke of the 'symbolic behaviour that such behaviour functions as signs. But as we come to human communicative behaviour, more and more the word 'symbolic' becomes relevant. The most typical symbolic behaviour of man is his *verbal behaviour*, namely, his *language*. The characteristic nature of man is revealed by language; it may be called his specific behaviour i.e. The behaviour of man as man, as distinct from all other animals. All the same language is symbolic, a characteristic which we partially attributed to the sensitivity of animals. Just as responses to and interaction with the environment point to the sensitive nature of animals, language as specific to man points to man's fundamental capacity to deal with *abstractions*, and subsequently to his mind.

Language is symbolic not only at a single level : it functions at a two-level representation. Linguistic behaviour (stimuli) is symbolic in the sense that the stimuli represent something more complex than themselves. The two-level representation consists in the units of a language (e.g., a word, a phrase etc.) symbolizing some content of the speaker's mind, namely, a concept, and the content of the mind in turn symbolizing some feature of the speaker's experience. This two-level representation of language in terms of the mental content and the feature of experience renders it a more complex system than the mere sign representation (in terms of sense-images) working in animals.

The animal brain, as we have seen, is the sole arbitrer of all sense experiences that animals undergo. The pose a faculty or principle beyond the biological mechanism in these lower organisms is beyond question. All the same, the human brain of itself cannot account for all the abstract, calculating decision-making, insightful behaviour of man. Man is capable of involving in so superior a kind of behaviour, and of revealing the artistic, aesthetic, poetic, philosophical, scientific and mystical sides of his personality that it is thoroughly groundless to assign to the human brain the role of the role arbitrator of human behaviour. This role can be assigned only to a *substantial principle* which is capable of co-ordinating and integrating the past, present and the future activities of the individual person, with a resonance of universality. Such a substantial principle is the human mind. The brain and the nervous system solely function activities of the human mind. It is true nature of language as a structured system and as a process can truly be understood.

# 9
# Language and the Mind

## 1. The Content of the Human Mind

Understanding the mind of man, its structure and its working is crucial and delicate because one can be easily misled. The crucial problem in this attempt lies in the fact that man can study the human mind only through the mind itself in two ways: (1) by an interior reflection of the observer's own mind, and (2) through the behaviour of other men which reflects the working of their minds. Philosophers of all times have studies the working of the human mind, mostly by means of interior reflection, and have reached quite contradictory conclusions, as are well known. This is only one side of the story; on the other we find that psychologists have discarded any direct reflection upon the mind itself which in fact they wished the mind itself which in fact they wished to reach, and started with the extrinsic behaviour of man. But the outcome as we know is a denial of any such intrinsic principle which is substantial enough to be called a *mind* as the common man understands it. Well, the positions in regard to the nature and working of the mind are varied and often contradictory. One can only term a deaf ear to those who require empirical proofs of the existence of the mind making use of which infact they deny its presence.

Sense perception, as we have seen, involves the possession of the senses and their arbitrer the brain. This as we find in infra-human organisms involves quite a complex process (Ch. 9 Sec. 4). The explanation of the role of neurons in bearing the sense impulses to the localized centres of the brain is all right. But it does not give all that we need to understand about the sense experiences of an animal in relation to the objects it encounters, and stimuli it receives.

Animal sensitivity involves the animal's interaction with some object or stimuli external to the animal, apart from the 'organic sensitivity' the animal experiences as part of the working of its own body (such as hunger, thirst sex-drive etc.). The animal, say, a dog sees an object in front. The senses of the dog becomes alert and existed. The dog's senses are prepared now to receive any corresponding stimuli from the object in front. The visual elements are perceived by the eyes i.e. the dog sees the colour, the size and other physical dimensions of the object. The auditory stimuli, if any, are received by the auditory receptor, the ears. Whatever quality the object possesses which are susceptible to the dog's senses are received. What happens now ? This is where we pause and think. What is the extent of the dog's cognitive perception which the dog is capable of as an animal?

It is significant that the dog perceives the particular object in its particularity and singularity. The essential limitation of the senses his in this that the senses do not go beyond the particular stimuli or sequence of stimuli. What the senses receive one *images*; the brain stores the stream of stimuli as images. Images as pictures are essentially *particular* and single, in the sense that an image is a replica of the thing it represents. An image is some kind of *sign*. The dog upon receiving the visual stimulus of the object as a whole, in fact, receives the stimulus as an image of the object with the extrinsic features represented. The image which in this particular case is visual will consist of the colour and the physical dimensions of the object. Similarly the image could be auditory, tactile etc. Every sense, thus, is capable of transmitting to the brain the stimuli required for the construction of the respective image of the object in front.

The particularity of the sense-image needs to be stressed again; it is against this background that we shall understand what have called the *concept* which constitutes the content of the mind as a unit of thought. We have to some extent seen the nature of the human infant's *first encounter* with the mother as the representative of the world outside. The human being like the animal is endowed with the five sense faculties. He encounters the world and interacts with the world through these faculties. The senses are the liaison agents with the external world. Man receives any extrinsic stimuli through the sense only.

The question is whether human sense experience stops with the senses and the brain themselves or do we have anything beyond? We have cast aside any doubts in regard to the presence of a substantial principle, the *mind* in man and said that the very question itself is sufficient proof of man's ability to think and hence the presence of the mind. If so what is the essential nature of human *cognition* which should account for both the sense and intellectual experiences of man? In man the cognitive faculties are *not* two isolated phenomena: one of the sense and the other of the intellect. But the *sense* and the *intellect* (the source of thought) are so conjoined and co-ordinated that the functions of the senses are over shadowed by the functions of the human intellect. It is too delicate a task to see in man where exactly the functions of the senses begin and stop. The intellect pervades the human senses in all cognitive activities. All the same there are possible demarcations that can be observed.

We have seen that all of man's fundamental knowledge comes from the world outside i.e. as a result of his sense experiences with the external world. It is significant to note how the first content of the child's mind is formed and what this content is. The child normally is born with the biological and mental (Psychological) faculties which are required for the child's interpersonal communion and interaction with the external world. The *biological faculties* include the brain, the nervous system, the sense receptors, and the vocal organs. The *mental faculties*, on the other hand include the intellect seat of thought), the imagination (seat of imagination), the memory (the faculty for storing, recalling and reproducing the content of the intellect and of the imagination), and the *will* (the faculty that is the arbitrer of a variety of human emotions and decision-making). The child's psychological development can be thought of primarily as the (i) development of these mental faculties and (ii) the development of the *content* of everyone of these faculties of terms of thought, imagination and memory.

The child comes face to face with the doll. This is the first time he looks at it consciously with his mind alert in terms of the new object in front, although he has seen the doll several times before without the capacity to identify the doll from, say, other things like his biscuits. We may say that the child's faculties have so far been relatively *dormant* which in course of months became gradually activated, having been aroused by the objects and persons around. In other words here is an experience for the child in which the doll for the first time has sufficiently activated his mind and aroused his curiosity.

Face to face with the doll, the child looks at it. His curiosity is aroused. His senses become active; the sense of sight has received the visual stimuli in terms of the colour and the dimensions of the doll. The child grabs the doll; the sense of touch at once receives the softness of the doll. The child brings the doll close to his face; the sense of small receives some light odour from the doll. Perhaps the child derives some pleasure by bringing it close to its tongue and it may be that some light taste too is received. What has in fact happened have? The child's entire cognitive faculty has become active in a moment: the senses and the mind are aroused. The senses as primary receptors have received the visual, auditory, olfactory, gustatory and lactile impulses. What is most significant in this process is that the child perceives the object, the doll, not as a collection of all these various stimuli, but as one whole and unified experience, the doll. The particular sense impulses have are co-ordinated by the brain and the child now receives a unified experience of the doll. So far the child has not known any name related to the doll, nor has he any thing as apart of his mental content.

One significant thing happens now. The sense-stimuli which the child receives from the doll as a *unified experience* at once feeds to the intellect a certain unit of content as a representative, (symbolic) unit of the 'unified experience the child has now undergone. This happens in terms of what we call a *concept*, an abstract unit of mental content which is representative of the doll as a 'plaything'. In other words, the child by merely obtaining the experience of this *one doll*, has *abstracted* the essential meaning of the object, the doll. In other words, the child now *know* the doll; the child has obtained a 'human cognitive experience' of the doll, by contrast to a dog's 'sensitive perception' of the doll.

But more things have happened. The child has obtained a 'unified experience' of *only one* doll and *understood* the doll as a 'play-thing'. The child has simultaneously obtained two things : (i) the *image* (as a result of the 'unified experience of the one material object), and (ii) the *concept*. The child has seen only *one doll* (possibly several times) and the image represents only this one doll. At the same time the concept the child has obtained is the result of a process of abstraction, as we have seen, and the concept as such is very different from the image of the doll. The child is now given a second doll (the figure of a puppy) and a third doll (the figure of a lion) while the first doll is the figure of a baby.

The three different kinds of dolls have fed into the imagination of the child three different *images* of the dolls (each representing the figure of the particular doll), while the *concept* the child has obtained from his experience with the first doll is now relevant to and true of any number of the doll so long as the object fulfills the nature of a doll as such including the child's expectations of a doll as a plaything. If the child goes and handles a puppy in place of a doll (taking the puppy for a doll) and the puppy bites back, the child's notion of the doll will not include the puppy because he perceives the puppy behaving very different from his dolls.

This leads us to the notion of the '*universality*' of concepts as the units of mental content. The concept as we have seen applies to all the objects of the same nature (as revealed by the behaviour), while an image is true of only one of the objects as we shall examine these characteristics in greater details in the following chapters. Such '*universal concepts*' form the content of the mind i.e. of the human intellect. Intellection, as a process of the mind (which includes all the activities of the intellect such as thinking, understanding, reasoning, etc.) has the concept as the basic unit. All forms of intellectual activity, in turn, take place in terms of concepts, while images while accompany intellection form the content of imagination. In other words the content of the human mind must be thought of in terms of *concepts*, on the one hand and *images*, on the other.

## 2. Universals and Language Development

The infant's first encounter with the mother, we said, is the beginning of a development which aims at the vision of humanity in terms of (i) cognitive experiences, (2) socialization and (3) linguistic development. The intellect which the child is endowed with of birth is in potency for a great development which knows no bounds. There is no known limit to the knowledge and understanding which the intellect is capable of. Man's perceptive capacity can stand up to any manner and extent to which the universe will reveal itself. In other words there is a dimension in the intellect which makes it capable of a universal vision which penetrates all individuality and particularity.

The formation of concepts in the mind is such an instance. Just as the mind is capable of penetrating the *individualities* of humanity (which a spatially and temporarily limited thing like the brain cannot do) and see the humanity in terms of its universality, and as the mind is capable of penetrating the *particularity* of human cognitive experiences and reach the universe as such, the mind is capable of penetrating the particular aspects of the stimuli from an object and reach the 'object' as such as a 'unified experience' of reality. For these reasons we hold that the mind is in search of the universal aspects of material reality.

Matter is particular, molecular, essentially atomic. It is varied and dispersed. It is important to note that some *form* or other holds matter together to be this or that particular reality. So far as every unified thing say, the doll or the dog, is concerned this form that holds matter together is realized at two levels; (1) the extrinsic *shape* and (2) and that aspect of the thing which makes it essentially different from another thing belonging to a different class i.e. the *nature* of the thing in terms of its 'behaviour'. Doll no. 1 doll no. 2 and doll no. 3 (see sec. 1.) belong to one and the same group of objects and possess a kind of shape with differences only of details in terms of its colour or dimensions. We call this 'shape' the superficial aspect of the *form* of the object. In terms of shape the dolls look partially same and partially different, but the differences one less compared to the objects belonging to a different class. Now, though the dolls are different on the basis of their shape and every doll is one particular object, the child's intellect perceives all the dolls as essentially of the same kind, possessing the same, identical nature (as compared to a table or a living dog).

Again, for the child puppy no. 1, puppy no. 2 and puppy no.3 make up another class of objects compared to the dolls he has at hand. The living puppy has a shape very different from a doll; the three puppies, on the other hand, possess similar shapes. The child's intellect now perceives all the puppies as essentially having identical nature (as compared to the 'behaviour' of the dolls or food). The child knows now that the dolls belong to one class the puppies belong to another class of objects around. As we saw in section 1. The child has obtained in his mind two things in regard to the dolls: (1) the *images* of all the particular dolls, and (2) the *concept* of the doll as such related only to the nature of the dolls as different from the natures of all other things around. The same is true of the puppies; the child has obtained the images of all the puppies (perhaps different in colour and some features), and he has obtained the concept of the puppy as such, as different from the natures of all the rest of the objects around.

What do these examples show? The child's mind has penetrated the particularities, specificities and space-time bound limitations of the dolls and the puppies, and reached the very nature of the objects which specify the class as different from some other. The child has perceived a big doll, a small doll, a white doll, a black doll, one looking like a baby, another looking like a lion: but all of them are understood as 'plaything' which he has no fear to manipulate, throw, and carry around. While he has perceived the puppies similarly as different, individual animals which makes noise, move around, play with him, eat food and so on.

The child's intellect has obtained what is *universal* among all the dolls of any colour, type or dimension, so long as they are dolls: the *concept* of doll. In future, so long as his memory will retain this concept and he will have the experience of seeing dolls he as a grown up man will recognize a doll as a doll and not as anything else. The same is true of puppies or dogs so far as the person's recognition of them is concerned. It is in this manner that the individual person confronts any object, vent or other features of experience, understands the object or feature of experience by obtaining of the concept of it.

We have seen that concept from the content of the intellect, images the content of the imagination, and both together in turn the content of the mind. *Concepts one universals* (it looks inadequate say that concepts are universal). This notion is very important later in our understanding of meaning as the content of language. When we say that concepts are universals we mean several things. First of all it means that concepts are not images, particular signs or names, as some would tent to call them. We have made a clear distinction between the *concept* of a thing and its *image* (see the concepts and images of dolls and puppies on the foregoing pages). While an image stands for the 'extrinsic form' of one particular object, a concept represents the nature (the terms 'essence' is avoided here for a variety of reasons) which we may also call the 'intrinsic form'. Therefore on no grounds can we consider images, names and concepts, as identical.

Secondly, when we say that concepts are universal we mean that every concept represents all the objects (individual members) of one and the same class the class of cats, dogs, trees, tables etc.) The concept of man is a universal in the sense that this concept in our minds represents all men of all times. On the one hand over imagination maintains the images of individual men and women whom we have met in our lives, while on the other, our intellect has the concept of man as such devoid of any particularity and true of all men and women as human beings. Our imagination can never have the image of the human being as such, because images belong only to the true, living men, their statues or pictures. The concept alone i.e. the intellect alone is capable of penetrating particularities and individualities and of representing the nature of man as man.

One of the best instances for illustrating the particularity of images and the universality of concepts can be had in what we know as 'weapons'. What is a weapon? No one can show us a weapon as such, just as no one can show the 'human being' as such. If ten people one asked to produce a weapon each, every one will produce a different kind of a thing: a knife, a dagger, a sword, a club, a spear, a pick-axe or several other things. We know well that a knife and things. We know well that a knife and a spear are very different, but all the ten people understood each as a weapon and produced a different kind of a thing. What is significant here is that 'weapon' is a concept which is true of every one of the things produced so far as its nature is concerned. The weapons became different in each case because the concept is realized in several individual objects all of which are in the last resort used for the same purpose. The ten people, on the other hand, had ten images (as we have seen) of weapons as an image represents only one particular object (say, a spear or a knife).

Understanding the nature and function of concepts as universals is difficult, indeed. Concepts as universals represent reality so far as the human mind comes to know it. Concepts are not object themselves as some early philosophers wanted us to believe. They are only *modes* of representation so far as we can understand them; they are abstract units of intellectual content which enable the intellect to operate in a variety of ways. Thoughts should consist of systematic stream of concepts in the intellect so as to understand, reason out, or spell out things. All the same concepts as mental units of thought are often complex (see Sec. 5. for details).

On the ultimate realm we have found *reality* as working on and affecting the intellect through the sense faculties of man. This takes place in terms of various features of experience (persons, things, events, quality, quantity, relations etc.) The human mind obtains in its working the *concepts* related to a particular experience with reality, as representing the universal mode of the particular experience. This is the second realm: the realm of thought (mind). Man as an individual person is born to a society and from birth, as we have seen, he involves in a variety of interpersonal communion with the members of society. As a result he is required of express himself *informationally* or *intentionally* (to know or convey some form of knowledge, or to do or get something done). To carry out this man has developed a system of verbal communication which we know as language.

The content part of human language is the content of human mind. Language is not in any manner rooted directly in reality. Language is not co-ordinate element of reality outside; language is immediately the co-ordinate element of the mind of man. It is at once related to the mind. *Language proceeds from* and *terminates in the mind*. For this reason we say that the content of language is identical with the content of language is identical with the content of mind. Both entertain the same *semantic content*, the concepts and their stream in an infinite variety of ways. But this ultimate units of further to find out what the ultimate units of the semantic content could be. We shall do this in section 5 of the present chapter.

## 3. Language and Thought

Language here is seen as a co-ordinate element of the mind by means of which the mind is able to communicate itself and establish contacts with the external world. When we said that language is not a co-ordinate element of reality outside what we meant was that language as such has not much-immediate to do with reality outside even though language forms part of that reality. There are many who consider language i.e. its units such as words as mere names or signs standing for things outside, without relating it any way with the mind. No such position can be justified in the context which we have been examining linguistic process.

Language is at once related to the mind more than anything else as it proceeds from and terminates in the mind itself. Language, as we know, is a layer of two factors: (1) expression and (2) content. The expression part of language establishes what we shall call a 'communicational link' between the speaker and the writer, on an intentional or informational basis. It is the expression part of the language, which is perceived extrinsically, that is produced by the speaker and listened to by the listener or recipient, and understood usually as language proper. What goes on behind expression is often overlooked.

The whole thing is easily explained out in terms of 'encoding' and 'decoding' functions. At the biological level these two functions take place in the brain as the co-ordinating mechanism. Not much care is taken as to what happens behind these processes and exactly what is encoded and decoded. Well, 'information' is used as a key-word in psycholinguistics and in the field of communication engineering (see Ch. 3. Sec. 3). What is further beyond ? The essential links have never been established convincingly. As if we always afraid of facing that one any serious thing: the mind !

The content part of human language is the key to the wholly mystery. We have been moving to the mind now from two different perspectives : (1) the object, and (2) language. Both we essential cues to the shrouding mystery of the human mind. The true, external object shows us the path to the mind, and on the other hand, language also, leads us to the mind. The content part of language takes us straight to the minds of the speaker and the listener. An observer different from the speaker and the listener (a third individual) is able to obtain insight into the working of the mind chiefly through language. But normally every human being is a speaker and a listener, as such he does not have to assume the role of a third extrinsic observer. All the same the parallel roles, of being a speaker-listener and an extrinsic observer can very well help an individual observer to be more objective. Where what we ordinarily call *introspection* as a very valid method of observing and studying intrinsic realities like the working of one's own mind will be rendered more objective when coupled with extrinsic observation of other speaker-listeners in society. Both introspection (turning over to the working of one's own mind) as well as the observation of the speaker-listener's verbal behaviour place us right on the realm of *thought*. Whether we move, as we noted above, from the objective reality outside the human mind, or from the language of the speaker-listener, we cannot escape the mind and the content of the mind i.e. thought (described above as organized 'streams of concepts').

Thought and language project a unified experience and the nature of this experience can be understood only if we know their relation as co-ordinate elements of the same experience. Language represents (reflects or symbolizes) the thought that is present in the mind (i.e. in the intellect). Functionally, thus, thought precedes language. The mind conceives an organized stream of concepts with reference to some experience (intrinsic or extrinsic). The organization of the stream of concepts may be in the form of (1) reflective thinking, (2) self-effective thinking, (3) systematic introspection (with a view to discovering the structure and working of the mind), (4) inductive reason, (5) deductive reasoning, (6) comprehensional thinking (to understand a thing, event, or some written material), (7) appreciative thinking (involving artistic, aesthetic aspects of reality), and (8) critical thinking (which involves deductive reasoning also).

*Defective thinking* by the intellect takes place when the intellect accompanied by the imagination rests upon accompanied by the imagination rests upon some extrinsic object and endeavour to discover more its nature and characteristics. It is a common experience that we sit down and without much mental exertion thinks about a particular event, say, an accident we have, witnessed. This can happen without the minding involving in any kind of reasoning as such. *Self-reflective thinking* takes place when the mind fixes to the subject as the 'reflecting' agent' and endeavours to discover more about the subject himself. This can be anything other than the mind itself (for instance, the moral aspects of one's life).

By systematic introspection we mean here the mind's attempt to know itself as what we shall call the 'thinking thought'. It is the most intense form of thought when the 'thinking agent' or the 'thinking thought' endeavours to know itself. *Systematic introspection* also includes the attempts of what we shall call the 'thought thought' (meaning the pure *content* of the intellect as distinct from the *agent* itself or the *activity* as such). The use of the terms 'thinking thought' and 'thought thought' in the present context aims at clarifying on the one hand the *abstract nature* of the mind (that the mind is so abstract as to resemble thought itself), and on the other drawing a contrast between the agent the mind, and the product, thought. Introspection, therefore endeavours to learn more about these aspects of the mind itself.

*Inductive reasoning* is an activity of the mind where the mind moves in terms of reasoning from one or more experiences (a particular experience) to a universal conclusion. This ordinarily results from the intellect's perception of the essential relation between the factors under consideration. The scientist's conclusions on the substance of a molecule of water is based on his analysis of only a limited set of instance rather than the entire world of water. But his statement in regard to the nature of water holds true of all water. *Deductive reasoning* is, again a stream of intellectual process where the mind moves from something universal and established as a fact to a particular instance. Once a scientist has established through experiment the substance of a molecule of water and proved it true of all water, for later scientists it is a deductive reasoning process where they take for granted that the substance of all water is $H_2O$, and more down to one particular molecule of water. They do not hesitate to ascertain that the substance of the once particular molecule is $H_2O$, without further analysis of water. All scientific processes involve inductive and deductive thinking at various stages of development.

By *comprehensional thinking* we meant the activity of the intellect in understanding some extrinsic object, event or some written material. While reflective thinking aims at a deeper understanding of some object by means of a concentrated application of the intellect. Comprehensional thinking as an intellectual activity precedes reflective thinking. We read a passage accompanied by comprehensional thinking and reflect upon the content of the passage for deeper understanding without again caring for the passage as such.

*Appreciative thinking* as an activity of the intellect concentrates on the artistic/aesthetic aspects of reality. The working of a poet's, painter's or artisan's mind at the time of same creative production is some how different from all other forms of intellectual activities. Lastly *critical thinking* concentrates on discovering the truth with an objective and unprejudiced bent of mind without under emotional attachment to aspects of reality related to the truth the mind is after.

By thought we mean such a variety of ways as seen above in which as stream of concepts may be organized by the mind depending on the need of the situation in which thinking takes place. All the ways of conceptual organization seen above are but the content of the mind; any expression of it in any manner possible for communicative purposes or otherwise requires a concrete medium through which the content of the mind can be conveyed. The two ways of achieving this communication we saw in ch. 3 sec. 1. as verbal expression (communication or behaviour) and non-verbal expression (communication or behaviour). Language is in fact the verbal outlet of the conceptual organization or stream of concepts that takes place in the mind.

For this reason we have said that language as at once related to the mind than to outside to reality. The mind reaches reality outside through the senses; language is a manner in which reality can be reached so far as society is concerned. Language is not symbolically related directly to objects and features of experience. Thought at once represents reality and it is only through the medium of thought and language symbolizes any aspect reality. This is how language becomes subservient to human thought and subsequently to the mind.

All the same the primacy of thought over language has quite considerable limitations. This primacy is relevant chiefly at a horizontal level, name, in terms of individual speakers. At a vertical dimension language often commands considerable priority over the thinking of the individual. This happens because the individuals of all times have been able to know the thoughts of others primarily through language. It means that the verbal categories (the categories of language) predominate and influence through, and individuals are often introduced to categories of reality through categories of language. As we shall see in detail in the following section the thoughts and language is the child develop in a simultaneous manner mutually influencing each other.

## 4. Development of Symbolic Behaviour in the Child

It is again quite a delicate thing to trace the development of symbolic behaviour in the child. In Ch. 7, we found that the first experience of the child with outside reality, in fact, is his encounter with the mother. The reason we saw for this was significant. The child is born with (1) the biological faculties which include the brain, the nervous system, the sense receptors, and the vocal organs, and (2) the mental faculties which include the intellect, the imagination, the memory and the will (see Sec. 1.). Apart from these and other 'principles' and faculties with which the new-born organism is specifically oriented, there are no reasons to believe that the mind of the infant possesses any content at all at birth in the form of concepts or images. This 'tabular rasa' theory has been held valid by most thinkers on child psychology. Any experience of cognition of the respective faculties. This excitement of the child's consciousness cannot be caused at this stage by some intrinsic experience is powerful enough to rouse the child's cognitive faculties. At this initial phase the only experiences of the infant are the *organic sensations* such as hunger , thrust or lack of warmth. These are all intrinsic experiences which are not powerful enough at this stage to rouse/excite the sense organs of the infant.

It requires therefore an external agent to cause this excitement which is the first step to an act of sensation. Again, the very first agent to cause this arousal of the child's sensitivity cannot be an inanimate object as its passive state cannot be sufficiently causative to act upon the child's senses. It needs to be a sufficiently animate, active and dynamic agent to cause this first arousal of the infant's consciousness. This is how the mother or who ever takes the place of the mother becomes the agent to cause the first arousal of the child's consciousness and enable the child to recognize her as an object different from he himself. From the moment of birth the mother's bestowed on the child, and the figure who thus has continually stooped over the infant becomes the very first *figure* for the infant to recognize as an external object.

Again, another significant stage and one very proximate to the recognition of or encounter with the mother is the recognition of the self as something different from the smiling, stooping and affectionate figure of the mother. It is from the moment of this recognition of the self, possibly, that the organic experiences (hunger, thirst etc.) of the child are recognized as those of the self as different from the mother.

The awareness of the child's organic experiences together with the recognition of the self as a unified experience for the child to achieve more intense awareness of himself as the centre of all that goes on around. This is the beginning of a development which knows no bounds within the range of human experience. In the present analysis it may be noted that cognition in the sense of experience with an outside agent is given precedence over language so far as the child's development is concerned. Language experiences at all levels are built on the basic cognitive experiences with which the mind becomes conversant. It is to extrinsic reality rather than to language that the conscious child is first of introduced.

Once the initial cognitive experiences are established, the child's development becomes a parallel process of three things as noted in chapter 7, namely : (1) cognitive, (2) sociological, and (3) linguistic experiences. Language development is essentially correlated to the child's cognitive and sociological developments. The child as an individual person growing up in society is in continuous interpersonal communion with other members of society; and this he achieves and carries out by means of the language he has mastered. Here language becomes somehow subservient to the cognitive and sociological ends.

As the first experience of the child with outside word expands in dimensions corresponding to his growth, we find that the child encounters continuous pressure and need to acquire the language of his community to the best of his capacity. This pressure to cope with the requirements of personal and communal life should be looked at from two view points : (1) the mental greater complexity as years go by, and (2) greater need for communication as an extrinsic requirement arises. The individual obtains ever greater cognitive experiences as he meets new persons new events and new features of experiences. As his cognitive experiences increase, the thought streams by way of conceptual organization attains added intensity. At the same time the individual becomes able to carry out intellectual activities in greater intensity in terms of the seven forms of thought we mentioned above.

All this may be looked at as the development of the child's symbolic experience. The manipulation of symbols is a corollary to rationality. It is the ability of the human mind to operate with universals which are capable of symbolizing all the members of one class. Development of symbolic activity would mean, again, that the mind of the child has reached the stage when he can grasp reality represented by the symbol. The mind instead of reaching and receiving reality directly, employs the concrete medium of symbols to reach reality. The whole operation of employing symbols as a medium of the mind is built on basic sensitivity which the animal world shares in. We have found that animals receive in their perception of stimuli particular images of stimuli one signs which do not posses the characteristic of universality as these signs do not represent all members of a particular class, but the 'extrinsic form' of the single (particular) object only. All the same it means some form of representation without, perhaps, the animal obtaining a unified experiences of the object as a whole. It is because of this representative quality of signs, that animal cognition is often called 'symbolic'. But symbolic experience as representative of universals, namely, concepts is applicable only to human cognition, more specifically, to the activity of the intellect. But there is no anomaly in saying that human symbolic experience is founded on sensitivity as sense experiences still remain the foundation and starting point of all human knowledge.

Coming back to the child, we find his early cognitive experience flowering in a triple direction: cognitive, sociological and linguistic. As the child's cognitive experience expands in the context of his meeting new people, things, events, relations, and other features of experience, he obtains an over greater grip over his verbal symbols. The range of the verbal symbols (words and expressions) that he acquires at every given phase of development has also rational behind it. In his acquisition of verbal symbols for communicative purposes, we find two distinct dimensions at work: (a) the acquisition of more words and expressions which means a 'quantitative expansion' of child's language; and (b) the acquisition of greater depths of meaning in the language he has already obtained, namely, a connotative and denotative expansion of his language. These one the two levels at which language development will take place in the individual. A few of the major cognitive experiences of the child of home one the following: a growing understanding of the parents' behaviour, of the behaviour of other members of the family, an understanding of the behaviour of children of similar age, and perhaps the presence of children younger than the learner under consideration. Again, the child confronts other animate and inanimate objects in the family: dogs, cats, cattle, dolls, furniture and things of day-to-day use. Among the sociological aspects of development we find the child being required to interact better with others in the forms of give and take; he notices social relations among the family members, and between the family and those who often visit the family; he notices all sorts of give and take among the people around. Thirdly, there is the linguistic dimension as such; the child more and more pays attention to aspects of language (words and expressions) he has not hither to noticed as a learner. These cognitive, sociological and linguistic experiences form the bases of the development of symbolic behaviour in him.

'Mummy' and 'Daddy' meant for him only two individual who were related only to him as the centre of the world around. Now he finds that the sense individual are 'mummy and daddy also for others in the family 'mummies and daddies outside his home who are so for the children he often meets. This is a 'denotative expansion' of his language (the members of the class for which a word stands find extension).

The child, as we have noted above, also comes to acquire greater depths of the meaning of the words he already knows. This is the 'connotative expansion' of the his language. The word 'mummy and daddy initially meant only those who often put him, care for him, care for him, and feed him. But as he grows up the two words (relating to the two people he meets and those whom he meets outside) assume new shades of meaning. The words (mummy and daddy) mean greater things to him now than what he conceived so far. He understands what parental relation is without, perhaps, knowing its full implications. This becomes true of the entire range of the verbal symbols at his command. He now knows greater expressions, deeper meanings and greater command over the organization (syntax) of his language. It all a mutual influence of the maturity of his thoughts, (the content of the mind) on the one hand, and the maturity of his language (the expression of the mental content) on the other. The development of symbolic behaviour, thus, is two-dimensional.

## 5. The Semantic Content of Language

Considerable attempts are made in present-day linguistic to codify the semantic content of language. Such attempts have often been proved clumsy and onerous because analysts have seldom cared to look at the *content of language* from the perspective of the *content of the mind*. One seldom comes across a work in which a unified and comprehensive view of the language process is attained and a proper understanding is reached in regard to the identity of the content of language and the content of the mind.

The 'content of the mind' is a product of over understanding of the structure of the *mind*, while 'the semantic content of language' is a product of our understanding of the structure of *language*. The content of the mind we call 'conceptual content', while the content of language we call 'semantic content' (or meaning). These are merely looking at the *same* thing from two distinct perspectives: language and the mind. What we should not hesitate to recognize is that at the deepest core of the human mind and human language lies the universals, namely, the *concept*. All our further understanding of language and the mind has to be built on this very some foundation of concepts.

At the same time an understanding of concepts as the content of the mind, and of meanings as the content of language is not so easy a task to undertake as done by ancient or medieval thinkers of languages.

First of all the words and expressions of a language, in other words, the meaningful units of a language and the respective concepts in the speaker-listener's minds do not have exact one to one correspondence. This is the most significant thing to understand in the consideration of the 'meaning of meaning'. Thinkers of ancient and medieval periods who held such views talking of the meaning of words, wanted us to believe that for every word there existed in the mind a corresponding concept. It sounds all right to the question 'what is meaning ? We have found one unique answer that meaning is the content of language which represents the content of the mind. It remains mere verbal gymnastics if the real problems involved are overlooked. Certainly, the content of language are meanings, and meanings are concepts and their organized streams in the form of thoughts. In other words, *concepts* certainly stand at the meeting point of language and the mind functioning as the content of both.

The real issues related to the 'meaning of meaning' lie in what are called to day *semantic specifications.* The treatment of the semantic implications of language has become the most life issue present-day structural linguistics. The semantic content of language is very complex. How are word-forms and concepts related (here concepts and meanings seen as identical)? Does one word-form signify one single concept? What are 'shades of meaning'? What could be the nature of the *minimum units* of meaning if they are broken up? How are meanings as larger units of meaning consist of concepts in a one to one correspondence? There are only a few of the questions pertinent to the study of the meanings of language. Just as human thoughts consist of a realm of limitless complexity for man to examine, the content of language which takes us directly to the realm of thoughts is expected to pose similar complexity.

A quick glance through a dictionary of English tells us that a description of the *meanings of a word* is not an easy task. Why does a dictionary list the several meanings of one word? It is because one word is seldom, if ever, related homogeneously and unambiguously to one meaning. The dictionary is witness to it. One English word (just as in case of any other language) signifies several meanings; one word signifies several shades of meaning. Again, one meaning is signified by several words with perhaps difference of connotations from word to word. Further we see that words share meanings in part and new meanings are derived when compounds or phrases are formed. Half a dozen prepositions added to the same action word yield half a dozen entirely different meanings. An analysis of such factors show that the variations are limitless, and to discover an adequate descriptive rationale for all these factors pertaining to the organization of meanings is next to impossible with the kind of descriptive tools which are available to us. It is to reach such a descriptive adequacy that structural linguistics is resorting to mathematical logic and similar methods of description.

For present purposes of understanding the structure of the *semantic content* of language we may examine a few dictionary entries, and see the role concepts play in such entries and subsequently in language. Every word in the dictionary can be looked at as a combination of semantic specifications. Let us examine the word '*milk*'. What are the semantic specifications of milk? The semantic content of this word can be examined at different levels.

(1) A dictionary entry No. 1 reads like this: 'white linguid produced by female mammals as food for their young'...... The individual who for the first time obtains an experience of milk at a conscious level and makes it, an object of his sense experience comes to know milk as milk either on his own or with the help of other members in society, obtains the concept of milk. Usually this first experience with milk will also be accompanied by the verbal symbol for it, 'milk', used by the mother. This happens as part of the *third phase* of each language acquisition (Ch. 2. Sec. 3). In other words in this particular case the formation of the concept is accompanied by the presence of the *object* (reality) and the *verbal symbol*.

But as we notice, we find that milk is not an 'elementary object' of the senses and it consists of several *component qualities*. Consequently the concept that represents the object, milk, too cannot be a 'micro conceptual element'. The concept of milk should, therefore be a 'macro-concept' which consists of more than one micro-conceptual elements. At the language end, as the content of the linguistic unit, milk, we label this macro-concept as *meaning-unit* ('unit' is added here because the word 'meaning' is quite an unspecified term). Now, what are the elements of this macro-concept of milk? An analysis of the object, milk, will yield these component elements of milk. We find, therefore, that milk is composed of component qualities such as included in the dictionary-entry: 'White liquid produced by female mammals as food for their young......'. Milk therefore consists of qualities such as *whiteness, liquidity, sweetness nutritiousness* having its origin in *mammalic glands* etc. In regard to the macro-concepts of milk, 'whiteness', 'liquidity', sweetness' and 'nutritiousness' having its origin in 'mammalic glands' are the component qualities and each of them is labeled here as a micro-conceptual element. These may be considered elementary and basic units which enter into the making of macro-concepts. In usual descriptions of the semantic content we lable all these elementary qualities, again, as *meanings* only; but as done in structural linguistic descriptions we shall lable them as *semantic specifications*.

(2) Second, the semantic specifications or micro-conceptual elements of the macro-concept of milk can be viewed from another perspective adding to the number of semantic specifications or micro-conceptual elements of milk. Present-day structural linguists analyze semantic specifications in terms of '+ — ' features (e.g. +Animate, +human etc.). The semantic content of milk, we find, is specified in a number of ways other than what we have seen above. Milk as an object belongs to a specific class Milk can be classed as (1) *material*, (2) *inanimate*, (3) *liq[illegible]* 4) *edible*, etc. Everyone these specifications of milk can be feature as + or -x depending on the class it belongs to. The '+' entry of a class leaves out all its alternatives as opposites, and a '—' entry shows inclusions of any class other than one mentioned. Again, the specifications shown above are the micro-conceptual elements of the macro-concept of milk.

(3) Apart from the two levels of micro-conceptual elements we have seen, there are several more that are more accidental, peripheral and related to the socio-cultural dimensions of language. 'Milk' as a linguistic unit has socio-cultural connotations which add to its semantic specifications. For a child 'milk' goes with the image of the mother; for a villages milk, goes with the image of the cow; but for an urban individual the cow is seldom thought of in relation to milk, but it is the 'dairy' (where milk gets processed) that normally goes with the notion of milk. Again, in some societies milk invariably forms part of a meal, while other communities never drink milk during meals. For some milk, again, is vegetarian while for others it is non-vegetarian. These, for instance form the third level of micro-conceptual elements (milk + mother, milk + cow, milk + meal, milk + vegetarian food) etc. which form peripheral components of the macro-concept of milk. A *fourth level* of micro-conceptual elements, too can be explicated in terms of the 'idiolectic specificities' of language depending on the experiences of given individual (e.g. for many milk goes with tea or coffee; never is milk taken alone). This is how a concept becomes socially, culturally and idiolectically bound at the peripheral level, even though the essen-

tial features remain the same.

An examination of any linguistic unit (say, a word) shows that most such units represent a rather complex phenomenon (reality) through the medium of correspondingly complex *mental content/ semantic content*. The mental and semantic contents are, therefore, two different perspectives of the same content labelled as *concepts* in terms of the mind and *meanings* in terms of the language. Three very essential levels of the human mind that we may therefore pose are:

(1) *Micro-conceptual elements* which form the basic building blocks of all mental content.

(2) *Macro-concepts* which in fact function as unified conceptual symbols of individual objects, events, and relations in reality.

(3) *Organized streams of concepts* which make up all forms of thoughts that the mind is capable of entertaining.

All level of meanings (of words, phrases, sentences,) in the last resort result form an interplay of micro-conceptual elements in limitless combinations into the larger units of macro-concepts, further getting organized themselves into streams of concepts which we have called thoughts.

# 10
# Deviant Language Behaviour

## 1. Physiological and Psychological Background

Chapter 10 has made it clear to us the extent to which language as a major behaviour of man and the mind which is the immediate functional principle of language are related. In Chapter we saw to what extent the *neurological structure* of man including the brain and the nervous system, and the vocal mechanisms form the biological substratum of human language. Language as it is clear is the product of the co-ordinate functioning of (1) the mind of man, and (2) his physiological mechanism. When either of these co-ordinate principles (mind and physiological mechanisms) do not function properly and language is affected the resultant behaviour we term as *deviant language behaviour* (also known as *speech-disorder* and *speech pathology*). The dimensions related to such behaviour are far too many to deserve mention in such a treatise. Deviant language behaviour in the form of language abnormalities can be traced back to (1) physiological disorders, (2) mental disorders, (3) physiologic disorders causal by mental abnormalities, and (4) mental disorders caused by physiological abnormalities.

Any abnormality, congenital or otherwise, of the physiologic mechanisms of language can cause abnormalities of speech. The role of the brain and the nervous system in the production of language is examined in Ch. 9. The central physiological mechanism of language activity consists of the *neurological structure* with its (1) central nervous system, (2) peripheral nervous system and (3) sympathetic nervous system. The central nervous system consists of the *brain* and the *spinal cord*; the peripheral nervous system consists of the incoming and the outgoing nerves linking the central system with the peripheral mechanisms, the sense receptors. The sympathetic nervous systems, further, carries out the autonomic (reflex) activities of the human body.

Language activity in man not only involves the co-ordination activities of the central nervous system, but also the receptive and productive language functions of the peripheral mechanism. These peripheral mechanisms include (1) the *vocal organs* for language production, and (2) the *auditory organs* for language reception. Speech at the same time involves, several *motor activities*. Speech production involves the manipulation of the diaphragm, the lungs, the muscles of the chest, the *vocal cords*, the mouth, the tongue, teeth, and lips. The vocal cords consists of two membranes stretched across the interior of larynx, a box-like structure. As we know, this lies at the interior level of the adam's apple visible outside. The function of the vocal cords is to produce 'voice' effected by the vibration of the two folds inside the larynx and make speech audible. The less active the vocal cords are the less aloud speech becomes. Speech would turn out to be a *whisper* if the vocal words are not at all active. As we shall see later, speech function would be greatly impaired, if the vocal cords are not active. Sometimes disease necessitates the removal of the larynx with the vocal cords, resulting in total inability to produce voice except whisper.

Apart from the lungs, the wind-pipe and the vocal cords almost every part of the mouth helps the production of language in a co-ordinate manner. The *tongue* with its (i) tip (ii) front, (iii) middle and (iv) back portions is the chief functionary in the formation of the vowel and consonant sounds. The alveolar, hard and soft palates play a major role in the formation of consonants when the tongue touches these positions in the upper part of the mouth. The presence of the *uvula* at the back of the mouth controls the formation of nasal sounds. Again, the *teeth* on the upper gum, and the *lower lip* are important mechanisms in the formation of sounds that are the building blocks of language.

The ear with their internal structure form the auditory organs or organs for the reception of language. The ears function in a characteristically mechanical manner. Sound waves travel through the external canal and strike what is called the *tympanic membrane* (eardrum). Vibration of this membrane activates the *hammer* attached to it and further the *anvil* and *stirrup*. The stirrup precesses against the *oval window*. Movements of the oral window send the waves up the *vestibular canal* and the *tympanic canal*, both of which are filled with liquid, and further to *cochlea*. From the cochlea the sound vibration in its high or low frequency is conveyed to the associated nerve fibres; the stimuli concerned finally reaches the cortex of the brain. Each ear is connected with both sides of the cortex.

The auditory organs of man, unlike recognized often play such an important role in language activity. As it will be examined later, defects and abnormalities related to the organs of audition contribute to most serious set back in the reception of language. The ear constitutes the most sensitive of organs which help language behaviour and is prone to defects which make normal language behaviour impossible to man.

Deviant language behaviour can be the result, on the one hand abnormalities (congenital, permanent or temporary) in any part of the physiological mechanism we have examined now. Since language behaviour is not superficial biological behaviour, but originates from the very core of the personality of man, we have said, that the mind as a co-ordinate principle of language can also cause deviant verbal behaviour. Abnormalities of the mind often result in disorganized and deviant language behaviour in the individual. Psychological abnormalities are largely caused by (1) *faulty development* and (2) *excessive stress situations*. Faulty development may be *biological*, *psychological* and *sociological*. Again stress situations too may be *biological psychological* and *sociological*.

Biological disorders often lead to abnormalities of the mind, just as mental disorders lead to abnormalities of the body. But the type of adjustment man is achieving at any time is the result of the psychological (psychophysiological) development and stress situations which as social beings we part-take. In other words, anything that has led to faulty biological, psychological or sociological development or any thing that has caused stress situations of an excessive type brings mentally abnormal behaviour and subsequently shows out in language, so far as language behaviour is concerned. Over-whelming stress which the individual cannot withstand results in abnormal behaviour.

Faulty biological development as a cause of mental abnormality can be *hereditary*, namely, attributed to heredity, leading to probable bio-genetic factors. Faulty biological development may also be physiological or *constitutional* including physique, sex, temperament, endocrine function and blood type. It includes what we call *congenital* or *acquired* defects of the body such as deformities and disabilities of all types. While we are able to see good adjustment despite serve handicaps, while serve personality problems with only slight physiological defects. Faulty psychological development which led to abnormal behaviour include things like early deprivation of children, pathogenic family patterns that cause anxiety, inadequate background for proper development etc. Varying patterns of social organization with their unhealthy ways and attitudes breed several types of psychological disorders. Lastly, severe physiological, psychological and sociological stress, end up in mental disorders when it goes beyond individual's capacity to bear the situation that develops.

## 2. Physiological Abnormalities

Of factors which cause deviant language of any kind, physiological abnormalities of some kind rate high. By physiological abnormalities, as mentioned above, we mean any form of *defect* which the physiological mechanisms for language behaviour are subject to. A rather detailed listing of these mechanisms on the preceding pages makes clear the extent of such languages which can deviate the comprehension or production of language in some manner from normally. The following are some groupings of the major abnormalities and deviations that are commonly observed. Attempts are also made to provide alongwith some deviant language specimens wherever they are relevant and available.

**(1) Defects of the Central Nervous System :** A large variety of diseases, abnormal growth and other biological conditions affect the normal functioning of the nervous system, and give rise to abnormal behaviour including abnormal language behaviour. These disorders of the brain or the spinal cord causing *total loss* of language function or *partial impairment* results either form (a) *congenitally acquired* defects or (b) a permanent or temporary impairment of the neural function. The loss of or deviation in language behaviour is governed chiefly by the extent of neural damage and degree of emotional instability (in the case of adults). A slight brain damage would load to impairment of language function if the individual's emotional stability is less. Again as we shall see later, a brain damage leads to mental disorders (again, depending on the emotional instability) and further to total or partial loss of language. A person with a stable and integrated personality withstands a serious brain damage, and the subsequent impairment of verbal behaviour would be much less. But there are limits to the correlation between a person's emotional maturity and the loss of language. If the neural damages would directly affect the control centres of language in the brain, then the deviation in language functions is bound to occur (e.g. loss of memory and ability to recall). In short the several forms of *brain pathology* which result from brain disorders often result in the impairment of language behaviour as a direct result of (a) the damage of the brain and (b) the subsequent influence on the functions of the mind.

The broad group of language disorders resulting from neurological (brain) defects is generally known as *aphasia*. Generally, from the aphasia groups of disturbances are ruled out the various psychogenic disorders (of mental origin), language deficiencies caused by the defects of the sense organs, and those disorders resulting from defects of purely auditory or vocal mechanisms. Language disorders resulting from aphasia would extrinsically consist of impairment of all aspects of comprehension (variably distributed in different cases), and production language symbols. Adequate conceptualization and semantic organization are difficult with aphasia patient depending on the severity of cases. Aphasia patients exhibit discrepancies in almost all areas of language comprehension and production characterized especially by impaired memory, adequate intellectual perception of cognitive experiences, shorter span of retention, reduction of functional vocabulary, problems of auditory, visual and often motor activities related to comprehension and production and language.

(2) **Defects of Vocal Mechanisms:** Apart from the impairments and abnormalities of the brain, deviant, language behaviour is caused by defects in any part of the vocal mechanisms all of which

contribute in a co-ordinate manner to the production of language. If defects or abnormalities of the Brain can effect hurdles in the production and comprehension (reception) of language, the defects of any part of the vocal mechanisms would result only in the impairment of *speech production*:

1. ***Lungs*** : The lungs are known as the billows of speech function. It is from the lungs that the breath necessary for the production of speech is made available. There are several diseases that affect the lungs. The volume of air that can be made to pass into and out of the lungs is termed the vital capacity of the lungs. This *vital capacity* is reduced by disease of the lungs, by heart disease and by the weakness of the muscles engaged in the act of breathing. This loss of the vital capacity at once influences speech production. The individual will no longer be able to push up the breath necessary for speech production. This will result in 'laboured speech', 'impaired speech' or 'incomplete speech'. Such deviant behaviour is observed in persons suffering from tuberculosis or asthma. Especially in times of severe attack speech becomes almost impossible. The immediate cause is such person's lack of control over their breath. Again coughing and violent respiratory efforts after hard labour of any kind result in temporary inability of speech. Basically these are all related to the respiratory activity of the lungs which feed the breath necessary for speech.

2. ***Vocal cords:*** Section 1 of the present chapter provides a short description of what the vocal cords are. Defects of these horizontal folds in the larynx, or the laryx as a whole (the box-like structure behind the Adam's apple) results in speech disorder. Infections of these vocal folds can cause permanent or temporary speech disorder. It becomes necessary for some patients to get the whole larynx removed when such infections become acute. Also acute exertion of the vocal folds due to raising the voice beyond its capacity level can paralyze these folds and impair speech. This will occur in degrees depending on the extent the vocal folds are affected. Voice will be affected by the extend of the damage.

3. ***The tongue:*** Another major area which is noted for causing impairment of speech production is paralysis of the tongue.

It has been noted that in serious damages of the brain, epileptic attacks, or abnormal physiological conditions the tongue is highly susceptible and would be the first to be affected. Serious stress *situations* effected by biological, psychological or sociological conditions have left people 'speechless' paralyzing the activity of the tongue. Speech is partially or wholly affected depending, again, on the extent of the damage caused to the tongue. We have seen abnormal conditions where the individual makes all attempts to express himself, but it unable to activate the tongue and articulate speech. Even if the lungs or the vocal cords are damaged the individual still manages to produce at least 'laboursome speech' or whisper; but in case of serious paralysis of the tongue complete loss of speech would result.

Most deviant pronunciation of speech sounds, especially the *diphthongs* and *consonants* in children below the school-going age can be traced back to their ability to manipulate the *tongue* the way required by the particular sound. Substituting | I |, | r |, or | s | respectively with | w |, | d |, and | tʃ |, and | e: | for | ei |, for instance, has been observed. The following is a set of sentences noted as part of the pattern of behaviour observed from the ten children whom studied.

1. Doggy going vely kean (very clean).
2. That chichor (scissors) is broke.
3. Please, sit up the chair (in).
4. We'll sit on the dable for food (at the table).
5. Moob the chair out (remove).
6. Daddy coming to home lately (coming late).
7. You don't dok fastly (talk-fast).
8. I have so much clothes.
9. Do you wunted me to see (wanted)?
10. You are not habby at me (happy).

The most interesting aspect noted is the nature of the deviation. The ten children studied were mostly able to use the same consonant later in one position which they were unable to use in another. While some could say 'sun' with | s | in the initial position prefixing a vowel, they failed to use words such as 'blouse' where the final | s | was substituted with | tʃ |. In several cases we observe the 'baby talk' being carried over to some extent to later years chiefly because of the inability of the tongue to form the set of sounds in an exact manner.

The *loss of teeth* (either from the upper or lower gun) often leaves children and adults helpless in the articulation of certain sounds. The loss of front teach affects especially the articulation of sibilant sounds, such as found in *sun*, *shun*, *same* and *shame*. Lastly, deformity of the *lower lip* as an important organ of articulation often causes language deformity in terms of articulation. The deformed lip will be unable to stop the breath in co-ordination with the upper-teach in the production of, especially, the labio-dental sounds. Deformity of any part of the articulatory (vocal) mechanisms as seen above, affects language corresponding to the seriousness of the deformity; but none of these defects can so seriously damage language behaviour as it would be in the case of those mentally retarded or mentally ill as would be examined in the following section. Therefore the deviation in any of these particular cases will consist of the individual's inability, in terms of given physiological condition, to produce language partly or fully. But disorders at the *syntactic* or *semantic* level of language production or comprehension do not occur in the cases described above as those would reflect disorders at the deeper level where the mind plays the major role of linguistic organization. Where the mind is normal and the language is acquired properly such linguistic disorders do not occur.

**(3) Defects of the Auditory Mechanism :** The basic functioning of the auditory mechanism, the ears, is examined in section 1. The role of the auditory mechanism is often underestimated, just because research into this part of the human speech organs has very limited scope; and phoneticians have not reached very far in the study of auditory phonetics as they have done in case of articulatory phonetics.

There lies an intimate physiological link between the *auditory* and *articulatory* speech mechanisms. Infants begin listening to language stimuli months earlier than when the first linguistic unit is produced. Listening and recognition begin very early in the child's life. The most significant fact is that the entire language behaviour is built on the early *listening* which the child is subject to. For these reasons we find that children who are cogenitally *deaf* will not learn language and subsequently their speech capacity remains fully retarded. The learning capacity of such individuals will depend entirely on the visual (and tactile in the case of those who are *deaf* and *blind*) senses.

Deformity in any part of the organs of audition causes partial or total *deafness* and gesticulation alone become the possible means of ordinary communication with such persons. All the same difficulty with audition cannot be solely attributed to defects in the organs of auditions alone. Problems of audition can, intact, result from more than one causes: (a) patients suffering from aphasia can experience loss of hearing as aphasia affects almost all aspects speech capacity; (b) those who are congenitally deaf; and (c) post-natal deformity of a permanent or temporary kind can cause partial or complete loss of hearing.

Aphasic patients as clinical findings show, exhibit (1) an inability to recognize the meaning of spoken words (known as '*word-deafness*), (2) this inability to recognize words may stem from their inability to *differentiate sounds*, (3) inability to *comprehend* the whole meaning of a discourse, (4) inability to *recall words* to complete their sentences, and (5) *confusion* where trying to express themselves at length. But in such extreme cases of aphasia, it is reported, that a patient recognizes voice as voice, but nothing more; he recognizes language as such but cannot recognize what is said, and he hears things and can repeat, but does not understand what he says. All the same, analysis of aphasia as such does not make clear except for specific tests of audition whether failure to respond to language is the result of auditory damage or general neural disorders. In cases of clear deafness, naturally, auditory remains fully or partially impaired.

## 3. Psychogenic Speech Disorders

In the preceding section we discussed speech disorders (language deviation) of physiological origin including defects of the vocal and auditory mechanisms. It is necessary, further, to distinguish such speech deviations of physiological origin from speech deviations resulting as a direct result of *mental disorders*. What we notice in patients of speech pathology or in people suffering from any form of speech disorder is that they are incapable of functioning normally in their linguistic behaviour, if not a total loss of speech function. This phenomenon, all the same is rather apparent since speech as such is externally clearly observable.

In several cases it is difficult to make a clear distinction between speech deviations of a physiological or psychological origin. This is true especially if the physiological disorder stems from brain abnormalities or other physiological sources which cannot be easily diagnosed. The principal cue in such cases would be the presence or absence of detectable symptoms which would accompany the speech disorder. Again, when symptoms of serious physiogenic disorder are present, to trace the speech disorder back to the mind will be difficult since the speech disorder could be the result either of the physiological damage or directly of the disorder of the mind. But the sources of the disorder is very significant from the viewpoint of therapeutic measures. Depending on the sources of the disorder treatment has to be drawn from (1) *medical* sources. (2) *clinical* sources or (3) *psychiatric* sources.

Serious *physiogenic disorders* that affect speech, apart from what we discussed in section 2, mostly stem from brain abnormalities. Among such brain abnormalities include;

1. disorders such as the following (1) *Brain infection*, which usually result from the activities of bacteria or viruses that invade the brain causing;
2. damaging to the nerve tissues, (2) *Brain tumors* which involve an abnormal enlargement of neural tissues and cause serious hurdle to the normal;
3. functioning of the brain. (3) *Head injuries* which often result in chronic brain disorders and seriously affect the normal functioning of the brain;
4. (4) *Metabolic disturbances* which directly affect neurological functions, such as nutritive deficiencies imbalances in the functioning of endocrine;
5. glands etc. (5) *Epilepsy* as a disorder in the nervous system featured by sudden and repeated convulsions;

6. and lapse in or loss of conclusions. (6) *Senile brain diseases* which result from a degenerative neurological changes effected by old age. (For a comprehensive account of brain disorders, see Coleman (1964). Permanent or temporary, complete or partial handicap of language behaviour is the definite outcome of these disorders of the brain depending on the damage such disorders directly cause to speech activity and the extent to which the working of the mind would be affected by such disorders.

But from the physiogenic disorders that affect the mind and subsequently language behaviour, we distinguish those disorders that originate directly from the mind, affecting and upsetting the normally of the mind. Such abnormalities and disorders that stem directly from the mind are called *psychogenic disorders*. The following are some of the major disorders of psychological origin:

1. *Traumatic reactions* to war situations which resulted from heavy military combat experienced especially during world war I and II. This consisted in temporary or permanent neurotic or psychotic reactions, developed mostly from general combat situations, physical fatigue, threat death or mutilation and severe psychological shocks.

2. *Traumatic reaction* to catastrophies that occur in civilian life. Catastrophies such as plane crashes, getting trapped in a burning building, automobile accidents, explosions, firs, floods, earthquakes etc. have left people with personality disorders as a result of the thematic experience they underwent.

3. *Chromic situational stress* result as a reaction to situations when an individual continues for a considerably long time under threat, fear or serious dissatisfaction. This can also happen to people put in entirely new situations where things become intolerable for the individual to continue in normally. This has happened to newly married women with intolerable treatment from the in-laws.

4. *Psychoneurotic disorders* are found in those who have had a long faulty development of a biological, psychological or sociological kind. In the face of stress situations such individuals experience severe anxiety and subsequently develop neurotic reactions such as phobias.

5. *Psychophysiological disorders* are developed as a result of chronic emotional tension. A large variety of such ailment result from a repression of emotional tension and its discharge through visceral organ systems. Such disorders have a psychological origin but show out in physical ailments in any part of the body.

6. *Psychotic Disorders*: This group of mental disorders originate from psychological stress situations, organic brain disorders or from an interaction of both. In psychotic disorders, patients manifest a thoroughly deteriorated personality and a marked loss of contact with reality. The layman calls all these psychotic disorders by the term *insanity*. The Psychotic disorders are of two major types: *functional* psychoses and *organic* psychoses, the latter being associated to brain disorders as we examined above. Delusions, hallucinations, schizophrenic and paranoid reactions are a few of the instances in psychotic disorders. Schizophrenic and paranoid groups are distinguished on the basis of the patient's relative 'relationship with reality' and relative withdrawal from society. (For a comprehensive treatment of psychogenic disorders, see Coleman. 1964).

We confront a remarkably complex issue when any attempts is made to provide a systematic description of speech deviations related to psychogenic disorders. One is required to make a number of categorizations based on diagnostic reports which are available. The following list shows the areas of language and speech activity which are usually affected by psychogenic disorders.

1. *Impairment or loss of speech activity* as a whole would result from chromic brain disorders, and attacks such as epilepsy or from very acute traumatic reactions to war or civilian catastrophies. The same would be the result if psychophysiologic disorders affect the nervous system in such a way as to cause damage to the brain centres.

2. *Lack of conceptual organization* is a corollary to psychogenic disorders of depending on the severity of the case under consideration. By lack of conceptual organization we mean the patient's inability both (i) to comprehend spoken language or written language in the form of discourses, as well as (ii) to communicate himself in logically and sequentially

organized content material. Meanings tend to get mixed up and confuse the conceptual flow of the listener.

3. *Lack of comprehension* often results from cases of psychological disorders of most kind. This is observable in patients who listen to speech intently but understand not much of what is spoken to them. The level of comprehension depends on the diffusion of the patient's intellectual function, psychological distance from reality and the extent to which he shows tendency to withdraw himself from society. All forms of psychotic disorders, especially schizophrenia and paranoid cases manifest acute loss of touch with reality in various degrees and consequent loss of ability to understand what others have to say to such patients. Such patients are also disoriented in space and manifest their inability to recognize pictures and written material.

4. *Loss of memory in general* is another specific characteristic of psychogenic disorders. Both neurotic (nervous disorders) and psychotic (levels of insanity) cases exhibit loss of memory depending, again on the severity of the case. This affects language activity most seriously. Loss of memory may be in the form of the patient's inability to understand certain words used by the speaker, to maintain the *link* that needs to be established in listening, to say, a series of sentences, to remember the required vocabulary to speak a sentence, to recall the name of an object seen in front and so on. In fact the loss of memory in varying degrees affects the entire range of linguistic comprehension and production.

5. *Impairment of audition* is often exhibited by patients of psychophysiologic disorders which affect the brain or the organs of audition. This can be the result of total or partial deafness or of the impairment of nerve functions. In almost all patients of aphasia a degree of impairment of auditory process is seen. In fact this goes with 'lack of comprehension', but the symptoms in case of auditory disability are specifically related to the processes of audition. Lack of comprehension can be due to general intellectual disintegration, specific neural disorder to auditory disorder as such.

6. *Impairment of visual functions*, do occur in psychogenic

disorders just as in physiogenic cases as discussed earlier. Visual disorder at once affects visual patterning and organization. Such patients perceive words (as sequence of letters) and sentences (as sequences of words) as confused. Visual configurations become a hard task for such cases to recognize. When such persons write, the letters and words are bound to get confused.

7. *Disorder of sensory-motor functions* is another area where speech disorder manifest themselves. Patients suffering from psychogenic disorders are often unable to move their tongues for the production of speech, or speech becomes laborious, hard, slow and jerky for the patient. Articulation of certain sounds becomes hard; fluency in such cases will be beyond the patient's capacity. Sensory-motor impairment may also exhibit in terms of the accompanying gesticulatory use of hands or in the movement of the patient's eyes. All this point of a degenerative control of the mind over the body or move specifically the disintegration caused by the disorders of the brain-centres.

Much less specific manifestation of psychogenic disorders in terms of language activity occur in the area of *syntax*, *semantics*, and *articulation*. Errors of articulation, errors of syntactic organization of sentences, and errors in the organization of meaning occur as patients suffering from psychological disorders make attempts to speak, read or write. As in the case of aphasia, neurotic or psychotic patients of all categories exhibit some problem or other in the areas of comprehension and production of language in terms of the activity, as well as in the aspects of language such as in sound production (articulation), syntactic organization and semantic configuration necessary for spoken or written communication.

## 4. Deviant Language Behaviour and Home

In the beginning of the present chapter we attempted an explanatory definition of 'deviant language behaviour' and said that when either the mind or the body (mental and physiological mechanisms of speech) as the co-ordinate principles of language activity do not function properly, what results is deviant language behaviour. This explanatory definition covered, as we have seen, language deviations resulting from—

(1) physiological disorders excluding those of the brain,

(2) brain disorders of organize origin,

(3) brain disorders of functional origin,

(4) psychoneurotic disorders of from shocks and traumatic experiences,

(5) psychophysiological disorders resulting from chromic emotional tension, and

(6) psychotic disorders of insanity type. Everyone of these is characterized by (a) partial discrepancy in the functional aspects of language (say, memory), (b) total loss of the functional aspects of language, (c) partial discrepancy in the formal aspects of language (for instance difficulty with syntax), (d) partial disorder in the semantic content of language, or (e) total loss of language activity as such, in extreme and severe cases of disorders mentioned above.

There is yet another aspect of *linguistic deviation* that requires attention in the present context, namely, the kind of deviant language that is characteristic of the *$L_1$ learner at home*, and the *$L_2$ learner in the classroom*. A question may arise as to the validity of labeling the language of children with the usual mistakes as *deviant language*. The answer to such a query is clear by now; any form of language activity (either from the functional or content view-point) that is deviated from 'normal language behaviour' would very well form part of deviant language behaviour. One must indeed like care not to label this deviation as cases of speech pathology' which have been discussed above.

Home as the citadel of language development also provides us with a variety of cases in language disorder. Two major categories of language deviation we shall distinguish in relation to home environment are: (1) language deviation which forms part of the normal development of children, and (2) language disorder which is the result of some form of physiogenic or psychogenic disorder. This distinction is important to be kept in mind considering the wide range of causalities of deviant behaviour. We become aware of such problem-cases in language acquisition process when we discover that some children do not acquire language in pace with the normal language development in other children.

Again the problem of deviant language behaviour of children is complex to deal with. Problems are varied and considerably overlapping for any satisfactory classification and description. Most of the classifications we have made in the preceding section is relevant to the present purpose, but language problems of children do not include the extreme cases we examined above. First of all we shall be concerned with the deviant language behaviour of *normal children* who do not experience any conspicuous developmental problems. The following are a few of the language problem of children with a normal developmental record:

1. **Delayed manifestation of speech**: There are those children in whom speech process as a whole begins later than found in other children of their own chronological age. Is this the result of slow mental development? Certainly, we have left out for the present the group of children who are mentally retarded with significant behavioral manifestations of retardation. Also the group of children included above do not show any signs of slow psychological development in their non-verbal behaviour. The only significant behaviour is that speech is delayed noticeably but all the same begins with marked normally. There are serval factors related to this. In some such cases the random articulation phase goes on for a much longer period with normal intensity while in others the random articulation shows a marked lack of vigour and intensity. In some the production of one-word utterances counting for a much longer period than usually noticed but others do not make progress in one-ward production at all. A major percent of such cases of *delayed speech* later comes to be grouped under sub-normal cases, if not fully abnormal such as mental retardation. Research results shows that *deafness* causes the major percent of language delay in children whose mental age is marked normal. *Aphasia* with some congenital trouble to the nervous system marks the second biggest group; relative *mental deficiency* is considered the next important factor which delays speech delay. Delayed speech as exhibited by normal children, as research results show, stones, from:

(1) sociological factors such as the attitude of the parents

(2) the child's relations with the rest of the children of the family,

(3) lack of sufficient motivation as related to type of personality be tends to develop,

(4) isolation from which several children suffer in the hands of parents both of whom are employed and

(5) slight personality disorders caused by biological or sociological backgrounds.

**2. Defects in articulation:** Defects in the articulation of children's speech is something most observed in homes. Articulation defects are most common and are post of the normal language development. Articulation defects are not only restricted to children of lower ages, but are common even among school-age children who exhibit some form of deviant language behaviour. It is noted that *stutter* forms a co-feature of articulation defects when such defects are found to be considerably serve. A large number of school-going children in India suffer from some degree of stutter the reasons for which are attributed to their psychological growth and upbringing. But defects in articulations as such without the element of shuttering are considerably universal also with normal children. Defects in articulation where no physiological (organic) disorders are present can be traced back to :

(1) Lack of parental attention in making proper corrections on time,

(2) parents reinforcement of the child's wrong use of sounds by always repeating such forms for pleasure, (thereby the child hardly gets an occasion to distinguish his wrong use of the sounds from their correct application),

(3) isolation of some kind where the child mostly grow up on his own without occasions available for contrasting his language with those of other children, and

(4) delayed speech of which articulation defects from a part.

1. The *penchil* is nod here (pencil -not)
2. Mama is *coogging* now (cooking).
3. *Doont* talk to me (don't).
4. My *kair's* gone long. (hair).
5. You can *bold* it up (fold).

The sentence given above illustrate the type of articulation defects usually found in the language of children. Defects of articulation affects the consonant sounds more than vowels; it is because it is in the production of consonants that individual articulators are more involved and where greater motor-sensory control becomes necessary.

**3. Syntactic Deviations:** Just as in defects of articulation, syntactic deviations in the language produced by children often show out to be a feature in later school-age too. There is nothing significant about children at the early linguistic developmental stage making incomplete, disorderly sentences as part of their developmental process. But just as in the articulation of normal children who prolong such mistakes into later years compared to children of their own age, syntactic mistakes as exhibited by such children are prolonged into later school-going years. Such syntactic deviations include: displacement of nouns and verbs, use of nouns without placing the required articles, use of transitive verbs without objects, use of verbs of perception like *think*, *understand* etc. always in progressive tense, and use of broken phrases in speech. The mistakes in syntax will be detected as part of a form of language disorder only when such mistakes are prolonged beyond the age when they ought to disappear.

**4. Semantic defects:** A major area where language deviation in children occurs is the organization of meanings in the formation of sentences. For reasons of vocabulary shortage in such children, the sentences they form tend to be slow, lingering and confused. The syntactic and semantic disorder occur hand-in-hand and make the sentences lose their possible significance. It is chiefly from the accompanying gestures and from the context that the listening adults of members of the peer-group are able to comprehend what such children try to say. Semantic defects are also caused by the child's disability remember the links within one sentence and between sentences.

**5. Fragmentation of Sentences:** Fragmenting and disjoint sentences form part of language disorder even in otherwise normal children. It is very characteristic of children to produce sentences in broken, unrelated units of words which lock the required fluency.

Lastly there are those who are doubtlessly categorized as *abnormal* children with marked physiological or psychogenic disorders. This group of disorder cases may not so much be related to the ordinary home. Among such children include (1) the mentally retarded, (2) those with abnormal brain developments, (3) the deaf, and (4) those with defects in the vocal organs. An examination of the speech specimens of these children show degrees of language deviation from severe articulation defects and disorderly speech to complete loss of speech. The comprehension ability of such children is again markedly varying factor. From partial comprehension of the speech by adults, comprehension by these disorder cases cover degrees of comprehensions accompanied by gestures, and come to complete lack of response to any verbal stimuli in extreme cases of mental retardation and deafness. Deviated language behaviour has such a wide range of possible subnormal and abnormal variations that any description of it is bound to have limitations. A sheer reporting of a study of group of retarded children is purposeless as a mere listing of sentences they prepuce.

## 5. Language Disorder and the Classroom

Very little has been thought and said about the problems of deviant language behaviour in the classroom. The classroom, as it is clear, is an extension of home; and as such the problems of the $L_1$ learned at home is inevitably carried over to the classroom. As he moves over from home to school the language learning experiences acquire a new dimension, namely, his language learning takes place in a different set of cognitive, and sociological factors and experiences. Successful adjustment to and assimilation of these cognitive and sociological factors require a balanced and normal personality with no physiological and psychological handicaps.

We have observed three broad categories of learners in the classroom: the bright learner, the average learner and the slow learner. Again, in terms of adjustment we sub-grouped them into: the motivated bright learner, average learner and slow learner, and the unmotivated bright learner, average learner and the slow learner. Of these cognitively, sociologically and linguistically the most advantageous is the *motivated bright learner*, and the most disadvantageous is the *unmotivated slow learner*. Between these two extremes the rest of the class can be distributed in terms of their learning and adjustment.

Linguistic attainment along with better cognitive experiences and sociological adjustment stands out to be a major component of the child's performance in school. It is in this regard that deviant language behaviour becomes significant in the school-life of a child. The child with language behavioral problems may belong to any one of the groups mentioned above. All the same, the successful adjustment or maladjustment of a particular pupil with marked speech disorder of same kind will depend on to which group or sub-group the pupil belongs.

All forms of speech disorder and all degrees of such disorder will not be part of the usual classroom. The usual classroom as we have it in our schools is meant exclusively for those who are supposed to be physiologically and mentally fit and 'normal' enough to obtain necessary adjustment in the kind of present-day classroom patterns. Therefore disorder cases such as the mentally retarded, children with chronic brain diseases, the deaf etc. do not form part of any usual classroom. Mentally retarded and deaf children receive separate educational treatment in situations that are congenial to their unique requirements, which in ordinary cases are not available in the usual classroom.

Consequently, speech disorder as a linguistic factor becomes relevant to the classroom only so far as a few unique disorder problems are concerned, as we shall examine below. However limited the range of these problems which school-going children face, these problems of deviation have considerable influence on their successful adjustment to the 'classroom community'. The child who suffers from any such disorder will be in the best position to find adjustment if he belongs to the *motivated bright learner* subgroup. The reasons for this are several: The all-round performance of this subgroup is expected to be comparatively high and this must be the 'floating group' in the class. As such the language disorder any individual child in the subgroup is suffering from is counteracted by the performance of the child in all areas of study and co-curricular activities. Again, the intelligent attitude the child assumes towards his studies in general and language learning in particular enables him to make up in several ways for the defect of speech that he exhibits.

If the child belongs to the *unmotivated bright learner* sub-group, his attitude towards his defects in speech cannot be so positive and constructive as it is the case with the first subgroup. In this unmotivated bright learner who may have a few problems of adjustment, the learning attitudes in regard to the speech disorder would take two directions. While some would not care about what happens to his language and takes a stern attitude towards his language learning process, others of the subgroup would be certainly conscious of the defect and would wish to overcome the defect, but no serious learning-efforts would be made as he has only a low-level motivation to improve himself.

With the third subgroup which consists of the *motivated average learners*, the problem is not so desperate as in the second subgroup mentions above. This group of learners, like the first subgroup, is both conscious of the disorder and is in a position to make hard attempts to overcome the defects once such a thing is brought the notice of these children. Since they have not so much an intelligent bent of mind to attack the problem as the first group, they will obtain the results of overcoming the disorder, wherever possible, more slowly than the first group would. It is the positive, motivated attitudes that come to the aid of such children even if their efforts would be slow.

The fourth subgroup which consists of the *unmotivated average learners*, tend to show much less effort in overcoming the defects, if possible, than the unmotivated bright learners of the second subgroup. The chief problem with the present group is that the individual lacks, on the one hand, the mental vigor with which to attack and overcome the defect, and on the other the motivation and adjustment which would otherwise make up for much of the lack of mental vigor. Since there is considerable lack of both intelligence and motivations in these children, their problem remains more acute than would be in earlier cases.

The fifth subgroup consists of *motivated slow learners* who exhibit considerable motivation in learning, but lacks the necessary intelligence for learning. The low intelligence of this group coupled with their insignificant all-round performance gives rise to considerable stress and strain in regard to their language deficiency. There may be children who do not at all feel embarrassed about their deficiency even if it is apparent; but there can be those in the group, who feel deeply about their poor role as slow learners in class.

The sixth and the last subgroup under consideration consists of the *unmotivated slow learners* who exhibit a lack of motivation in learning together with low intelligence. When these two factors co-exist, they become in fact hopeless cases for learning purposes. Again there can be those who are sensitive to their speech deficiency, but the whole thing becomes clouded in their attempts to cope with the least demands as classroom learners. Their inability to speak well becomes a part of their experience as slow learners in class, and they learn to be more or less insensitive in the long run to all these demands. This is how we find children for whom it becomes impossible to show any progress whatsoever in their performance in general and language learning in particular. It is kind of 'negative acclimatization' to the demands of the classroom when they become insensitive to any kind of treatment such as punishment or leasing.

As mentioned above, all speech disorder problems do not become relevant to the classroom situation. There are a few unique disorder problems which are often found especially in the very early years of schooling. Such problems often escape the notice of the ordinary teacher who has his own day-to-day problems teaching to solve and who mostly tend to overlook if and when there are children in his class suffering from any form of not-so-acute speech disorder. The following are some of the major forms of deviant language behaviour which school-going children exhibit:

1. **Auditory Disturbances:** Deafness would include a post-natal development of auditory disturbance which in early years have perhaps gone unnoticed but become a hurdle to learning in the classroom. Naturally an acutely deaf child would not be admitted to school and such cases cannot form part of the classroom. The auditory disturbance may range from difficulty to recognize anything which the teacher says, to difficulty in recognizing many words of what the teacher says especially when the teachers position are not directly facing the child.

2. **Problems of articulation:** Problems of speech production caused by some defects of the organs of articulation or points of articulation are the most common of the deviant language behaviour of children in classrooms. Articulation defects of a wider range has been discussed in section 4. Articulation defects will range from any serious *handicap* of the vocal organs to varying degrees of paralysis of these organs. The

*paralysis* of the tongue, especially, makes articulation very difficult depending on the severity of the paralysis. Again defects in articulation range from the child's inability to pronounce certain consonants and vowels, to disability to produce any word with correct articulation. Stutering in varying degrees, too is no stranger to the classroom.

3. **Visual Disturbances:** Visual disturbances are mostly noted while the child is asked to do reading while the child is asked to do reading aloud. One can be sure that the child experiences difficulties with his vision if he confuses letters, word and sentences. Visual disturbances will remains a serious hurdle in reading and writing activities.

4. **General Motor Disturbances:** Problems with motor control of the child's vocal and related organs can cause speech disturbances as indicated in the preceding section. This phenomenon is noticed in learners in the classroom. Again, to demarcate everyone of these so far as deviant language behaviour is concerned is difficult because of the considerable overlaps which often appear.

Impairment of speech, auditions, reading and writing behavior manifest themselves in varying degrees in classroom learners just as such behaviour does occur in learners at home. What is important in this regard is to keep a careful eye on the learners in our classrooms and find out the extent to which any one of them suffer from such speech disturbances however minor and insignificant the case may be. Any such disturbance in the learner's language behaviour is bound to have resonance in his learning behavior and adjustment to classroom-life as whole. It is the teacher's responsibility, in such instance, to trace the history of these disturbance in such individuals and recommend them to proper sources for necessary therapy or treatment. Deviant language behaviour, thus, is so extended a phenomenon in terms of the varying degrees in which it can appear, that it invades not only mental hospitals but classrooms also.

# 11
# The Teacher and Usage

## 1. The Problem of Usage

Psycholinguistics as an investigation into the functional aspects of language acquisition, development and production, is concerned also with certain linguistic specifications of language production related to the individual and the community. This leads us directly to the problem of *usage*: What is the extent of the individual speaker's freedom in the production of language? What aspects of language remains unchanged as its core to which the individual speaker is compelled to adhere ? What relation do we recognize between the language specifications of the individual, a group, a community, and the larger linguistic society? Several Such questions need to be answered for us to know what exactly linguistic usage is.

Broadly speaking, there are three different levels at which an individual exercises language. The *first level* consists of those aspects of language which we call the 'core language' (core grammar), and the individual speaker enjoys no freedom in manipulating this level except that he has the choice to employ one structure or another as part of his efforts to communicate. This level may be said to remain mostly unchanged in the history of language development. The *second level* consists of those aspects of his language which he has some freedom to change, but once the change has been accepted by the community, the individual is again conventionally found to use the newly introduced forms. At the *third level* the individual speaker enjoys full freedom to employ a choice of his own from among the several alternatives that may be available to him.

The *three levels* we have mentioned above are very significant in our understanding of two aspects of language, namely, (1) freedom of the speaker in the production of the language, (2) the freedom which a language as such enjoys in terms of the historical changes which it undergoes. In the last resort it is solely the individual speaker who uses language, and language, however, complex a system it has become, is only a functional tool in the hands of the individual speaker who employs it for various purposes. The three levels seen above and the two aspects mentioned are highly correlated so as to yield a number of insights into the working of language. The *first level*, we have said, consists of the core aspects of language. This level has three distinct dimensions : (a) core phonology, (b) core grammar and (c) core semantics which the speaker of the language has no freedom to manipulate at will. These three dimensions, in particular the core phonology and core grammar are re-statable in terms of specific sets of *rules* which will describe the competence of the speaker. By *core phonology* we mean the sets of phonological rules which remain fundamental and consistent in the language from the viewpoint of aspect (1) and aspect (2) above, namely, the *individual's freedom to change* elements of language, and of *language change* as such. The consonant sounds, monophthongs, diphthongs and triphthongs, the basic rules for the formation of clusters and sequences using these sounds, certain patterns of stress and intonation etc. are instances of the core phonological rules that have mostly remained part of English language through out its history: the old English period, Middle English period and Modern English period. The manner in which the English sounds are articulated by contrast to the sounds of another language, say of Hindi, is a typical component of core phonology. Historians of English language note that the tutonic barbarians of the Pre-English period, some 1500 to 2000 years ago, spoke words such as *arm*, *finger*, *dumb*, *grass*, *heart* and *hand* in a way very different from the way we speak them today.

By *core grammar* we have meant the morphological (inflectional and derivational) and syntactic rules of language which remain consistent through out and do not undergo any significant change, again from the point of aspect (1) and aspect (2) above, namely, the freedom of the individual speaker and linguistic change. In fact the core grammar rules are more significant and elaborate than the core phonology or semantics. It is most basic to the language in ordering the semantic elements which reflect the conceptual store of the linguistic community in terms of the communities experiences. We may further view the core grammar from three dimensions : (a) lexical morphology, (b) inflectional morphology, and (c) syntax. As we examine the history of English we find that in all the three dimensions we find material that is most fundamental and unchanged through out its history also as we examine the present-day language in its horizontal dimensions (as used by the community), we discover stable and unchangeable core grammar rules an all the three dimensions mentioned above. These rules are known in present-day linguistics as *obligatory rules* (In contrast to optional rules).

Instances of core grammar would include: the third singular suffixation ([s], [z],[iz]), the plural suffixation ([s],[s],[iz]) the past tense and participle suffixation ([t], [d], [id],) rules of morphonology (Sandhi), the placing of the English noun, the placing of the verb, patterns of questions, rules for patterning the passive etc. These are morphological and syntactic rules which have both vertically and horizontally remained the same without change in the essentials. Neither does the language in course of years, exercise freedom to bring in changes in these rules, nor is the individual at a given time permitted to manipulate these rules the way he wishes. These are the core rules of the language which render stability and consistency to the language.

By the *core semantics* of a language we mean all the essential semantic specifications of the set of meanings (for details, see Ch. 10) which constitute the content of the language of a community. This is an important notion in understanding the first level of language we are talking about. The linguistic community as the total population which employs the language, has at its disposal a set of meanings representative of its total experiences, and a set of lexical items (lexicon) to symbolize these meanings. (see ch. 10 for details). All the same, the core semantics consists of the meaning specifications (what is called earlier conceptual elements) which the particular language *shares with* the meaning specifications of another language in conceptualizing the same set of expediences. The core meanings of a language leaving out all the superficial semantic specifications contributed by the community itself, constitute the *core semantics*. In the example of 'milk' examined to chapter 10 sec. 5 the core meaning specifications consists of the first and essential set of conceptual elements mentioned. These do not change from language to language. These are universals which equally hold good wherever the particular feature of experience is available.

The three core dimensions described above: Core phonology, core grammar and core semantics, thus, constitute the *first level* of language we have been talking about. The *second level* we said, consists of those aspects of the language which the speaker has the freedom to change, but once the change has been accepted he is conventionally bound to use the new forms. The second level is, in fact, what we shall call *usage*. In regard to aspect (1) and aspect (2), namely, the freedom of the speaker, and linguistic change, the second level is highly characteristics. While the first level remains constant and keeps the language unified retaining its fundamental features (phonological, grammatical and semantic) as a language, the second level enables two things as above (1) and (2) : it permits the language to have dialectical (horizontal) variations (1), and it permits structural change in all dimensions of phonology, grammar and meanings as part of its historical development (vertical) (2).

The *third level* consists of the complete *linguistic freedom* that the speaker is permitted to have a member of a dialectic community and further of the linguistic community at large. The second and third levels on one hand possess closer affinities while on the other they are considerably different. The second level is what makes *dialectal variations* within the linguistic oneness that the first level retains, and makes *historical change* possible for any language. The third level is what makes, as we shall call, *idiolectic variations* within the oneness, first of all, of a dialect and secondly of the language at large. The relation between idiolect, dialect and language will be discussed in section 3.

If we attempts a rationale of distinctions on the basis of what is seen above, it may be said that the first level of core elements of the language is *Grammar*, the second peripheral properties of language as a whole constitute *Usage*, and the third level of the most superficial freedom that is permitted is the *Use* of language. These distinctions are meant only to help us understand and explain the three levels which cannot escape the notice of any student of language. These are not water-tight compartments, and the demarcations between grammar, usage and use is the way we shall look at the structure of a language from a functional viewpoint.

As some would tend to think, everything in language is not in a state of continuous flux. There are very stable elements which in the last resort makes a language distinct from any other and render it unique in terms of structural features. It is the *Grammar* of a language and core semantics that renders it this unification and uniqueness. Students of language may learn it with confidence and the linguist can describe it in full faith that this will not change by the time he completes the learning or description of the language.

Everything of a language all the same is not stable and unchanging. As decades go by we notice things changing for a variety of reasons, and we also notice that various communities within the larger linguistic community speak, the larger linguistic community speak, as though, differently using different forms and semantic differentiations. This is the *Usage* part of language which makes the vertical and horizontal variations possible. The student of a language and the linguist have to be careful in learning or describing these features of usage because of the possible variations and change. Lastly, there is the individual speaker who alone infact 'uses' language for instance as a father, as a teacher and as a neighbour. This is the realm where most variations and changes take their origin, and variations of all sorts co-exist. This is the realm of idiolect or the language of the individual speaker, the *Use* of a language, with all the stylistic specifications.

## 2. The Grammar of a Language

The term *Grammar* is used here in its very special sense as seen in the preceding section, meaning the very fundamental structure of language with its phonological, syntactic and semantic dimensions. This has to be looked at from different perspectives. Every language in the world spoken by a variety of communities possesses a substantiality of its own which somehow or other make it different from others. This is why in modern times the fact that language are unique has been stressed. Linguists in the first half of the present century stressed the uniqueness of language so much that they almost lost sight of a very important aspect of language, namely, its fundamental *universality*. But in present-day linguistics the notion of *universals* is, again given sufficient attention so as to make up for the past neglect. What is significant in the present context is that the grammar of a language, as seen above, consists of two levels. We have been trying to get into the very core of language and now we find that the *first level* mentioned in the preceding pages consisting of stable and unchanged elements at the core itself is again a complex thing. What constitutes this core (as seen above in terms of 'core phonology, core grammar and core semantic - Grammar') and (1) *a set of universal* and (2) *a set of differential features.*

The set of universals as the former features are called, consists of all aspects of the (a) core phonology, (b) core grammar and (c) core semantics i.e. of Grammar, which are the same in all languages among mankind. This notion is very characteristic. It would mean that there are things at the very substratum of every language (apart from the set of concepts which we have called universals, see Ch. 10 sec. 2), which are the same or identical all. However few these universal features (phonological, grammatical and semantic) may be, they are there as the very foundation of human language as the product by the members of the same human species.

These universals, further, do not entertain any variation in terms of any of the aspects we examined above: dialect, idiolect or historical development. So long as it is men who speak language, the universals are bound to sustain their universality as applicable to one and all languages irrespective of the socio-cultural, or geographic backgrounds, of the respective communities. As mentioned, the phonological, grammatical and semantic features of the Grammar constitute the universals. Each of the three aspects have a lot to do with the very nature of language as related to the nature of man.

The universals in *phonology* would include aspects such as (i) the structure and functions of the mechanisms for articulation and audition, (ii) the point and manner of articulation of a specific sound as distinct from those of another sound, (iii) the nature of vowels of sonorous sounds, (iv) the nature of consonants as a results of some constriction in the month, of the flowing breath, (v) the characteristics of nasal sounds as resulting from the flow of breath through the nostrils, and (vi) the articulatory specifications (distinctive features) of | p |, | b |, | k |, | g | and others sounds which are part of the phonological (phonetic) system of all languages. This is a more restricted sense is also called *universal phonetics* when the concentration is exclusively on the objective articulatory features of sounds themselves. It is not necessary that a language should include a given sound, say, | z |, but the phonological universals which form a restricted set must be found in all languages spoken by man. An inventory of the universal aspects of phonology shared by a particular language would include, surprisingly perhaps, more such elements than would be otherwise.

The universals in *grammar* (core grammar) as an aspect of the Grammar of a language would include elements such as the following which would be true of all languages.

Universality, in the sense we understand it would mean that certain elements (features) under consideration are present in and true of all language of the world. The most fundamental and authentic part of the universal phonology consists of the phonetic structure of sound production which is shared by the speakers of all languages in terms of the distinctive features of specific sounds. And the differential features which are not part of all languages (unique only to a given set of languages) enable a particular language to retain only a finite set of phonetic units as the sounds of the language. In other words there can be *more or less* of features in a language compared to other languages, but whatever universals are present they retain the same characteristics in all languages. The following are a few instances of the inventory of universal grammatical features, which are more concerned with the basic syntactic framework (structure) than specific rules of the grammar of a given language.

(1) Lexical items constitute the building blocks of a sentence.

(2) The sentences of every language are linear sequences of lexical items ordered in a definite manner.

(3) The sentence as unit of a discourse is the surface manifestation of a kernel sentence of the deep structure which consists of phrase structure rules.

(4) The deep structure sentence is the product of the process of

generativity governed by the creative capacity of the speaker.

5. A Kernel sentence is the linguistic base at the deep structure level from which the surface sentence is produced by means of a process of transformation.
6. The sentence at the surface level as a product of transformation (complex sentences, questions, passive sentences etc.) is phonologically set, and further articulated in terms of the phonetic rules or written in terms of the orthographic rules of the language.
7. Every language has a phonological structure which is the immediate base of the individual's speech or writing. It is at the level of the phonological structure of a language that a discourse takes turn into speech or writing, as sun above.
8. Just as a discourse consists of sentences and a sentence consists of phrases (noun phrase, verb phrase, prepositional phrase), a phrase consists of words.
9. Every language has a suprasegmental system consisting of tones (in tonal languages such as Turkish or Chinese) or intonation (in intonational languages such as English) which help differentiate and specify the meanings of sentences.
10. The listener of a discourse undertakes a process of tallying the semantic content of the discourse (sentences) with the semantic content he as a speaker possesses, and comprehend the meaning of the discourse depending on the extent of semantic specifications which constitute the content that has in mind.

The few instances mentioned above constitute part of the inventory of universals elements at the level of the grammar of a language. All the ten instances examined above are fundamental aspects of all language because these are components of the very nature of language as such which constitute its structure. As we more closer to the peripheral level which concerns more with the organization of elements in the sentences of a language, we find that there are elements which may not be found in all languages. While a formal distinction of some kind between a noun a verb is part of the structure of all language, we find that a formal distinction of prepositions, case forms, or articles, for instance, the way we find them in or the language (prepositions in English or distinct cases in Latin) do not form part of the all languages.

Third, we have the universals of semantics as part of the grammar of a language consisting of all aspects of the core *semantics* which are true of all languages. It must be noticed that all the universal aspects of language the most significant set of universals is constituted by the core semantics. It is here that we find the true sense of the term *universals* realized. All the same the notion of universals adds to its complexity as we apply to it the level of semantics. The core semantics consists of two levels of universals. They are (1) *functional universals* and (2) *content universals*. By functional universals is meant all the functional aspects of language at the level of semantic which are concerned with the *organization of meanings* to constitute the sentence at the deep structure, and with the relation between the features of experience and the concept. Content universals are concepts and conceptual elements (see ch. 10 for details) which constitute the semantic component as the content of language. The two sets of universals together constitute the core semantics of language. The functional universals are universals by virtue of the fact they are true of all languages. These universals are intimately bound with the very properties of language as such. Language as human behaviour with a semantic content (symbolic by nature) cannot be thought of except in the context of the functional universals and content universals as elaborately discussed in ch. 10 of this book.

The *Grammar* of a language consists not only of the two *sets of universals* (1) examined above, but also a set of *differential features* (2) as mentioned in the beginning. If by universals, of the Grammar we meant aspects and elements which are stable and unchanging on the one hand, and found true of all languages on the other, the differential features of the Grammar of a language consists of those features which on the one hand are stable as above, but on the other *unique* to the particular language (not universal). The differential features are stable elements and form part of the Grammar *like* the universal aspects, but *unlike* the universal aspects the differential features are unique to the particular language and are not in the same manner part of the languages. A differential feature of the Grammar of English, for instance, consists of its basic *sentence patterns*, with main 'to be' 'to have and 'to do' verbs, intransitive verbs, single and double transitive verbs etc. An inventory of such differential features would include of a major part of English grammar, unless one is able to prove that any of these one part of the grammar of all languages.

It is on the basis of this significant notion of the *Grammar* of language that we shall understand the *Usage* and the use aspects of language. It is the grammar consisting of the core phonology, core grammar and core semantics that provides any language the kind of unification and substantiality which it manifests as a unique form of human behaviour. The grammar enables both to identify a language as distinct from other languages and at the same time define the language in terms of its structural features.

## 3. Usage and Language Change

The *usage* and the *use* of a language, as seen above, are built on the *Grammar* of the language. Usage entertains its freedom for change in two aspects, as seen in sec. 1. (1) the speaker's freedom at the horizontal level, and (2) the freedom of the language at the vertical level i.e. language change in its historical development. Usage constitutes that level of language which is on the one hand, built on the grammar of language, and on the other permits the speaker within a given range to divide from the established norms of the linguistic community. Usage infact forms the second level of the speaker's language, the first being the Grammar, and the third being use.

The notion of usage as such is quite modern. With the onset of descriptive structural linguistics the descriptive structural linguistics the traditional understanding of grammar as something 'prescriptive' (by contrast to 'descriptive') came to be widely depreciated. Language is considered no longer a phenomenon consisting solely of unchangeable and absolute elements and rules as it had been traditionally held, and as something over which the grammarian of the language holds absolute authority. Instead, present-day grammars are expected to be *descriptions* of the grammar of a language in such a way as to *explain* how the speakers of the language use their language. In more technical terms, the grammar of a language is expected to explains the *linguistic competence* of the speaker. (see Ch. 4.)

In trying to provide an explanatory accounting of the linguistic competence of the speaker of a language, the grammarian (linguist) is expected, again, to base his accounting (theory, grammar) as a product of *introspection* , and inference on the *observation* of the speaker's performance. In other words the higher the correlation between the grammar (accounting) and the speaker's *performance*, the better the grammar ought to be. What is required is an accounting of the data on the language oriented to a comprehensive theory of language, which is neither a plain product of the grammarian's introspection without correlation to the data, nor a sheer presentation of the data. This in fact is the solid basis and rationale of descriptive grammar, where *introspection* and *observation* are expected to yield an accounting which will further add to a comprehension theory of language.

The *theory of language* is the ultimate aim and final product of any grammar in which all aspects of language as seen in the present sections will be taken care of. The *theory of language* which the linguist aims at will, thus, include following aspects described above but schematically presented below:-

| | | Language<br>1<br>Grammar<br>↓ | | |
|---|---|---|---|---|
| sets of<br>universals in<br>phonology<br>grammar<br>semantics | Compe-<br>tence | Core<br>phonology<br>grammar<br>semantics | level<br>of<br>stable<br>elements | sets of<br>differen-<br>tials in<br>phonology<br>semantics |
| | Compe-<br>tence<br>perfor-<br>mance | 2<br>Usage<br>↓<br>phonology<br>grammar<br>semantics | level of<br>historical<br>change | |
| | Perfor-<br>mance | 3<br>Use<br>↓<br>Phonology<br>grammar<br>semantics | speaker's<br>level of<br>options/<br>stylistical | |

On the basis of all that is seen above we may ascertain that it is at the level of usage that the speaker (vis-a-vis the listener) as the sole agent of any language activity functions as the 'agent of language change'. Although for purposes of adequacy we differentiated aspects (1) and (2) above as the speaker's freedom and language change, it can be seen that the speaker's freedom at the second level of language called usage as a horizontal and spatial factor is the same *force* working behind language change as a vertical (historical) and temporal factor. In other words, the speaker is the ultimate agent of (1) historical as well as (2) dialectical ('dialect' considered in its broadest sense) variations.

Usage as the second level of language enables the speaker consciously or involuntarily to introduce newer forms for a variety of purposes. These purposes will include better communicative adequacy, better artistic expression, euphemism (choice of new word to avoid certain undertones, e.g. *expired* for *died.*) and creative needs. Any such newer forms and expressions will in course of time be accepted by the community so long as such forms with the grammar of the language (seen in the preceding section). The level of usage permits the introduction of new forms and expressions ultimately providing the language the kind of flexibility that is required for any language to develop and adapt itself to the changing needs of a given period. The level of usage covers a considerable portion of all aspects of language which somehow are liable to change without affecting to grammar of a language:

1. *Sound changes* have happened in the history of English. English sounds as we use them today have a traceable history. The great vowel shift was concerned with the 'long stressed vowels' of English during the middle ages. The high vowels became diphthongs. The middle English ride | i : d |. became modern English ride | raid |. This vowel shift affected hundreds of English words such as *life, hide, wide, side* etc. The sound | e : | became | i : |, | o | became | u | or | u | in words such as *reed, heel, queen, deep* and soon, *mood, shoot, cool, fool* and *took, look* etc. affecting the vowels of hundreds of words in English.

2. *Changes in spellings* : Spellings constitute an area where English language has undergone in its history amazing transformation, chiefly contributing to the present-day flux in

orthography. This transformation becomes clear if we examine a few sets of words the old English, Middle English and Modern English:

| Old English or (Old French) | Middle English | Modern English |
|---|---|---|
| ābīdan | abide | abide |
| āfx̄rd | afred (e) | afraid |
| æfter | after | after |
| banere | baner | banner |
| bær | bare (bair) | bare |
| befallan | befalle | befall |
| ceallian | call (e) | call |
| chaine | cheyne | chain |
| eild | child (chylde) | child |
| ealle | alle | all |
| fæder | fader | father |
| modor | moder | mother |

3. *Grammatical changes:* The grammar of English changed in many aspects from old English to Middle English and further to Modern English. So far as usage is concerned the changes at the level of grammar is the most significant. Grammatical changes have occurred in (1) *structural items* (function words) such as the pronouns and the definite and indefinite articles, (2) *inflections*, especially the plural suffix and past-tense suffix, (3) *derivations* in their prefix and suffix forms, (4) *compounding* as a principal device for the formation of word-units to designate new meanings, (5) continuing shift of 'strong' *verbs* in to their *ed* (weak) forms in the formation (6) certain developments in the formation of *tenses* such as the progressive *are doing* and the negative, *do not*.

Such forms were not part of the Old, Middle or early Modern English. One of the classical ways to note and study changes in usage is to examine the translations of the Bible which belong to various periods. A close examination of materials which belong to different ages in the historical development of English would reveal that there have been *syntactic changes* also. Modern usages such as : *What they are doing* in place of the older *what they do*, the present-day use of the modal auxiliaries (could, should would might, must, ought) without any relation to the past which the form in fact designates, and changes which have occurred in the structure of English *verb phrase* in a number of ways, are all instances of syntactic changes that have come as part of the development of English language.

4. *Semantic Changes:* Apart from what is mentioned above, the second level of language which we have called *usage* as the domain of change and development also affects the *semantic component* of language. Semantic changes in language should be seen against the background the structure of the semantic component as projected by the present book. By semantic changes we mean the following:

(1) addition of a meaning specification to the semantic content a word in terms of a *conceptual element*, e.g. the word *cloud* designating the clouds in the sky assumes an added conceptual elements which signifies a similar state of mind in the expression '*the mind is clouded*'.

(2) the addition of a different meaning specification to a word in terms of another *concept*, while retaining the already existing signification. The word *trunk*, already employed in designating a number of features of experience such as an elephant's trunk, tree trunk, a trunk for keeping clothes etc. now comes to designate another concept 'a *trunk-call*'.

(3) an increase in the *denotation* (extension) of the meaning of a word by applying the word to include the members of a different class. The word *father* already designating the biological father (father of a child), comes to include as part of its denotation *Fathers* meaning spiritual (religions) father. Here we find the signification undergoing an extension, not a deepening (designated by the term 'connotation'). Both would mean 'begetting', fathers in the biological sense, and fathers in the spiritual sense.

(4) an increase in the *connotation* (depth) of meaning of

conceptual elements to the word and the resulting semantic content would have a deeper sense. *Beauty* which usually designates physical beauty comes to mean deeper aspects such as the beauty of 'thought', 'life', behaviour' and 'imagination'.

(5) a substitution of already existing designation of a word with a different concept. In other words the word assumes an entirely new meaning deleting the old. While *meat* once meant 'any food', it has come to mean exclusively 'the flesh of animals'. *Galaxy* which once referred to 'milk', now has an entirely different meaning in Modern English.

(6) The creation of a new word to designate something which has not been part of the experience of the community. This mostly happens with inventions and discoveries. It may be an entirely new word like *Kangaroo* formed out of, perhaps, some expression which the natives of Australia used, something which had no relation to the animal with a pouch for carrying its young one. It may be the result of coinages by an interplay of classical prefixes or suffixes and English roots or vice versa, as found in *miniskirt, aristocrat, lavishness, imperishable* etc. Such new forms also originate as a result of *compounding* of forms already in use, such as *black market.*

(7) the use of a word to designate exactly the opposite of what the word stands for. The utterance 'Wonderful' or 'excellent' is equally used to designate opposite meanings in relation to a context, especially with a touch of sarcasm.

(8) the formation of phrases and idioms which would mean different firm what the co-elements mean. Instances for this are the numerous phrases and idiomatic expressions used in Modern English. The word *put* has generated forms with very different semantic specifications as found in *put on, put off, put out, put up with* and so on. English verbs have proved very fertile in designating new *specifications* with the addition of a different preposition.

In short, as the conceptual clarity of the linguistic community increases, and as ways of expressing new features of experience become increasingly required there occurs ever *newer organization* of the set of symbolic forms which the community uses. New thinking (new conceptual organization) by way of better understanding of reality, origin of new concepts, the need to discard irrelevant concepts and the addition or deletion of conceptual elements in terms of semantic specifications are what constitute semantic change in a language. The root of semantic change lies in the very mind of man, and subsequently his need to represent new sets of experiences that he confronts. But old reforms are preserved because of linguistic continuity and become available to subsequent generations, which in turn reflect the semantic transformation.

## 4. Usage and Linguistic Strata

Usage, as seen above, consists of the changeable aspects of language (the second level) and its vertical dimensions (in history) consists of phonological, grammatical and semantic changes which we discussed in the preceding section. Usage has another dimensions which is realized in a horizontal (spatial) manner at a given time without considering it from a historical viewpoint. This latter dimension of usage, noted above as aspect (1) (see, Sec.1), we label as *linguistic strata*.

More important than the historical perspective of usage, 'linguistic strata' constitutes in present-day linguistics an area of special interest. A linguistic community(society) is a far outstretched group. Such a community usually consists of a number of subsidiary communities which are geographically or locally separated. The notion of what is usually called a 'linguistic community' is very complex and ambiguous today due to large scale inter communion that it taking place at the international level. The same language (say, English) is spoken by not only a variety of communities in one and the same geographically unified country, but the same language is spoken by communities living in far off countries. Therefor in this context we are confronting a kind of linguistic variation that is peculiar and different from what we examined as historical variation.

By *linguistic strata* we mean the linguistic variations present among the communities speaking the same language at a given time. The term *dialect* is usually applied here, but dialect in present-day linguistics has a very restricted sense as we shall see below. The notion of 'language', in fact, is some kind of an abstraction in the same sense as we understand 'society'. Taking for granted the unification offered by the grammar (sec, sec. 1) of a language, we find that what we call language is a configuration of several 'sub-languages' to put it so, which are further divisible into sub--languages, unit we come down to the actual speaker who produces a unique language of his own. Subsequently, the variation that a given period is considerably large. Strata linguistics (known also as area linguistics) studies the phenomenon of such variation in language on a geographical basis.

Considering what we saw in connection with the *Grammar* of a language is sec. 2, which we labeled as the *first level* of language, the *second level* is what offers variety and change in the structure of any language. This second level we called *usage*. In other words, if termed historical *language change* as aspect (2) of usage, we shall term *linguistic strata variations* (including dialectical variations) as aspect (1) of usage (sec sec. 1.). In the context of aspect (1), thus, usage becomes the kind of variety in forms and expressions which a language at any given time exhibits on the basis of its geographical distinctions.

How do variety in forms and expressions (more specifically, in the phonological, grammatical and semantic aspects of usage) occur in a language? The linguistic community is highly dispersed group. The language of the 'original group' in the historical development of a language undergoes considerable change, especially the peripheral level, as the original community gets further and further dispersed into different communities in the distant regions of the same country. The closer these groups speaking the same language are, the least the differences become; and the further the groups are, the greater are the differences bound to be. Geographical separation and the nature of communal interaction in terms of business and cultural relations chiefly govern in the differences between the language of two given communities within the larger linguistic community.

The language of every one of the sub-communities we have mentioned with the linguistic variations they develop or retain, we call a *dialect*. Dialects are, thus, the language of the geographically separated sub-communities of a linguistic community, which in course of time retain or develop certain forms and expression that are not part of the language of other sub-communities.

The *level of comprehension* based on the *oneness of the language* should be considered as the criteria for differentiating dialects. A speaker mores away from home; initially he finds the language of the people around fully comprehensible, and no form is found different from what he speaks: he is in a region where his own dialect is spoken. As he goes further he finds the language comprehensible but forms and expressions which are strange to ears become more common: he is in a regions where different dialects of his own language is spoken. He moves further and finally comes to a region where not only strange forms occur in the language of the people, but he finds the speech fully strange and *incomprehensible*: he is now in a region where a (dialect which belongs to an entirely different language is spoken. Here all speaker is in the midst of another language. He understands earlier dialects not because he has further learned them, but they belong to the language that he speaks.

Linguistic strata not only includes dialects, but (as so characteristic of English today) the some language spoken in *another country*, which cannot be called a dialect of the language. English today is an international language and it has long ago crossed the geographic and national boundaries of its original linguistic community of English people. English is spoken as the first language ($L_1$) in the united states of America, Australia, Canada and New Zealand.

Apart from the British Isles; while in most other countries such as India English has become the language of the elite as a second language ($L_2$). The use of English at all these levels has given rise to additional problems of linguistic strata. While we do not label Australian English as a dialect of English, we may conveniently call it a *regional variety* of English. Indian English even-though not spoken as $L_1$ becomes a regional variety of English Language the moment we take into consideration a set of specificities which can be called uniquely Indian and not found in other regional varieties. All such regional varieties becomes part of the linguistic strata of a language. An important consideration, in this regard, is that every such spoken at the $L_1$ level, can have different dialects. Both at the level of native dialects and at the level of other regional dialects any one dialect in course of time gains prestige and will be accepted as the *Standard Dialect* of the language in which all formal learning takes place.

Apart from *dialects* and *regional variations*, linguistics strata has a third dimension, which consists of the levels at which a language is used. A distinction can be made between *standard language* and *non-standard* (or dialectical) *language*. In English, for instance, standard language consists of the Received Pronunciation and standard English usage which have been internationally followed. Non-standard English consists of the various dialectical and slang usages of English. As mentioned above standard language develops out of the most prestigious dialect of the language. Standard English developed from what we know to day as the London dialect spoken in Southern England.

The standard language is further seen at two different levels: *general language* and *special language* (technical language). By general language we mean the language used by the general *media* and in books of non-specialized nature. Special language which goes with specialized fields of knowledge such as the sciences, is built on the bases of general language. A comparison may be made in this regard between a book on 'social studies' for a high school class IX and book on, say, 'machine design' for students of engineering. While the first reflects general English, the second will reflects special English.

A further consideration takes us to the division between *formal* and *informal* language. General language is the basis, again, for this consideration. An educated English man employes his general English for two distinct purposes namely to function outside as a professional, and to function of at home as member of his family. The language an educated individual employes at his professional (formed level is known as formal language, while what he uses at informal situations (say, home) is informal language.

While considering the third dimension of linguistic strata, we have (almost unknowingly) stepped into the *third level* of language which we have labelled as *use* (see sec. 1.). We thought of the *Grammar*, *usage* and *use* as the three levels of language based on notion of linguistic *variation*. What, thus, constitutes use, as the individual speaker's *freedom* ultimately to employ one form or expression for another in course of his language activity. The Grammar at a given context specifies the essential rules of the sentences the speaker should produce, the usage of the language permits the speaker to employ one expression for another as the content of the pattern that the Grammar specifies, while use permits him, as a speaker not only to choose between a number of formal units of similar that are at his disposal, but also to *deviate* in a very personal manner from the norms of production and style which other speakers follow in their own way. In other words use is the *idiolectic manner* of language production characterized by very personal aspects of phonology, grammar and semantics. This is the final realm of language *unification* as well as *variation* realized at the level of the individual speaker.

In fact, the scope of the *use* of language as a principle of variation is illimited. It all depends on how many levels the individual speaker as a member of a complex society can function. The speaker is, for instance, a professor, a father, a husband, a friend, a brother, and he is expected a to play numerous of roles in the context of his community apart from the fact that he belongs to socially and economically upper class. Every one of the roles call for a different set of forms and expressions drawn from his general language store. If being a professor requires formal language, when he functions at the level of a friend he is called on to employ an informal set of forms of his language. Any closer examination will show that the individual's use of the language has the most characteristic phonological, grammatical and semantic specifications which are based on his socio-economic background, features of physiological speech mechanisms, mental development and general upbringing and temperament. All the same the speaker's *use* of the language is based on accepted *usage*, and further built on the foundations of the *Grammar* of the language.

## 5. Usage in the Classroom

The notion of usage has much relevance to the classroom. The language teacher whether of $L_1$ or $L_2$ should be in a position to view the language he teaches from the *three levels* of language that we examined in the preceding sections. This will help him to function as judicious arbiter that he is expected to be in class. His attitude towards language and the rules of grammar will not strike any extremes provides he is conversant with the fact language is not so simple a set of rules for the pupils to commit to memory. He knows what the *Grammar* of a language is, and to what extent this Grammar (as distinct from the broader aspects of grammar) should be enforced in the teaching of the language. He learns to distinguish this fundamental grammar from all other more peripheral aspects chiefly from his experience with and insights of the language.

Now the teacher knows that the entire grammar of his language is not to be enforced with one and the same love for rules. The teacher, as it often happen, need not get worried over what is often labelled as 'craze for change' which he finds with the latest trends in the language. He knows that all the change and the kind of nauseating variety which his language exhibits are all part the usage level of the language which we have thought of as the *second level.* The level of usage, though permits change has again a substantiality of its own. Usage allows new forms to come in and get settled as part of the language, but once the forms are accepted by the community the speaker is expected to use the new forms and expressions.

The general texture of the word *dimension* (to examine only one instance) with the number of sounds, the rules of the sequence that is realized, the articulation of the vowels and consonants, and the possible phrases which can be formed out of the word is part of the Grammar (core phonology) of English language, while we find the word pronounced differently in different regional varieties of English. The principal varieties are found as part of American and British English. Americans pronounce the word as I dimenʃn I while the British speak it as I dimenʃn I with chief difference lying of the word. The peculiar nature of the first and the second syllabus of the word has given rise to a number of specific variations in regions where English is spoken at the level of $L_2$.

Again the same word *dimensions* spoken by individual speakers who belonging to the United States, Britain and India exhibit a large variety of specific differences in pronunciation which when grouped under general heads give us the averages of specificities belonging to these three regions. By *use* we have meant exactly these differences at the level of the individual speaker, and the choice of the word *dimension* of form a noun phrase from among numerous other forms which are available to him with more or less similar meanings.

We may also examine an instance from the core grammar of the Grammar of English. Traditionally it was held that the form *among* goes with several, while '*between*' goes with only two. This was indeed part of the classroom grammar of our good old days. But today the teacher gets more puzzled than ever when he discovers that *between* has come to be used to designate a relation of 'two' as well as 'several' members of a class. 'Among' has assumed another specific semantic role as found in *They chose three 'from among' ten*. The basic phonological grammatical and semantic texture of the expression (between, vs among) belongs to the Grammar of English, while more specific application of the two forms as *variants* in surface sentences belong to the level of usage. Lastly, the constructions that an individual speaker produces, the variety of phonetic specifications of the forms, the semantic shades which the speaker introduced using the two forms as an expression of his own creativity are all part of the use of the forms, or the use of the language by the speaker as part of his idiolect.

The distinctions which the teacher draws in this regard are of considerable help to him in his classroom practices from the viewpoint of (1) his own linguistic convictions, (2) his attitude towards the problems of variety and liberal usage, and (3) the learners' attitudes to grammar. He knows that language that the necessary fundamental stability that it requires, and at the same time it is not a set of absolute rules from top to bottom, that as the content of human behaviour language has also provisions for change, adaptation, variety and even ambiguity. Everything is not so neat and clear in terms of grammar as a classroom practitioner wishes it to be.

Our understanding of language in terms of the three levels of the Grammar, usage, and use (each level consisting of its phonological, grammatical and semantic aspects) renders our view of 'grammar' more realistic, plausible and liberal. It is not an authoritarian attitude that serves, but a better insight into the working of the grammar, usage and use at three different levels exhibiting the structural specificities of language in three different ways.

The understanding of language of terms of the three levels helps us view with greater sympathy the roles of the linguistic community and the individual speaker. The traditional and authoritarian views hardly did justice to the two agents. Today we view language no longer as a awe-inspiring and objective system which has nothing to do with the community and the speaker. Instead, the very structure of language allows key and active roles to the speaker as an individual and the community as a whole. The grammarian should observe the true usage of the people, accepted by the community at large, is the mean of a set of variants used by individual speakers specified by their own linguistic backgrounds. Languages are not primarily properties of textbooks but of living communities which are rooted in specific cultural behaviour. This awareness of the living and evolving nature of language in socio-cultural setting must enable the teacher to deal with it not a sterile, untouchable commodity, but with a living and sensitive touch.

The teacher is required to shape and re-shape pupils' language patterns to accommodate them among the large-scale adaptation which the pupils as speakers are expected obtain. Usage has communal acceptance (group norms) as its foundation. As seen above, the linguistic community at large can be brought down to sub-communities and sub-groups until we reach the level of the individual speaker. It is the speaker who ultimately plays social roles where large-scale adaptation to group and communal situations in called for.

The effectiveness of the substantiality offered by the Grammar and the group norms and their variants offered by usage come to be concretized only at the level of use by the speaker who, in turn, adapts the whole thing as suited to particular situations. Here as speaker he confronts large-scale options in terms of forms on the basis of accepted usage and the fundamental Grammar. Just as the 'competence' of the first language learner develops and reaches maturity in a given language environment through his (1) cognitive (2) sociological, and (3) linguistic experiences by means of the processes of abstraction and conceptualization, the students in our classrooms should have the keen sensitivity to observe the language used in and out of the class and deduce norms regarding the basic Grammar and, usage.

It is a matter to stress much that the students must be led to fit his communication to accepted patterns of usage. This is the only way to keep the language in our classrooms and of the students outside alive and dynamic. It is interesting to note that a pupil who can answer questions in class perfectly and a teacher who would communicate to his pupils well, fail equally to perform outside in actual communicative contents for which a language is exactly meant. Most people fail to use their language effectively at an informal situation where formal, academic or textbook language cannot easily come to his service.

The unit of a language is not the components with which a sentence is constructed, but the total perception, the 'linguistic gestalt' to be transmitted to the listener. The sub-components are subservient and oriented to this whole. As scientists we approach language in two ways: analytically and synthetically. We anatomize language, pick out its components and minutely study the phonological, morphological, syntactic and semantic aspects which are concretized at the three levels of language we have just examined. This is the way like a surgeon operating on a patient, the student of language operates. But the success lies in the synthetic part of the student's operation. The linguist on the one hand is expected to built up the blocks into a theory of the particular language comprising of the phonological, grammatical and semantic aspects which will indeed add to a comprehensive *theory of language* (comprising only of universals), and the *teacher*, on the other, like a practical linguist students to help them build up the blocks of their language (which they have analytically segmented for learning purposes) and achieve the total perceptions of *language as discourse* in all its beauty and purposefulness. This approach, as we shall examine more in detail in the last chapter, will make the teaching and learning of language more realistic, concrete, enjoyable and personal. The usage-oriented learning of the language with an age on the total linguistic perception (linguistic gestalt) will enables the learners to employ the language with equal competence both on the stage and in the market-place, instead of parrotting a few sentences committed to memory from the textbook. The paramount aim in this regard should be to make language learning at the $L_2$ level a pleasant and welcome experience.

# 12
# The Phenomenon of Error in Language

## 1. The Nature of Errors in Language Behaviour

Our understanding of language requires also an insight into the nature of errors that occurs at various levels in language. A variety at various levels in language. A variety of answers are given to the problem of errors, and certainly errors constitute a difficult area to investigate. To begin with, language should be seen at two levels: (1) as an objectively structured phenomenon which is (2) acquired and used by the speaker. A distinction of this kind leads us exactly to the relation between the *speaker* and *language*. The speaker and the language he speaks (produces) are not identical; they are distinct, and as the foregoing chapters make it very clear, language has a *substantiality* of its own, independent from an individual speaker even though at a functional level we shall not think of language as an objective phenomenon separate from the speaker. Considering the two levels mentioned above, one may pose the question as to where errors occur, supposing for the present we know what errors are. Errors as a phenomenon related to the use of language do not and cannot occur at level (1). Instead errors occur, if and when they do, only at level (2). This is an important notion in our understanding of the nature of errors.

What does this distinction mean? Level (1), as such a complex notion, renders languages an independent factor with some substantiality of its own. As such language is a built-in symbolic system consisting of its own phonological, grammatical and semantic representations and rules which developed into an objective system of components by the consensus of a developing community. It is not something with which the individual members of the community are born; instead the members, 'learn', 'pick up', or 'acquire' the language for themselves to make it subservient to their instructional needs.

An objective system of this kind of certainly equipped with all that it requires for proper functioning as a medium of behavioral interaction and interpersonal communion. As a behavioural device for communion among the members of the community, language undergoes a natural development in line with what in fact the community requires in a given period of time. As think that such a system can have errors of any kind in it. To think that language itself can have errors is certainly a contradiction in relation to the nature and purpose of language. Again, it has never been pointed out in the history of language analysis that any language contained *errors* of any kind from the viewpoint of the linguistic community which the language served. For these reasons are may safely hold that errors never form part of the very structure of any natural language (by contrast to artificial symbolic systems which the linguist may construct).

It is at the level (2) of language, we say, that *errors* occur. The level (2) as mentioned above, consists of the individual speaker's use of language. What is the structure of the level (2) as mentioned above ? In fact the answer to this one question is the gist of what has been discussed in the present book. The level (2) as the individual speaker's use of language consists of : (a) the speaker's linguistic competence, (b) the speaker's performance on the one hand, and on the other, (c) the acquisition of the Grammar of the language, (d) the acquisition of use, and (e) the speaker's actual use (production) of the language. Again, the level (2) has the dimensions of (a) language production and (b) language comprehension. An other words, the speaker's use of language has numerous aspects under consideration all of which have something or other to contribute to our understanding of what we have called *error.*

If errors are a matter of the speaker's side of language (the level 2), what then is error? Errors are *deviations* from linguistic norms (phonological, grammatical and semantic) which occur in the speaker's *use* of language. Whatever be the linguistic background of some error occurring in a speaker's use the language, it is significant to note that errors as a phenomenon occur *only* in the speaker's use of language. This rules out a number of alternatives: 1. Errors do not occur as part of the speaker's linguistic competence. 2. The process of internalization of language does not render itself to the formation of errors as part of the child's language (level 1). 3. We do not consider under errors any 'deviant language behaviour' (see Ch. 11) which occurs as a result of organic or functional speech disorder. 4. Errors do not occur in the child's acquisition or core phonology, grammar or semantics which constitute a system of rules.

If so, what are the areas where errors occur? What areas of language behaviour should form the contest of a description of the phenomenon of errors in language behaviour ? Errors, we have said, are deviations from the phonological, grammatical and semantic norms of a language. A significant question closely related to all that we discussed above is whether, errors, as deviations of some kind which figure in the speaker's *possession* language or the actual *exercise* of it. This at once takes us back to the above alternatives which we have ruled out. The terms competence, 'internalization' and 'possession' of language designate that the individual speaker has made his own a fundamental *linguistic system* which is the heritage of the community that the speaker belongs to. It is this fundamental linguistic system (known also as the theory of language, or the grammar of language. See also Ch. 4) that the $L_1$ learner acquires for himself in the process of learning his language. We therefor assume that the child makes his own the fundamental rules of his language without any error creeping in at the level of his competence which he acquires as a result of the long acquaintance with the language of the adult speakers of the community. (See sec. 2 for the detailed discussion of this aspect).

In other words we may safely assume that errors occur only in the speaker's actual *exercise* of the language. This exercise of language, more technically we have called *performance*, constitutes the level (2) mentioned above. A closer examination of error would require a number of distinctions of linguistic performance, namely, the areas where errors in language behaviour will chiefly occur.

Three broad categories which we shall consider one: formal errors, functional errors and conceptual errors.

1. ***Formal errors*** are deviations of language performance at the level of the formal units of language. Errors of this category can occur both in speech and writing. This include the formal units of (a) sounds, (b) graphics (c) morphemes, (d) words, (e) phrases, (f) sentences, (g) discourses, (h) stress, (i) intonation, and (j) punctuations. Of these errors in sounds, morphemes, words, stress, intonation, phrases, sentences and discourses occur as part of the child's speech behaviour, and errors in graphics spellings morphemes, words, phrases, sentences, discourses and punctuations occur as part of the child's writing behaviour.

A child a pupil instead of saying *ball* uses the form I pɔl I we say that he has committed an error in sounds. Although I b I and I p I are part of the sound system of English, and the child has produced I p I correctly, the error consists in the substituting the consonant I p I for I b I. Again, instead of saying *oxen*, the pupil employs the usual plural suffix 'es' with ox and says Iɔksis I. Both the morphological units (ox and es) are part of the morphological system of English and such are not themselves wrong. But the error consists in the combination of both in places of the exceptional form lən I. Spelling errors occur as a very usual phenomenon in the writing even of adults. The pupil who spells the word wrongly and writes m-a-t-e-r (mother), we say, commits an error in spelling. Both in speech and writing pupils make use of wrong words when either the correct words are not known to him or he finds it not possible to recall the correct forms. In the sentence *My front has gone home* the pupil uses *front* in place of *friend*. We call it a lexica error when we know that it is not a matter of sheer pronunciation. All such errors occurring at the formal level can be categorized under formal errors.

2. ***Functional errors*** occur in the language behaviour of pupils at the level of the language *skills* which we have described as 'functional moulds' with a specific linguistic content. In fact it is difficult to distinguish functional errors in this sense from formal errors described above because the skills of listening, speaking, reading and writing cannot be thought of except in terms of the language content. (An English sentence for instance) that fill in the mould. All the same formal errors are usually tagged on to the skills

of listening, speaking, reading and writing, although these errors specifically occurs in terms of some formal unit or other which will constituent the content of the skill. Unlike the communication skills of speaking and writing, the recognition skills of listening and reading will exhibit distinctive problems of comprehension which we may not attribute exclusively to the formal level. Errors in comprehension (listening comprehension and reading comprehension), apart from failures in recognizing the formal units such as words, do occur at the semantic level as we shall see below. (see section 4 below for further details).

***3. Conceptual errors*** occur in children's language at the level of the semantic component. This is the third major area where errors can occur in language. Conceptual development (see Ch. 10) as a process of the formation of concepts on the basis of the cognitive experiences, and the denotative (broadening) and connotative (depending) development of concepts in terms of conceptual elements are a slow process in children. Acquiring the complete set of meanings and meaning specifications of a word takes years of learning. Consequently, inadequate use of words which should suit to a given context is common in the language of children. This results from several factors such as the extent of the child's vocabulary, his aptness in recalling a word, and ability to make the proper choice of a word for a particular expression. It is such inadequate conceptual development that chiefly contribute to problems at the level of comprehension. While reading or listening what primarily helps the pupil are the recognition of the formal units as such, and recognition of the semantic specifications which contribute to the contextual (special) use of such units in language.

The formal, functional and conceptual errors constitute the first dimension of errors which often form part of the pupils' linguistic performance. Errors, on the other hand have something to do also with the three levels of language discussed in Ch. 12, namely, the *Grammar*, *usage* and *use*, the three levels posed as part of the child's linguistic performance. The child acquires the Grammar of the language which in turn consists of the core phonology, grammar and semantics, as the fundamental level upon which to build his usage and use of the language. The Grammar must be looked at from two viewpoints : competence and performance. The child's linguistic competence guarantees the possession of the

Grammar of the language; his performance involves the exercise of the Grammar.

Competence as the acquisition and possession of the Grammar in the form of a basic. System of rules and patterns as discussed above, and as we shall examine more in detail later, cannot involve error because the learner acquires the Grammar on the basis of what he directly listens to from the speakers of the language. Since by the Grammar we have meant the core aspects of the language which on the one hand consists of the universals and on the other consists of what is fundamentally unique to the language (namely, the differentiate) there is little possibility of any error occurring at this level. The level of the Grammar constitute principally of the basic sentence patterns, formal, functional and conceptual elements which are universals and differentials, these patterns and elements as rules and functional norms themselves cannot render themselves to any error whatsoever in the usual communal context of the language acquisition.

Performance as the actual exercise of language involving the Grammar of the language, may have a number of factors as will be examined below, which render performance at this first level itself to error. In other words the errors which occur (in a variably at the level of linguistic performance) cannot be traced back to the child's acquisition and possession of the Grammar as constituting the competence of the language. Instead, satisfactory rationale must be searched level of linguistic performance as involving the exercise of the Grammar of the language in terms of the skills of listening, speaking reading and writing.

## 2. Errors, Grammar and Usage

Looking about for a set of rationale for the occurrence of errors in language, are might find the following factors:

1. Errors occur primarily as a result of wrong transformation which the pupil undertakes as he attempts to produce a sentence in speech or in writing. As we know, transformations are processes by means of which one or more kernel sentences at the deep structure level are converted into surface sentences (phonologically set and further phonated or converted into graphic forms). While the kernel sentences forming the content of deep structure are

simple, declarative and active sentences, the transformation takes place in terms of negative, interrogative, passive or explanative sentences. The linguistic competence of the child as the basis of all linguistic functions is infact 'a built-in syntactic structure' in the sense that it is capable of generally the kind of sentence that the speaker's situation requires.

As part of the competence the child possesses the rules for the phonological, morphological, syntactic and semantic patterning of sentences (described above as the Grammar of the language). This patterning which constitute the 'syntactic structure' of the language yields the correct and necessary pattern of phonological grammatical and semantic sequence which alone will constitute the fundamental kernel sentence. So far things are all right with the child's language; he has not made any errors whatever, nor has he the possibility to commit any error at this level. The reasons for this being that all that the child as speaker is required to do is to fill in the *functional slots* of the patterns at the deep structure level (which the phrase structure underlying the deep structure sentence consists of).

The phrase structure rules as the functional slots will look like the following :

1. S NP + VP
2. VP V + AP
3. AP Aj + Compv
4. NP N

as the deep structure basic of a sentence like *He was tired enough to sleep*, at the surface level. It is in the conversion of sentences from the underlying deep structure base to the surface level that errors occur. This conversion of kernel sentences into any of the surface expressions such as negation or questioning we have called *transformation*. Errors occurs in the process of transformation when the speaker's cognitive structure draws out the surface sentence from the deep structure level.

2. As part of transformation itself errors are caused by a number of factors. While the deep structure sentence or sentences are more of an automatic kind springing automatically from the child's cognitive base in the mind, the formation of the surface sentences would be greatly determined by the child's (i) mem

(ii) imagination, (iii) creativity, and (iv) linguistic resource (the level of the child's linguistics attainment). While at the deeper level, the sentences are mere *strings of slots* to form patterns required as the intrinsic structure of the would be surface sentence, the surface sentence is the result of the strings of slots (expressed earlier as a linguistic mould or framework) being filled in with the formal units of the language. Therefore it happens that errors do occur in the final production of sentences when the child's (i) memory fails in terms of retaining or recalling a given form, (ii) imagination does not at one feed the image required to accompany a given concept, (iii) creativity has limited range to allocate a substitute form, or (iv) linguistic resource has too limited range to include a given formal unit of expression. The child's surface sentences fail in case of any one or more of the above instance and what results are erroneous sentences at the surface level. Memory, imagination, creativity and linguistic resources especially in terms of active and passive vocabulary one factors which determine the on the spot product of a sentence at the surface level.

3. Errors in the language of the speaker can be the result of discrepancy at the level of phonological representation of sentences. Sentences as mentioned, are (i) generated at the deep structure level (ii) transformed into surface sentences (iii) phonologically set in terms of the phonological rules of the language, and finally (iv) phonated according to the phonetic rules of articulation and production. Sentences assume a definite *phonological* representation at the surface structure level after the syntactic structure of the surface sentences assumes shape. Errors creep in at this phonological level of production which can manifest both in speech and in writing (as for both the aspects of production the phonological level is the pre-condition and starting point. The phonological structure follows the phonological rules of the particular language (as different from the phonological rules of another language. By the time the child is capable of complete utterances, he will have mastered the phonological rules of his language. The phonological rules include the *selection* and *ordering* of the sequences necessary for the phonological representation of the sentences. In this selection and ordering of sounds the child can make mistakes. Such errors will take the shape of (1) using the wrong allophonic variant such as found in a form like | tiptɔph | *tiptop* where the final (p) should be an unaspirated sound with final release. When the plosive sounds

are used at the final position with aspiration as they should be at the initial position, this phenomena can be considered an instance of wrong phonological representation. It may be the use of (2) a wrong allomporphic variant as found in [dɔgs) dogs or [cætz] cats, (3) a wrong phoneme as such as found in [tɔfmaust] topmost where the phoneme [f] is employed instead of | p |; or (4) a wrong level of intonation such as an inverted question represented as a falling pattern of intonation. Inverted or 'yes'/no questions in English have rising tones while wh qucstions have fâlling tones in the usual pattern of conversation.

4. Errors, finally occur as part of the level of (a) *phonetic representation* and (b) *graphic representation* of language. In linguistic performance the two representations (a) and (b) constitute the final stage of the production of language. This may be considered in terms of skills as two levels: speech and writing, of which the first has (a) and the second has (b) as the final stage.

Errors in phonetic representation may consist of the following. It may be an error in the *articulation* of vowels or consonants, more specifically in the *manner* or *point* of articulation of consonants, in the *length* or *position* of vowels, and in aspects like *nasalization*. The error may consist in substituting one sound for another, for instance, the short | i | for the long | i: | as in | spi:d | speed pronounced as | spid |. Errors can be in the areas of *stress*, *pitch* or, *tonal contours*, or *junction*. Children are prone to misplace the primary and secondary stresses, placing and secondary stresses, placing for instance the stress of the first syllable in the second or third syllable, of word. At the level of phonetic representation the most usual error is the placement of broken phrases. Children do find it difficult to put phrases together in difficult to put phrases together in speech. This is true especially of idiomatic expressions with the proper placing of the primary stress of the phrase as a whole. It may be a noun phrase like *the black dog*, a verb phrase such as *get along with* or a prepositional phrase like *on the way to the market*.

Error occur also at the level of graphic representation (writing) just as in phonetic representation (speech). Such errors include the wrong shaping of a letter, mistakes in spelling, substitution of one written from for another, mistakes in putting down compound words and phrases, leaving inadequate space between words, errors in capitals, punctuations etc.

In short, errors in linguistic performance occur for reasons of discrepancy at the levels of (1) transformation, (2) phonological representation, (3) phonetic representation and (4) graphic representation. We have attached to this as causative factors memory, imagination, creativity and linguistic resources including active and passive vocabulary. The rationale we have drawn up to explicate the phenomenon of error in language should be closely linked to the grammar and usage, first of all, and then to use. The grammar as constituted as by the fundamental sets of universals and differentials has more to do in the final analysis with linguistic competence than with linguistic performance. But usage as the second level of language which permits variation, though goes as part of language as the 'objective possession' of the child (again, competence) has more to do with linguistic performance than otherwise. The first level of language, the grammar, comes to be represented and realized at the second level, usage which ultimately consists not of basic rules, patterns and universal elements but of definite and rule-governed organization of sounds letter, words, phrases, sentences and discourages. The rationale of errors which we have notice above while are not immediately relevant to the grammar of the language, are certainly and immediately relevant to the second level which we call usage.

## 3. Errors and Use

If the Grammar of the language is assigned a role within competence, and usage is assigned a role part within competence and partly within performance, we may ascertain that use is assigned a role within performance. It is an issue that has revealed itself in course of all that we have so far seen about language behaviour. By use we mean, as mentioned above, the third level of language which offers the speaker the freedom to pick and choose from all his linguistic resources the elements required for the final output of a sentence or discourse with the kind of phonological, grammatical and semantic specifications unique to the speaker by contrast to the speaker by contrast to the other speakers and individuals. Use, in other words is a level of language which we have assigned to the performance of the speaker, as its content.

Use is the level at which errors have maximum relevance. A

sentence which is phonologically, grammatically and semantically patterned in terms of the strings of slots at the Grammatical level, is further filled in at the level of usage in terms of formal units which are changeable but are subject to the norms of the community at a given time, is final represented at the level of use when the speaker concretely produces the sentences in speech or in writing. The level of use fully corresponds to surface grammatical, phonological, phonetic and graphic representations. Consequently all errors which were found arising out of the various levels of representation must be grouped together partly under usage as sharing in performance and partly under use which is fully assigned to performance.

Errors can occur at the phonological aspect of usage when some discrepancy occurs in the formation of the phonological representation of a sentence or discourse. This has been examined in the preceding section under the aspect of the errors at the phonological representation of a sentence (3). From the viewpoint of usage, again, errors will occur at the grammatical aspect of usage when some discrepancy causes any disorder in the organization of the formal units at the grammatical level. This grammatical level corresponds to the more peripheral aspects of the surface structure. This includes errors in elements of morphology such as the formation of wrong inflectional, derivational or lexical units (for instance *walked* [d] instead of [t], *cooker* meaning cook (N) derived from the verb *cook*, or the use of *house* for *home*). Again, errors occur of the semantic aspect of usage when some discrepancy creeps in at this level of more peripheral aspects of meaning attached to the surface level of the sentence. Under this we group errors resulting from the formation of phrases, misplacing a phrase or a word for another, using a word which has inadequate denotation (extension) and connotation (depth) with less semantic coverage, displacement of synonyms with considerable semantic differentials, or of homophones with a formal happens is the wrong use of a word which has more or less or different conceptual elements as compared to the word which would be required to express the actual meaning. Instance such as *His home is on fire* (instead of house) or *He is ploughing the farm* (instead of field) show how such semantic discrepancy can occurs. All this is an area of usage.

In the same manner errors at the level of use can be categorized under its sub aspects. Errors occurs at the phonological aspect of use when in this aspect any specific idiolectic differentiation in this aspect made by the speaker crosses the structure of the usage. In British English | labɔ:rətəri | laboratory is pronounced with an indistinct (weak) secondary stress which occurs at the penultimate syllable. In American English, on the other hand the primary stress falls as usual on the second syllable, but a strong secondary stress is put on the penultimate syllable of [la'bɔ:rə,tɔ:ri] *laboratory*. But individual speaker do use their idiolectic differentiations and in their use of the word minor changes in the vowels especially within in the broader norms of usage can be found. But a discrepancy occurs when a speaker stretches, the idiolectic freedom too much and says ['læbɔ rətə ry] or [ləbɔ:rə'ta:ri] he goes wrong in his *use* of the word.

As part of the phonological aspect of use, we may distinguish the phonological and phonetic representations. This has been already discussed in sec. 2, but in a different context. Errors in phonological representations include (i) the wrong use of an allophonic variant as in [kait] instead of $k^h$ait] kite as initial occurrence of [k] should be aspirated by nature, (ii) the wrong use of a free variant as in | aiðər | instead of the correct forms [aiðə] or [i :ðə] either, (iii) the wrong use of a phoneme as a in | pikækz | in place of | pikæks | *pickaxe*, (iv) wrong stress placement, (v) wrong use of the pitch phonemes, (vi) wrong intonation and so on. Errors in the phonetic representation of sentences include (i) wrong manner of the articulation of a consonant, (ii) wrong point of articulation, (iii) wrong voicing of a sound, (iv) wrong position and length of vowels, (vi) wrong lip rounding which would change the nature of a vowel, (iv) wrong nasalization etc. Nasalizing sounds where it is not required is an idiolectic phenomenon commonly found among speakers which comes directly under use, as an individual characteristic of language production. So long as such errors do not exceed the limits and remain within the bounds of idiolectic use, they do not affect and change the usage that the speaker employs. If the usage itself is altered, then the meaning of the sentence under consideration will either be marred or altered.

Errors occur as part of the grammatical aspect of use. This too is quite significant an area for our consideration as most errors occur in the concrete use of grammar in particular. Under the aspect of grammar at the level of use we include only the most peripheral grammatical aspects which are characterized by the individual speaker. Idiolectic variations which are part and parcel of the speaker's use of language are not errors as usage is constituted by the average of the use specifications of the speaker. Errors occur only when such variations cross the limits of one elements of usage and get blurred with another element or go totally wrong. Grammatical errors under use inched (1) the wrong of these structure words such as the articles of prepositions, (2) wrong use of concord and agreement, (3) wrong use of prefixes suffixes for word formation, (4) wrong use of infectional suffixes, especially misplacing the allomorphic variants of past tense suffix -ed or third singular (plural) suffix -s, (5) wrong compounding in speech or writing, (6) disorder in patterning a phrase, or sentence, such as the use of *cope up with* instead of *cope with*, (7) the wrong use of question tags such as found in *you are going home, do you* ?, and (8) mistakes in tenses which mostly occurs in conversation.

Errors occur also in the semantic aspect of the individual's use of language. Such errors are closely linked to the speaker's possession of conceptual specifications in relation to a feature of experience. Also the speaker's or writer's displacement of meaning may not be understood by the listener or the reader. Again, this concerns only with the most peripheral aspects of meaning which will occur in terms of addition, deletion or alternation of conceptual elements which go into the making of a concept. Errors at the level of use occur, again, only when the idiolectic (individual) use of sounds, grammar and meaning at the surface level cross the limits of sheer variations and effect the structure of a particular element of usage and alter or blur the meaning of the formal unit.

## 4. Error Analysis—I

**Error in $L_1$** : Error in fact is a reality in the classroom with which the teacher is actively concerned. There is no use levelling the fact that children make mistakes. Errors in language are caused by numerous factors and errors occur at different levels of language behaviour as examined above. As a learner in the classroom the child is initially concerned with errors in the mother tongue ($L_1$). It is possible to think of errors in language only after an individual speaker has attained a level of mastery. At the earliest learning phase, there is no sense in talking about error when the child's linguistic competence is only at the early phase of formation and hardly any performance at the period is exhibited. Therefore we may think of the errors of a chid in two phases, first, errors in the first language which the child uses in the classroom for communicative and learning purposes, and second, errors in $L_2$ (for instance English) which becomes acute problem for the teacher and the pupils as the second language learning gathers momentum.

By the time the child joins school, he is in a position to communicate himself effectivity in case of all practical needs. We say that by the age of five or six an average child acquires satisfactory mastery of the language and he is never at a loss to float in ordering social situations. All the same there are arrears of the first language where he is a neophyte. Writing is such an area which the child is ordinarily introduced to only in school. Just as in the learning of the second language, learning the writing system of the first language creates problems for the child. Errors in graphics, spellings (or the constituents letters of a word where spellings are not relevant), in the formation of words and phrases, spacing of the words in a sentence, punctuations, a construction of a paragraph etc. form parts of errors in writing.

Apart from *writing* the learning of $L_1$ at this early phase of schooling has problems like (i) the need for greater passive vocabulary, (ii) the need for such active vocabulary, (iii) errors in the construction of phrases and idioms, (iv) errors in the inflectional and derivational aspects of words, (v) errors in the construction of varied types of sentences and (vi) errors in the social etiquette aspects of language mostly form part of the child's mother tongue at the early part of the schooling. The child's performance of $L_1$ is in no way devoid of errors, not to mention the handsome variety of dialectical usage which are part of the child's language if the child does not belong exclusively to the standard dialect. Certainly, such dialectical forms and expressions will not be considered errors although these are deviations from the forms used in the standard dialect of the language. This aspect is clear from what we discussed above under the section on usage.

**Transfer of Habits :** Any speech disorder resulting from functional or organic disorders of any kind in the individual child would equally affect $L_1$ and $L_2$ behaviour. The same need not be said of errors that arise in the first and second language of the child.

Errors in the two may occur in totally different areas of the languages of the child rather than having any correspondence in both in the strict sense of the term. Errors, all the same, can have simultaneity in both the languages when such errors are part of the functional system, namely the skills. Just as any organic or functional disorders (see Ch. 11.) would affect performance in both the languages, the functional features related to the skills can affect performance in both the languages equally. *Comprehension* resulting from listening skill which is a properly to the $L_1$ and $L_2$ can be hampered by low intelligence and memory, and limited range of cognitive experiences, which in turn limit comprehension both in the first and second languages. *Comprehension* resulting from the skill of reading may have hurdles such as poor eye-sight, low intelligence etc. as above, and poor reading speed and other reading habits and consequently reading in the $L_1$ and $L_2$ suffers equally from these respects.

Speech habits of one language have both positive and diverse effects on another so long as these habits are not identical with the intrinsic structure of the first language or the second. Speed of speaking, clarity of voice and articulation, features of enunciation, fluency of speech (partly), nasalization if found in excess, or anything that is *not* part of the intrinsic structure of a language (such as the vowel of consonant systems) will affect both the languages which the child acquires and such habits will be transferred from the $L_1$ to the $L_2$. Also, the characteristics (idiolectic by nature and form part of the speaker's *use*) which constitute a vowel or consonant sound in the $L_1$ will also be found true of the same vowel or consonant sound in the $L_2$ if such sounds are not structurally different in the languages. Such identity of features may also be part of sounds which are not identical but only similar as in the case of several English and Hindi Sounds. Excessive stress or lengthening of such sounds be part of the both the languages, if such sounds occur in the same phonological environment. For these reasons, we observe that a given sound unit in the first language becomes an obstacle to the child's acquisition of a sound unit in the second language when both the sounds are not identical or different but part both i.e. *similar*. A voiced, nasalized or aspirated sound in the $L_1$ can be an obstacle to a similar sound in the $L_2$ but do not posses the above features. The unaspirated initial [p] in Indian language makes it difficult for an Indian learner of English the use of [$p^h$]

the initial English {ph} which is normally aspirated.

**Reading habits** related to the reading skill can be as usual looked at from the view points of (i) comprehension, and (ii) speed of reading. There are, again, several functional aspects of the reading skill related to both the above factors, which do not constitute part of the intrinsic structure of the particular language. Aspects such as feasibility of eye-movements over the written material, distance of the book from the eyes, other related habits such as vocalization and sub-vocalization, the bulk of material that an eye-span of the reader can cover, the speaker's intelligence and memory level and a number of other functional aspects which constitute the reading skill will be common to which have found development at the instance of the $L_1$ will either promote or hinder the reading of the second language. Functional errors the reading skill such as vocalization and sub-vocalization found in the reading of $L_1$ will be at once transferred to the reading of $L_2$ unless such habits one spotted and controlled in the beginning itself.

**Writing habits** which constitute the writing skill, similarly exhibit functional areas which cannot be attributed to the intrinsic structure of the language as mentioned in the case of other skills. Among the functional writing habits are may include aspects such as the motor pliability of the fingers and the hand, habits of holding the pen or pencil, position of the hand, sitting posture, eye-sight, general neatness of the letters, speed of writing (partly controlled by the command over the language), again as in other cases the levels of intelligence, memory, creative imagination and characteristics which do not form part of the intrinsic structure of any one language. Such habits will be easily transferred from the $L_1$ to the level of $L_2$ in the acquisition and performance of language. Transfer of habits in other words is not something applicable equally to all areas of language, at the same time there are the functional areas of language skills where transfer of habits from one language to another becomes relevant. These are areas especially the knowledge of one language helps or hinders the learning of another.

**The Teacher's Role :** The factors discussed above have much to do with the teacher's understanding of the phenomenon of error as it is present in the language of children in the classroom. The knowledge of deviant language behaviour (Ch. 11) and the intricacies of error as something which the teacher has to persistently tamper with helps him understand better the linguistic requirements of the pupils. By *error analysis* we mean two distinct things in this context : (i) an attempt to obtain greater insights into the phenomenon of language acquisition and development by an enquiry into the errors in language (as has been the attempts in the preceding sections), and (ii) an attempts on the part of the *linguist* for theoretical purposes and the *teacher* for practical classroom purposes, to analyse and study systematically the errors which children commit in their spoken and written language.

Error analysis at one level or other needs to be carried out by the teachers especially of second and foreign languages. Error analysis in both the senses given above is relevant to the teacher so far as his (i) general classroom observation of errors and (ii) some systematic attempt to error analysis, are concerned. The teacher of English, for instance, with a practical bent of mind should be in a position to undertake occasional error analysis of children's spoken or written language and shape his attitudes to the teaching of languages with a view to meeting the variety of learning needs of the classroom. A particular, practical situation is at the teacher's disposal and his success lies in fully exploiting this situation to have better yields. As we shall examine in further details, error analysis is very scientific approach and a useful *action research* for the teacher as a classroom practitioner to undertake to meet the variety of learning problems with which he is expected to deal.

## 5. Error Analysis—II

**1. Introduction :** The present section attempts to present a scheme of error analysis for the teacher's use in the classroom, which would include all the steps required for an action research of this kind. Error analysis could form part of a broader action research or it could be made an attempt itself to under take more effective teaching once the relative position of every pupil in the class is known. The material for the teacher's analysis could be from *spoken* or *written* language, or both. Written material could be gathered in two ways: (i) getting a set of exercises or assignments written by all the pupils or (ii) getting a select set of home assignments or class work which have been completed, as part of the regular work. Either of the two would serve the teacher's purpose here. Material from the pupil's spoken language could be gathered by (i) getting the material tape-recorded, or (ii) by any kind of oral exercise which could include the aspects of the language which the teacher specifically intends to test. The exercises such as short answers to questions (depending on the level of the pupils) could be spoken out and the teacher mark the mistakes in columns meant for specific errors (as will be shown below). Taking into consideration the elements of time and other facilities, using oral material for error analysis will be more tedious a task except when the teacher may want to analyse specifically the pupils oral language.

**2. Areas of Error:** Before the teacher undertakes the actual work of analysis, it is necessary to spot the number of language areas where he expects the pupils to be probably weak. This would take the form of an inventory of specific areas where mistakes would occur in the pupils' language. This inventory should consist of details depending, again, on the level of the pupils. Deciding the areas of errors in anticipation fixes a definite direction for the teacher's work of analysis. The areas of errors decided could later be worked out into a chart. The following could be specific example of such an inventory of areas where errors would occur:-

I. Graphics

1. Too large letters
2. Too small letters
3. Poor shaping of letters
4. Letters too slating
5. Clumsy writing
6. Poor neatness
7. No capitals

II. Spellings

1. Letters missing.
2. Letters misplaced
3. Wrong letters
4. None-sense word.

**III. Punctuations**

1. Punctuations missing
2. Wrongly placed
3. Wrong punctuation.

**IV. Lexical Errors**

1. Wrong word used
2. Partly correct word.

**V. Grammatical Errors.**

1. Errors in agreement.
2. Errors of articles.
3. Errors of prepositions.
4. Errors of conjunctions.
5. Errors of auxiliaries.
6. Errors of progressive tenses.
7. Errors of simple tenses.
8. Errors of perfect tenses.
9. Errors of passive construction.
10. Errors of reported speech.

An inventory especially of errors in the area of grammar can not be exhaustive as the details can be limitless. Therefore it depends on the teacher to include aspects of grammar which the facts will be relevant to the class where the analysis is carried out.

3. **Proportion of the Chart:** Once the listing of the areas where errors would most likely occur (judged from the experience of the teacher) is complete, the next task is the preparation of a chart for marking the actual errors during the analysis of the pupils oral or written work. The chart makes the teacher's work easier than one would except. The following is a miniature of the chart which the teacher has to work out at length for marking in a consolidated manner all the errors found in the exercises:

| S. No. | Names of Pupils | Gra- phics | | | Spell- ings | | | Lexi. Errors | | | Gra- mmer | | | Organi- sation | | | Totals |
|---|---|---|---|---|---|---|---|---|---|---|---|---|---|---|---|---|---|
| | | 1 | 2 | 3 | 1 | 2 | 3 | 1 | 2 | 3 | 1 | 2 | 3 | 1 | 2 | 3 | |
| 1. | | | | | | | | | | | | | | | | | |
| 2. | | | | | | | | | | | | | | | | | |
| 3. | | | | | | | | | | | | | | | | | |
| 4. | | | | | | | | | | | | | | | | | |
| 5. | | | | | | | | | | | | | | | | | |
| 6. | | | | | | | | | | | | | | | | | |
| Totals | | | | | | | | | | | | | | | | | |

The chart helps the teacher mark most specific errors with amazing speed. All that the teacher is required to do is to put a tally (i) in the respective column against the name of a particular pupil while analyzing the pupils material. It may not even be necessary for the teacher, for the specific purpose, to mark the errors in the notebook or in the material prepared by the pupil. The teacher will straight away mark the error under the respective heads. The earliest way to the marking is by means of tallies which could later on subjected conveniently to simple statistical counts.

**4. Analysis of Errors :** After the chart has been prepared the teacher undertakes the analysis. he has gathered by now a definite number of books or assignments from all the pupils either worked out for this purpose or got written earlier as part f the regular work. The teacher systematically goes through the material and marks the errors on the chart. By means of tallies the errors of every pupil is presented on the chart the way shown on p. 213.

The tallies are presented as clusters of five which makes the counting easier and the presentation accurate. Depending on the level of accuracy and specificity the teacher expects from the analysis, the details of the inventory of items which constitute the chart could be more or less. If the analysis should include or be specifically concerned with the spoken area of the pupils' language, the

| S. No. | Names of Pupils | Graphics 1 | Graphics 2 | Spellings 1 | Spellings 2 | Grammar 1 | Grammar 2 | Totals |
|---|---|---|---|---|---|---|---|---|
| 1. | | II | II | II | III | | II | ..... |
| 2. | | IIII | IIII | III | III | II | III | ..... |
| 3. | | II | II | II | I | III | IIII | ..... |
| 4. | | | IIII | III | IIII | | II | ..... |
| 5. | | II | | IIII | III | | | ..... |
| Totals | | ..... | ..... | ..... | ..... | ..... | ..... | |

inventory which is prepared for the purpose could include or would consist of areas of speech.

**5. Drawing Conclusions:** Once the entire range of material worked out by all the pupils is read through and the tallying complete, the material on the chart will exhibit certain well-defined designs. The chart becomes representative of a number of features related to the performance of the class and the level of linguistic attainments. As the chart shows there are two wheelers of totals which reflects two distinct dimensions of the pupils performance. The *vertical* column of total errors reflect the performance of every individual pupil in the class; while the totals at the *horizontal* level reflect the overall performance of the class as a unit of learners by contrast to other such units. Conclusions may be drawn of serval levels from these two dimensions: (i) Individual clusters of tallies specifically shows the areas of individual's errors, the areas where the individual has committed majority of errors. If for student (i) spellings constitute the weakest area, for student (2) it may be grammar and for (3) it may be graphics. (ii) conclusions on the overall performance of individual pupils are available from vertical column which contains their total mistakes. At a glance it shows the individual pupil's rank in the group. For the average teacher it is possible to obtain considerable insights into the working and level of his class without subjecting the data to any form of more systematic and formal statistical analysis such as finding the mean, median, mode, standard deviation, correlation coefficient and so on which will provide several systematic cues into the nature of the group. (iii) The third set of conclusions the teacher may draw are from the totals of errors lying at the horizontal dimension. These do not directly reflect the performance of individual members of the group, but of the group as a whole. From these totals of errors, the teacher can say where the weakest area his for the entire class, where the group has performed best and areas where the teacher has to concentrate better to improve the entire class. Based on such conclusions the teacher could formulate the details of any *remedial teaching programme* the teacher will have to undertake.

6. **Reporting the Error Analysis** : The last phase of a systematic error analysis carried out by the teacher may consist of a report of the study that he has undertaken. Without getting into the details one can recognize the importance and utility of a report of this kind of the cause of education. A report of error analysis should consist at least of the following steps:

(1) A statement of *specific aims*, (2) a statement of the *areas of errors* which the teacher expects to cover in the course of his analysis, (3) a description of the *material for analysis* which is used as the basis of the present error analysis and of the actual work of analysis, (4) the *presentation of the chart* which exhibits the actual analysis done and the errors committed by the pupils, (5) an *inventory of sentences* in which prominent errors have occurred, which has serval objectives to serve as part of the report; (6) a statement of the *probable causes* which have contributed to the level of errors found in the group, and (7) a detailed report of the *conclusions and findings* of the teacher on the basis of the analysis in line with what we examined above. A report of this kind provides the work of analysis a scientific touch and renders the teacher's work most useful as concrete data for any further research along the line.

# 13
# Creative Aspects of Language Learning

## 1. Creative Behaviour

In connection with language acquisition and language process several times we made mention of the aspect of *creativity* which is considered to be in present-day thinking an intimate element of language behaviour as such. As we shall be examining below in the following section, language is essentially a *creative activity* which may be considered contrary to the view that language behaviour is as continuous a chain of S—R bonds (Stimulus—Response bonds) as any other form of behaviour. An initial understanding of what exactly constitutes 'creative behaviour' would help us apply the same notion in one form or another to language behaviour.

Creative behaviour would involve, naturally, what we shall call *creative thinking*. It is held that all great thinkers, scientists, artists, poets and inventors were men of extraordinary creativity. All such achievements which made history had creative thinking at its helm. In fact, both the common man and the specialist alike consider creative thinking as the central factor in great achievements in any field of life. Creative thinking consists of so many constituent elements that right from what a carpenter does in the preparation of a new wooden model to what happens in present-day space-technology come under creative thinking.

Creative thinking as a mental process involves the organization and reorganization of concepts alongwith the accompanying images in such a way that in course of time. Something relatively new is *conceived*. Creative thinking is, in other words, conceptual and imaginative organization leading to something relatively new. The new outcome (product) may be in the form of a theory (pure 'conceptual organization'), some genre of literature, any form of creative writing, some material product (as in the case of inventions) or what we shall for convenience *'problem solving'* which is involved in the creative thinking behind administrative or organizational enterprises. It is said that all creative thinking is essentially a matter of problem solving. This is true in the widest sense of *problem solving*. Any one of the areas where creative thinking is involved, has in its core some kind of puzzle or problem to solve or a major decision to take. The creative thinker deeply involves himself in confronting the problem and he thereby exerts his intellect and imagination towards the effect of finding a solution or meeting the given situation. There are said to be serval stages involved in creative thinking as problem solving. Creative thinking, from that view point is not a continuous process of creative production, but an 'Aha experience' or a flashing discovery of the solution to the problem. As leading to the solution of a problem creative thinking is said to undergo the following stages: (1) the *reflective stage*, (2) the *assimilation stage*, (3) the *discovery stage*, and (4) the *production stage*. This partly corresponds to the four stages commonly thought of as constituting creative thinking : (i) preparation, (ii) incubation, (iii) illumination, and (iv) verification. The pitfall of the four stages commonly thought of its that these are so restricted that they are applicable to creative thinking of a very limited range, such as in the solution of mathematical or scientific problems.

As mentioned above, creative has such a wide range of human behaviour falling under its scope that a restricted view of it cannot do justice to such a wide range of creative experiences. Only in very restricted sense of the term creative thinking can be equated to problem solving; the sameway, if problem solving is taken in its widest sense it can be synonymous to creative thinking. In any form of creative thinking leading to creative behaviour one finds that a person at the initial stage exercises a certain period of intellectual activity (1). This period of *reflection* follows, his need for or desire to 'produce' something. This something could be in the form of a theory, a thing, a book, a new administrative or organizational structure or more generally speaking, a solution to a given problem. This first stage of creative behaviour when the intellect and imagination exercise intense activity we call the *reflective stage*. It may be long or a short period of time depending on the nature of the creative production which it is concerned with. The reflective stage is applicable equally to a child sitting down to build a mud-house and a writer who prepares for the production of a book in whose case the four stages mentioned above are more simultaneous and continuous than phased.

The second is the *assimilation stage* (2) when the streams of intellectual activity (long or short) get settled down. It is a stage of synthesis while the first is more of analysis. The person's mind, having now looked into all possible pros and cons, and having reflected sufficiently on the creative object he has in mind, now settles down and consequently a process of assimilation of concepts (however short and momentary) takes place. This is the calm which prevails *before* the storm, namely, the 'Aha experience' commonly understood as the stage of illumination. This may occur shortly or only after a long series of 'trial and error' process is over. The most characteristic thing about the stage of assimilation is that the mind is not active the way it is in stage (1).

The third is the *discovery stage* (3) and the most important phase of creative behaviour. It may be a single and unique discovery as in the case of an invention, or it may be one of continuous and evolving discovery as in the case of a writer attempting to produce a work of art or science. This is commonly known as the stage of illumination. Discovery follows the intellectual calm that person experiences during which a conceptual and imaginative synthesis takes place in the mind. The kind of discovery we have in the present instance,is an *intellectual perception* of a *fact*, some *relation* as in the case of some scientific invention, any new *phenomenon*, some *design* that one may have been looking for a *solution* which has eluded the mind for quite some time. The term *discovery* here takes care of a wider range of creative experiences than the term *illumination* or *insight* does.

The fourth is the *production stage* (4) and the instance when creative behaviour manifests itself in terms of some extrinsic behaviour. Since any creative thinking needs to take shape in creative behaviour as its termination, one may not certainly stop creativity at creative thinking as are activity of the human intellect. The very end of creative thinking, therefore lies in the concrete *creative production* which the person undertakes. In a scientific invention or discovery this may correspond to the stage of *verification* when the scientist attempts to pool together fragments of the new 'discovery' he has made and makes sure that the relation he has established between two phenomena is experimentally or mathematically correct. In other forms of creative behaviour that last stage of production consists, for instance, in giving concrete shape to a theory, a painting, a poem, the design for a machine or a building, or a book. In fact it is at this level that creative thinking as an intellectual activity becomes creative behaviour in the overt sense of the terms, and the creative production becomes materialized.

The four stages discussed above constitute what we call creative behaviour, when such behaviour has a definite process of problem solving at the heart of it. As mentioned above, we do not consider creative behaviour (creative thinking) synonyms to problem solving; on the other hand creative behaviour is broader than and inclusive of problem solving behaviour. Creative behaviour in this broad sense has still the four stages considered above as the central factors, all the some the four stages of (1) *reflection*, (2) *assimilation*, (3) *discovery* and (4) *production* in this instance cannot be easily distinguished as sequential phases. Instead when creative behaviour is thought of in its broad sense, the four stages have more of a simultaneity and repeated continuity than would be in the case of actual problem solving. In other words human creative behaviour is not *simple* as to be neatly compartmentalized into four sequential stages. It is complex, prolonged and continuous as in the case of a creative writer who taxes his intellectual and imaginative potentials for several years before he comes out (produces) a good book. It involves a complex and continuous chain of reflection, assimilation; discovery and production before the final output is realized.

Creative behaviour, again is not a simple phenomenon or characteristic of the human personality. Just as it is complex in terms of the stages involved, it is also complex in terms of the constituent elements which constitute creative behaviour.

(1) **Intelligence** is the major factor which determines the level of creative ability that a person possesses. In fact, there are those who identify creative ability with intelligence for reasons of the major role that intelligence plays in creative behaviour. The level of intelligence certainly determines the level of the creative ability.

(2) **Imagination** is another important factor which determines creative behaviour. The human faculty of imagination makes thing concretely present to the mind in terms of the 'individuality' which every feature of human experience possesses. Imaginative organization is a process that goes at once parallel to conceptual organization both of which we have constituting the contest of sees as of creative thinking.

(3) **Memory** is another factor which goes into the making of creative behaviour as conceptual and imaginative analysis and synthesis (organization and reorganization) call for a corresponding level of memory.

(4) **Personal dynamism** is not in any way less important than the factors mentioned for creative behaviour. A high level of intelligence, imagination or memory goes for nothing if the individual does not posses a corresponding level of personal dynamism in which the *will* of the person is capable of exercising decision-making at a corresponding level. Creative behaviour is aided by several other minor factors of the human personality but they do not deserve mention in the present context.

## 2. Linguistic Creativity

Creative thinking, we said, is a mental process which involves organization and reorganization of concepts and accompanying images in such a way that something new is conceived. It is a conceptual and imaginative organization leading to something new. But this is creative behaviour in its most explicit form. The human being, all the same, is fundamentally and by nature *creative*. Apart from most conspicuous and higher levels of creative behaviour, man possess some fundamental and essential creativity, granted that he retains all the faculties which a normal man is endowed with. Every human being one way or other shares in this basic human creativity as part of his very nature.

*Linguistic creativity* is one aspect of the fundamental natural creativity with which man is endowed. What is the essence of linguistic creativity ? What constitutes linguistic creativity is the human person's built-in ability to produce (generate) an *infinite number of sentences* from the person's store of linguistic structure and lexicon. This is how the transpirational generative grammarians (linguists) have looked at linguistic creativity. Through out the present book we have examined the process of language production at its various levels. Rooted in the language atmosphere of the community, the child acquires the phonology, morphology, syntax and semantics of his language and builds up his linguistic competence. As noted in the section on language acquisition (Ch. 2.), the child's language acquisition is a development, at its initial phase, from the acquisition of the distinctive sounds of his language to the final acquisition of the syntactic patterns basic to the language followed by a mastery of the greater followed by a mastery of the greater semantic implications (specifications) of the words that is expected to the words that he is expected to use.

Competence is not a dose of language which he takes in within a day or two. Competence develops in course of years as the child gets acquainted with more and more complex patterns of the language (Ch. 4.). The development of linguistic competence in the person is seen in the last resort as the acquisition of the Grammar and the usage of the language which the person exercises in his use of the language. The concrete exercise of the language in terms of its four basic skills of listening, speaking, reading and writing is seen as language performance (Ch. 4.). In fact, the process of language production begins with the basic semantic organization to fill in the slots of the syntactic patterns of the deep structure level (Ch. 12) in which the person opts for communicating himself. The production of language which begins at this level reaches consummation when the person, at the surface level, phonologically specifies the language which finally gets phonated (spoken) or graphically represented (written).

Along the line of language production as seen above in short, basic creativity figures in at the deep structure level where sentences are generated to be further transformed into surface sentence (questions, negation etc.). Like the electric generator which as such has not electricity at its possession has the potency to produce an illimited quantum of electricity out of its mechanical structure, the person's cognitive structure is basically oriented to produce newer sentence out of its generative system. It is called newer and creative set of sentences because the sentences of the language which the persons gives shape to one not repetitions of earlier sentences which he himself has produced, or of sentences he has heard from others. Except for some formulas which are employed in social situations, his sentences are not formulas committed to memory and produced at an occasion.

It can be granted that language acquisition production may involve some level of imitation of adult language or repetition of elements. Imitation and may be conceded to at the level of sounds, words and phrases; the acquisition of these involves imitations and the use of these involve repetition. But the significant thing is that both imitation and repetition occur on the foundation of creativity. Linguistic competence, the level at which the child has developed it, is not a store of sentence of the language which he learned through imitation and repetition. Linguistic competence, on the other hand,is an underlying *linguistic structure* which consists of the phonological, grammatical and semantic rules (at the level of the grammar and usage) of the language. This underlying linguistic structure has the lexicon of the language as its content. This structure making use of the lexicon of the language as its content functions as the 'linguistic generator' in producing, as the speaker wills, the kind of sentences in terms of their organization, which the speaker has neither spoken nor heard before. Here lies the unique characteristic of the creatively produced sentences; and herein lies the creative capacity of the speaker.

The child, for instance, has acquired the pattern in terms of the underlying phrase structure rules:

1. $S \rightarrow NP + VP$
2. $VP_1 \rightarrow VP + NP$
3. $VP_2 \rightarrow Aux + V\text{–}tr.$
4. $NP_1 \rightarrow (Det) + N$
5. $NP_2 \rightarrow (Det) + N.$

The rules which constitute part of the child's linguistic competence functions like a generative mould consisting of the number of slots given above. The slots represent words or phrases, which together constitute a string (NP+VP). The generative structure (mechanism) of the child on the basis of this underlying set of rules will be able to generate sentences such as the following making use of the set of the lexical items which the child has acquired:-

1. He is drinking milk.
2. She is eating food.
3. You are playing cricket.
4. We are telling lies.
5. The boy is wearing trousers.
6. The girl is wearing a frock.
7. The dogs are eating meat.

The above sentences are a few instances of an infinite number of sentences which the rule above will generative with the VP transformed into its progressive form. With a simple change in the slot 'Aux' into its past form, the same rule will further generate sentences in the past such as *The boy was drinking milk* and the pattern remains the same. The same rule will generate yet another set of sentences in future tense of the phrase is transformed into its future form as in *The boy will drink milk*. We are concerned here not with the processes of transformation but with the underlying generative process. A simple instance as this without getting into the complexities of transformational progress, illustrates how a syntactic rule which forms part of the child's linguistic competence is capable of generating sentences which can always here a newer semantic content as a result of the newer set of lexical items which enter into the making of the sentences.

Again, the creativity of the individual speaker is active not only at the level of the underlying generative machinery in the speaker's competence but also active at further levels as the language is fashioned to be transformed, phonologically set and phonated. The sentence assumes complete shape (semantic, grammatical and phonological) only by the time its phonological representation is complete. The use of sentences by the speaker constitutes the last phase of the creative generation and production of language. The fact that the same set of utterances cannot exactly be produced in the same manner in all details is an idiolectic characteristic of use towards which creativity of the speaker certainly contributes. Linguistic creativity, in short consists in the openness and infinite possibilities of the person in the production of language.

## 3. Creative Non-verbal Behaviour

All through the book attempts have been made to view language behaviour as a creative and unitary phenomenon which forms part of the trio : (1) cognitive experiences, (2) sociological experiences, and (3) linguistic experiences. Language behaviour in man cannot be studied in isolation as it is dependent on and subservient to several other aspects of man's life. Language neither takes origin and develops as a factor in isolation from all other forms of human behaviour, nor is it oriented in terms of its function to itself as an end. The end of language behaviour is communicative, aesthetic, philosophical and so on and it is totally oriented to the manifold needs of man.

Language behaviour and non-language behaviour (non-verbal behaviour) have no clear-cut demarcations to make so far as human behaviour is concerned. Both mutually influence just as the trio of cognitive, sociological and linguistic experiences develop hand-in-hand. Human creativity as examined in sec. 1 of the present chapter has its roots both in verbal and non-verbal behaviour. Linguistic creativity, examined in Sec. 2, is the underlying generative power functioning as the principle of the production of language. Human creativity is a principle of human behaviour at all levels wherever the mind as the source of cognition comes into direct communion. In fact linguistic generativity shares in this fundamental creative aspect of human nature, as mentioned in Sec.1.

What then, is the relevance of non-verbal behaviour is the context of creative verbal behaviour? In what way does one influence and enhance the other? Observing the young child who is at the very initial phases of his language acquisition, one finds that there is a whole range of non-language behavioural patterns which has something definite to tell us about the child's language behaviour. As we have noted earlier, the child's communion with the world around is more behavioural and dependent more on non-verbal devices as we inquire down the developmental process to the earliest forms of behaviour. The child depends very much on non-language devices to communicate itself to the environment. By non-verbal and non-language in this specific context are meant all forms of behaviour except the use of symbolic language proper. Even though the infant cries have a lot to contribute to later language development it is improper to consider such aspects of the child's behaviour as part of the language proper. (see Ch. 10. Sec. 4. for greater details).

The most elementary and initial forms of creative behaviour in the child are found in his attempts to obtain communion with the adults by means of language behaviour. The child who picks up and brings a tumbler to his father at the mere recognition of the father's request to the mother without directly asking the child to do so, is a typical instance of creative non-language behaviour on the child's part. The father calls for a tumbler. The child is probabiy playing nearby; without any one being conscious that the child is naturally alert to anything that would be happening at hand. Instantly, the enthusiastic child who can hardly carry a tumbler carefully gets up runs to the kitchen and fetches a glass tumbler for his daddy. What underlying factor is involved in this behaviour? It is related to language because the child is responding to his daddy's request. It is considered non-language behaviour because on the part of the child it involves purely action and not speech. The creative part of the child's behaviour is quite significant. What constitutes the creative aspects of the behaviour are (1) the child's recognition of some language stimuli which is not directed to him as something which he himself could respond to; (2) the child's identification of the role of the mother as the listener proper (the target of the speaker) with his own; (3) the child's ability to recognize the fact that the semantic content of the request made by the father has relevance to his own situation; and (4) the extrinsic behaviour of bringing the tumbler to his father.

The child listening to the father's request to his mother and providing adequate response is (i) cognitive and (ii) sociological phenomenon which retains some specific (iii) linguistic value. The child's behaviour is certainly not explainable in terms of stimulus-response or trial and error formulas. For the chid it is a cognitive experience feeding into his world of knowledge coupled with its sociological and linguistic implications. The sentence, *please, get me a tumbler* as a unit of language has assumed, a new set of meanings for the child, namely, 'My father is need of a tumbler',

'I know where to finding a tumbler for you', I am here, why have you asked mama for the tumbler?' and so on. The child may have any meaning of the kind retained in his mind while responding to the father's request.

In the instance examined above, the relation between language and non-language behaviour is readily apparent. The child is responding, though silently, to a linguistic stimulus from his father. We may think of child who of his own dresses up his doll with cloth-pieces available round. Certainly, in part the behaviour is initiative of adult behaviour. Upon analysis one finds that the initiation part of the behaviour is very limited. What the child has seen a number of times is his mother or father dressing up and he himself being dressed up. He has, let's us presume, never been shown how a doll is to be dressed up. There is in fact very little of imitative parallelism between (i) the doll and the mother, (ii) the mother's dress and a few pieces of cloth, and (iii) the mother's behaviour of dressing up and the child's act of dressing up the doll. The same is true of the child's own manner of getting dressed up and what he goes with the baby

The creative aspect of the behaviour consists in (i) the child's taking note of the dressing part of other's behaviour, (ii) recognizing the fact that his doll doesn't have clothes on, (iii) projecting the adult behaviour and dressing up, in a rudimentary manner to the situation of his doll, and (iv) finding out cloth-pieces and carrying out the act of dressing up in a manner which has comparably little to do with the adult behaviour of dressing up. The child, we shall say, is capable of *organizing* (rather than merely imitating) a cognitive experience for himself in the context of some pattern of adult behaviour.

The significant dimension of creative behaviour consists in the *organization* of a new cognitive experience which can be built on the context of some pattern of prevailing behaviour. With human person, creative behaviour does not mean giving shape to something absolutely new. The novel part of creative behaviour is always relative and built on something already prevalent. The child who brought the tumbler to his father, and the one who dressed up his doll in fact built up some creative behaviour on some pattern of behaviour they had noted around as prevalent. We have examined in this instance some non-language behvoiour which has apparently nothing to do with language behaviour as such. It is purely a cognitive experience which has only remote sociological and linguistic resonance.

What is significant, however, is that any form of non-language behaviour which the child carries out in his day-to-day life has dimensions related at once to language behaviour. This is chiefly because man is essentially a 'talking organism', a fact which results directly from his rational nature. If any man does not talk, apart from temporary reasons, it is because his normal speech capacity is retarded. As we noted in the beginning the conspicuous relation between language and non-language behaviour is true especially of children who are only in the developmental phase of language acquisition.

The fundamental relation between verbal and non-verbal behaviour lies in the context of the both patterns of behaviour. Language leads us back to meanings in their conceptual specifications (Ch. 10) which further takes us back to reality presented to us in terms of the features of human experiences. Similarly, our cognitive experiences (sensitive and intellectual) lead us right back to their conceptual contest in our minds and further to reality presented to us in terms of the features of our experience. Both language and non-language experiences coincide in the content of our minds, namely, in concepts and their organization, and images and their organization. If such a fundamental factor as this is the point of departure between verbal and non-verbal behaviour, then the kind of creativity which forms part of either aspect of behaviour should have roots that equally spread into them both. The common roots as we are in a position to visualize, constitute what we have all the while called the *semantics*, the *meaning*, and the *concept* from respective viewpoints.

## 4. Aspects of Creative classroom Learning

The intricate relation between verbal and non-verbal aspects of creative behaviour is examined on the proceeding pages. It is found that there is a point where verbal and non-verbal behaviour coincide. This common ground is the *semantic content* of language and the *conceptual content* of non-language conceptual organization. Linguistic experience in the form of listening, speaking, reading or writing leads us to the ultimate mental content (concepts and images); non-linguistic experience in the form of cognitive experiences with persons and things of variety of kind leads us, again, ultimately to the content of the mind as their representative modes, i.e. concepts and images. This parallelism between the content of the mind in linguistics experience and the content of the mind in non-linguistic experience enable us to recognize how intimate and unified both these patterns of behaviour in man. For this reason we have say that understanding language behaviour in a compartmentalized manner having nothing to do with non-language behaviour is not the proper way of approaching language. The deep semantic roots of language and behaviour lie far spread in each other forms of behaviour.

This understanding of the essential nature of language and non-language behaviour come to our aid as we move into the classroom as the second, citadel of language learning experience, the first being home. The child is brought to school from a playful world of toys, objects, plants and animals with the intimacy of interpersonal communion hovering over every hour of the day. The learning of $L_1$ took place in the intimacy and pleasantries of home atmosphere; it will be presumptuous for us to think that the learning of $L_2$ can satisfactorily take place in a diametrically opposed class-room environment. Only attempts towards a creative learning of the second or foreign language can solve the fundamental problems which present-day classroom face. This chapter presents ways and means to turn classroom teaching into creative teaching-learning behaviour and ultimately it is in the hands of the teacher that we find the detailed aspects of creative classroom behaviour.

The following are the underlying characteristics of creative learning in the classroom :

1. Creative learning is a highly *motivated behaviour*. Among the six subgroups which constitute the class : (i) the motivated bright learner, (ii) the unmotivated bright learner, (iii) the motivated average learner, (iv) the unmotivated average learner, (v) the motivated slow learner, and lastly (vi) the unmotivated slow learner, we find that the subgroup (i) tops the list in performance because in them we find a blend of ***high level motivation*** and *high level intelligence*. This highly motivated group with good intelligence is found as the most creative of them all. Although intelligence, as mentioned, is directly

proportionate to creativity, what adds behaviours is the high level motivation the pupils possess. This motivation as relating to creativity need not be of academic nature as brilliant boys and girls do involve in a large variety of creative behaviour. Consequently those bright learners who are unmotivated academically need not be unmotivated in all other respects. Instead they may be more highly motivated in aspects such as games than the academically motivated bright learners are. In other words creativity shows out in those aspects of human behaviour which are motivated just as non-academic creative behaviour will be part of the unmotivated bright learner's behaviour. Creativity and motivation have deep correlations as part of the child's behaviour in the classroom.

2. Creative learning means *personal commitment* on the child's part. Creative production calls for deep involvement, not half-hearted attempt. Even as a young child at home this deep involvement is fairly visible. It is the individual person who with an intrinsic or extrinsic motive undertakes some creative activity. One need only to look at the child who builds his house in sand or imitatively 'reads' the news paper. There is a sense of commitment visible even at this early stage. It means generating the vitality and enthusiasm required for the creative work.

3. Creative learning would mean *intimate attention* with a view to discovering the new and making it one's own. Intimate attention to the details is an integral part of the creative learning like any form of creative work. The learner entertains full awareness of *the new* that he is expected to grasp from the learning activity and to make to his own. For these reasons the academically unmotivated lot of pupils belonging to all sub-groups of the class cannot tap their creative resources for the cause of learning because the characteristics mentioned above will not be presented in the context of learning.

4. Creative learning, means *personal initiative* for discovering the new aspects of learning. Like personal commitment in undertaking whatever class or home tasks given, the creative child manifests considerable degree of personal initiative for discovering the new for himself. The child does not develop habits of getting spoon-fed in all matters relating to his learning. For

him the class tasks and home tasks are his own business, he takes them with a sense of commitment as seen above. No one need to dictate to him or persuade him for doing his variety of tasks related to learning. This is the kind of personal initiative which is found at the heart of all creative behaviour in adults and children. It makes a world of difference in learning behaviour between those who are to be spoon-fed in everything, and those who exhibit high level of personal initiative.

5. Creative learning and would lastly, mean *originality* at a variety of levels. The creative learner cannot help but be original. Originality in varying degrees is an integral part of the creative learner's learning behaviour. This originality will be seen in his learning exercises, construction of models, in introducing variety in his learning acts, and in co-curricular activities in all of which the conscientious teacher cannot help taking note of the creative learner due to his active presence in class. The learners originality will be felt most in discovering the new pertaining to the learning behaviour.

The creative learner, in short, exhibits a variety of cues which throws lights into his creative behaviour. The aspects of creative leaning examined above cannot pass unnoticed as the learner of this sort will remain active in the classroom in varying degrees depending upon his level of creative enthusiasm. The foremost characteristics of such learners, as seen, are the high level motivation, personal commitment, personal initiative, intimate attention to the details, and originality. Everyone of these characteristics is correlated to the six subgroups mentioned above including all the motivated and unmotivated learners. Creative behaviour as part of learning is not only found in subgroup (i) but at lower levels too in comparatively varying degrees. But at lower levels the cues which the pupils exhibit becomes inconspicuous in the context of the classroom. At higher level, the creative enthusiasm of the learners is a thing for anyone to discover as this enthusiasm penetrates all aspects of their behaviour in the classroom and outside.

## 5. Creative Behaviour of the Teacher

Not much need to be mentioned about the creative role the language teacher is expected to play in the classroom for providing effective learning experiences. Just as the unmotivated and non-creative children would waste time and labour for the cause of learning, the non-creative teacher of languages will not be able to achieve anything significant from his routine manner of doing things in the classroom. The five characteristics we saw in connection with the creative behaviour of learners in the classroom are equally applicable to the teacher of $L_1$ or $L_2$ and these form the criteria to discover to what extent a teacher will be creative. Not much can be expected of the teacher who enters the classroom unaware of (i) the presence of such varied subgroups there, (ii) the role of creative behaviour which governs the success of their learning and (iii) his role as a guide to tap their creative resources in all learning experiences.

The creative teacher is not only conscientious about his roles in the class classroom but also the need to equip himself as much as possible with the knowledge of the intricate working of language. The present book is oriented to the needs of the creative and resourceful teacher for whom an effective classroom performance presupposes the proper knowledge about the functioning of language. As we apply to the teacher the five aspects of creative behaviour mentioned above we find that his creative roles can be defined well.

1. Creativity means *personal commitment* on the part of the teacher. This involves the commitment to a cause at every given moment. Creative behaviour and personal commitment are seen to go hand-in-hand. No creatively gifted individual is known to have achieved anything without this commitment. This would involve again taping one's personal resources for the cause of teaching with a view to providing every richer learning experiences. It is such commitment that provides the energy required for discovering newer aspects of learning behaviour and newer techniques of teaching.

2. Creativity means *high level motivation*. Creative ability in a teacher will remain a sterile thing without high level motivation on his part to boost his creative behaviour. In fact a truly creative person undertaking teaching cannot help being resourceful. It remains part of his make up; his sense of value will be questioned and challenged if he remains unproductive even if this would mean no added material benefits. The

creative and resourceful teacher without enough motivation to given him strength will only turn out to be an overloaded worker rather than an enthusiastic classroom practitioner. High level motivation is a powerful factor in taping the resources of the creative teacher.

3. Creative teaching would mean *intimate attention* on the part of the teacher who is entrusted with a large group of enthusiastic learners to have language experiences. A creativity oriented teacher cannot, again, help being close to the pupils in terms of their language learning experiences at least during the hours when they are entrusted to his care. This would mean intimate attention to all the details of their learning experiences including what tasks they carry-out at home which are somehow related to his responsibilities as a language teacher. The attention that he has on the variety of learning activities of his pupils will certainly enable him to discover their needs as learners and the ways and means to fulfil these needs. All this would mean activity on the part of the teacher.

4. Creative teaching further means *personal initiative* as a corollary to personal commitment. What mostly happens in classroom is that the teacher becomes a victim of routine and stereotyped work. As though there is no room for personal initiative in the normal run of teaching. A creative and resourceful teacher takes considerable personal initiative in making his teaching rather than be victimized by routine. No one need to ask the teacher to do something new to solve a new problem, add to variety in learning activities, or to comply with a new situation. The creative teacher has enough of personal initiative to find new activities to add to variety in learning and solution to problems that crop up in relations to classroom learning. He is in fact on the lookout for doing something new to give vent to his creative resources.

5. Creative teaching, lastly, means *originality* in the teacher's approach to the learning situations. Unlike the average teacher, the creative teacher always exhibits a touch of originality in his work. Originality is co-extensive with creativity and must be considered as the heart of creative behaviour. A creativity gifted teacher soon gets tired of doing the something over and again in the same old fashion. He soon looks for new ways of

behaviour to appease his creative enthusiasm. The teacher's originality is almost contagions and ipso facto influence the creative learning behaviour of the pupils. It would then need no extrinsic motivation to boost the pupil's classroom performance since the teacher's efforts in providing creative learning experiences at once function as the chief, though perhaps temporary, motivating factor in a particular learning situation.

The creative aspects of language and non-language behaviour are based on the factors that we examined above. We found a common basis shared by both the aspects of human behaviour, namely, the *content of the mind* realized in language as its semantic representation and in non-linguistic cognition as concepts and their organization. The counterparts of both these aspects are found in images and their organization. Both language and non-language behaviour lead us thus to concepts and images as the content of the mind and ultimately to aspects of *reality* as such in its myriads of manifestations. The creativity oriented teacher with all the enthusiasm he has in store will relate both the aspects of the child's behaviour and exploit the tremendous resources of the child's concrete behaviour patterns to provide him as concrete language experiences as possible in the context of the classroom and outside: leading him to considerable *cognitive*, *sociological*, and *linguistic* maturity.

# Bibliography

Adams, Jack A. 1967. Human Memory. New York: McGraw-Hill.

Arapoff, Naney. 1970. Writing : a thinking process. English Teaching Forum (Washington) 8, 3.

Argyle, M. 1972. Non-verbal communication, social interaction. In Hindi, R., ed., Non-verbal Comunication Cambridge University Press.

Austin, John L. 1962. How to Do Things with Words. J.O. Urmson. ed., Cambridge : Harward Univ. Press.

Ayer, A.J. 1958. The Problem of Knowledge. London : Macmillon.

-----------. 1966. Language, Truth and Logic. Gollancz.

Bach and Harms eds. 1969. Universals of Language New York : Holt, Rinehart and Winston.

Bandura A. and R.H. Walters. 1963. Social Learning and Personality Development. New York : Holt, Rinehart and Winston.

Bastian, H.D. 1898. Aphasia and other Speech Defects. London: H.K. Lewis.

Bellugi, Ursala : How Children Say No. Cambridge : M.I.T.

Bendix, Edward. 1966. Componental Analysis of General Vocabulary. Bloomington : Indiana Univ. Press.

Berelson, B. 1952. Content Analysis in Communication Research. Free Press.

Berko Jean, 1958. The Childs learning of English Morphology. *Word* 14. In Sol Saparta, S.,

----------. ed. Psycholinguistics, New York : Holt.....

----------, and R. Brown. 1960. Psycholinguistic research methods. In Mussen, P.H., ed., Handbook of Research Methods in Chiid Development. New York : John Wiley & Sons.

Berustein, B.B., and Brandis, W., 1970, Social class differences in Communication and Control. In Brandis W., and Handersen D., Social Class Language and Communication. New York: Routledge & Kegan Paul.

Berry, M.F., 1969, Language Disorders in Children : Their Bases and Diagnosis. New York : Appleton-Century-Crofts.

Bever, Thomas, 1969. On Semantic Problems of Semantic Representation. Foundations of Language 5.

----------, 1970. On Classifying Semantic Features. In Bierwisch and Heidolph, eds. Progress in Lingusitics the Hagne : Mouton.

----------, 1970. The Cognitive Basis for Linguistic Stratures. In J. Hayes, ed., Cognition and Development of Language. New York : Wiley.

---------- et al. 1975. An Integrated Theory of Linguistic Ability. New York : Harper & Row.

Bierwisch and Heidolt, eds., 1970, Progress in Linguistics. The Hagne : Mouton.

Bigge, M.L., and M.P. Hunt. 1962. Psychological Foundations of Education. New York : Harper & Row.

Birch, Herbert G. 1968. Health and the Education of the Socially Disadvantaged Child. Developmental Medicine and Child Neurology, 10.

Black, Max. 1949. Lanugage and Philosophy. Ithaca : Cornel University Press.

Bloom, Lois, 1970 Language Development : Form and Function in Emerging Grammars. Cambridge : M.I.T. Press.

Bloomfield, L., and C.L. Barnhart, 1961, Lets Read : A Linguistic Approach. Detroit : Wayne State Univ. Press.

Bolinger, Dwight. 1965. The atomization of meaning. Language. 41.

----------, 1968, Aspects of Language. New York : Harcourt, Brace & World.

Bonin, G. Von., 1950, Essay On the Cerebral Cortex. Charles C. Thomas.

Braine, Martin D.S. 1971. The Acquisition of Language in Infant and Child. In Carroll Recd., ed., The Learning of Language. New York : Appleton.

Brain, Russel, 1961. The Neurology of Language. Brain, 84.

----------, 1965, Speech Disorders : Aphasia, A praxia, and Agnosia, Washington : Butterworth.

Brandis W., and Hendersen D., 1970, Social class, Language and Communication. Routledge & Kegan Paul.

Brazier, M.A.B., 1967, Neurophysiological contributions to the subject of human communication theory. In Frank Dance, ed., Human Communication Theory, New York : Holt, Rinehart & Winston.

Browon, Judson S. 1961. The Motivation of Behaviour. New York : McGraw-Hill.

Brown, Roger, 1958, Words and Things. New York : Free Press.

----------, 1970, Psycholingusitics, New York : Free Press.

----------, and E.H. Lenneberg, 1954, A study in language and cognition. Journal of Abnormal and Social Psychology (      ). 49.

----------, and J. Berko. 1960. Word associations and the acquisition of grammar. Child Development 31.

----------, and Bellergi, 1964. Three Processes in the acquisition of syntax. Harward Educational Review. 34.

----------, and C. Fraser. 1964. The acquisition of symtax. Monographs of the society for Research in Child Development. 29.

Bruce, D.J. 1964, The analsysis of word sounds by young children. British Journal of Edu. Psychology.

Bulchvarov, Panayot., 1970, The Concept of Knowledge. Evanston: Northwestern University Press.

Burling, Robbins, 1959, Language Development of Garo and English Speaking Child. Word ( ) 15.

Burt, 1971, From Deep to Surface Structure : An Introduction to Transformation Symtax. N.V. Harper & Row.

Byrne & Shervanian, 1977, Introduction to Communicative Disorders. New York : Harper & Row.

Cantor, Pamela, 1977, Understanding the Child's World. New York : McGraw-Hill.

Carnap, Rudolf, 1965. Meaning and Necessity. Chicago : Chicago University Press.

Cattell, R.B., 1957, Personality and Motivations. World Book Company.

Cazden, C., 1968, The acquisition of noun and verb inflections. Child Development; 39.

Chafe, Wallace, 1970, Meaning and Structure of Language. Chicago : University of Chicago Press

Chandrasekhar. A., 1965. A New Approach to Language Teaching. Delhi.

Chauchard, P. (Translated by David Noakes), 1962, The Brain, New York : Grove Press.

Chomsky, Carol S. 1968. The Acquisition of Symtax in Children from 5 to 10. Cambridge : M.I.T. Press.

Chomsky, Noam. 1959. Verbal Behaviour (a review of Skinner's boak). Language ( ) 35.

----------, 1962, The Logical Basis of Linguistic Theory. Pre-prints of the Ninth International Congress of Linguists. Cambridge:

M.I.T. Press.

----------, 1965, Aspects of the Theory of Symtax.

----------, 1972, Language and Mind. First Published in 1968. New York : Harcourt, Brace Jovanovich.

----------, 1966, Cartesian Linguistics. A Chapter on the History of Rationalist Thought. New York.

----------, 1967, The general prospective of language. In Clark H. Millikan and Frederic L. Darley, eds., Brain Mechanisms and Underlying Speech and Language. New York : Grune & Stratton.

Clark, Herbert, 1973. Space, time semantics and the child. In Cognitive Development and the Acqusition of Lanugage. T.E. Moore, ed., New York : Academic Press.

Cook-Gumperz, J. 1973. Social Control and Socialization. New York : Routledge & Kegan Paul.

Cook, V. J. 1970. The Creative Use of Language. Audio-visual Language Journal (London) 8.1.

Cohen, B.H. 1964, Role of Awareness in Meaning established by classical conditioning. Journal of Exp. Psychology 67.

Cooper, Malcolm D. 1970. Measuring Lanugage Problems and Attainment. English Language Teaching (London) 25, 1.

Cooper, R.L. 1967. The ability of deaf and hearing children to apply morphological rules. Journal of Speech and Hearing Research. 10.

Critehley, M. 1970. Aphasiology and Other Aspects of Language. London : Edward Arnold.

Cruickshan, W.M. ed., 1963, Psychology of Exceptional Children and Youth. New Jersey : Prentice-Hall.

Cynthia, Shewan, 1978. Speech and Language Disorders : Selected Readings.

Dance, Frank. ed., 1967, Human Communication Theory. New York : Holt, Rinehart and Winston.

Davtiz, J.L. 1964, The Communication of Emotional Meaning.

New York : McGraw-Hill.

De Cecco, J.B. 1968. The Psychology of Learning and Instruction. New York : Prentice Hall.

Deese, James, 1970, Psycholingusitcs. Boston : Allyn & Bacon.

De Laguna, Grace, 1927, Speech, Its Function and Development. New Haven : Yale Univ. Press.

De Vito, J. 1970, Psychology of Speech and Language. New York : Random House.

De Vesta, F.J. 1966, A Developmental study of the semantic structure of children. Journal of Verbal Learning and Verbal Behaviour, 5.

----------and G.O. Bernhein, 1967, Some semantic relations among word associates : A replication. Journal of General Psychology, 76.

Dixon, Robert, 1971, A method of semantic description. In Steinberg and Jacobvits, eds., Semantics Cambridge : M.I.T. Press.

Dollard, J., and N. Miller, 1950, Personality and Psycho-therapy. New York : McGraw-Hill.

De Vito. J., 1976, The Interpersonal Communication Book. New York : Harper & Row.

----------, 1978, Communicology : An Introdúction to the Study .of Human Communication.

Drillian, C.M. 1964, The Growth and Development of the Prematurity Born Infant. London : E & S Livingstone Ltd.

Eisenson, John. 1963. The Nature of Defective Speech. In Cruickshank, W.M., ed., Psychology of Exceptional Children and Youth, second ed., Prentice-Hall.

----------, 1972, Aphasia in Children. New York : Harper & Row.

Ervin Susan, M., 1964, Imitation and structural change in children's language. In Eric H. Lenneberg, ed., New Directions in the Study of Language. Cambridge ; M.I.T. Press.

Ervin-Tripp, S.M. and G. Foster, 1960, The development of

meaning in children's descriptive terms. Journal of Abnormal and Social Psychology. 61.

Eysenck, H.J., 1960, Behaviour Therapy and Neuroses. New York: Appleton-Century-Crofts.

Flanagan, J.L., 1965, Speech Analysis, Symthesis and Perception. New York : Academic Press.

Fillmore, Charles, 1971. Types of lexical information. In Steinberg and Jackobnits, Semantics. Cambridge.

Fillmore, Charles and D. Terence Langendoen, eds., 1971. Studies in Lingustic Semantics. New York : Holt, Rinehart and Winston.

Fishman, J.A., 1968, Bilingualism in the Barrio. U. S. Development of Health and Education, New York.

----------, 1968, Readings in the Sociology of Language. The Hagne : Mouton.

Fodor, J., and Terrold Kutz, eds. 1964. The structure of Lanugage, New Jersey : Prentice-Hall.

----------, and M. Garret. 1966. Some reflections on competence and performance. In Lyons J., and R.J. Wales, eds., Psycholinguistic Papers. Edinburgh : Univ. of Edinburgh Press.

Forgus, R.H. and Melamed, L.E., 1976, Perception : A Cognitive Stage Approach. New York : McGraw-Hill.

Fowler, W. 1962. Cognitive learning in infancy and early childhood. Psychological Bulletin, 59.

Fraser, Colin, 1966, Disucssion of 'the Creation of Language' In John Lyons and Rojcr J. Wales, eds., Psycholinguistic. Edinburgh: Univ. of Edinburgh Press.

Fry, D.B., 1966, The development of the phonological system in the normal and deaf child. In Smith F., and G.A. Miller, eds. The Genesis of Language. Cambridge : M.I.T. Press.

Goldman-Eisler, F. 1968. Psycho-lingusitics. Academic Press.

Goldstein, K. 1939. The Organizm. New York : American Book Company.

Goodenough, Ward, 1956, Componental analysis and the study of meaning. Lanugage, 32.

Green, B.F. Introduction, 1966, Current Trends in Problem Solving, In B. Kleinmuntz, ed., Problem Solving. New York: Wiley.

Greenberg, Joseph, 1966, Language Universals. The Hague : Mouton.

Guilford, J.P. 1967, The Nature of Human Intelligence, New York: McGraw-Hill.

----------and Hoepfner, Ralph, 1971, The Analysis of Intelligence. New York : McGraw-Hill.

Haring, Norris G., 1967, ed., Methods in Special Education, New York : McGraw-Hill.

---------- and Phillips, E.L., 1962, Educating Emotionally Disturbed Children. New York : McGraw-Hill.

----------and Schiefelbush, R.L., 1976, Teaching Special Children. New York : McGraw-Hill.

Halliday, M.A.K., 1961, Categories of the theory of Grammar. Word, 17.

----------, 1969, Relevant Models of Language. Educational Review. 22.

----------, McIntosh, A., and Strevens, P.D., 1964, The Linguistic sciences and Language Teaching. London : Longman.

Holstead, W.C., 1947, Brain and Intelligence : A Quantitative study of the Frontal Lobes. Chicago : Uni. Chi. Press.

Hayes, J. ed., 1970, Cognition and Development of Language. New York : Wiley & Sons.

Hebb, D.O., 1949, The Organization of Behaviour : A Neurophysiological Theory. New York : Wiley.

Hendersen, D., 1970, Social class differences in form class usage among five-year old children. In Brandis, W. and Henderson, Social Class, Language and Communication. Routledge & Keyan Paul.

Herdan, Gustav., 1966, The Advanced Theory of Language as Choice and Chance. Heidelberg : Springer-Verlay.

Hetherington, E.M. and Parke, R.D. 1975, Child Psychology : A Contemprary View-point. New York : McGraw-Hill.

Helzron, Robert, 1971, The Deep Structure of the Statement, Linguistics, 65.

Hinde R., ed., 1972, Non-verbal Communication. Cambridge : University of Cambridge Press.

Hirsch, Katrina DE, 1967, Different diagnosis between aphasic and schizophrenic language in children. Journal of Speech and Hearing Disorder, 32.

Hockett, Charles F., 1963, The Problem of Universals in Language, Cambridge : M.I.T. Press.

Holsti, O.R., 1968, Content Analysis. In Lindzey, G. and Aronson, E. eds. Handbook of Social Psychology. Vol. 2. Addison-Wasley.

Hopper, Robert, 1978, Human Message Systems. New York : Harper & Row.

Hopper, Robert and Tia Naremore, 1978, Children's Speech : A Practical Introduction to Communication. New York : Harper & Row.

Householder, Fred., 1971, Lingusitic Speculations. Cambridge : Cambridge Univ. Press.

Hull, C.L., 1943, Principles of Behaviour. New York : Appleton-Century-Crifts.

----------, 1970, Child Growth and Development, New York : McGraw-Hill.

Hurlock, Elizabeth B., 1972, Child Development. New York : McGraw-Hill.

Irvin, O.C., 1952, Speech Development in the young child : 2. Some factors related to the speech development of the infant and the young child. Journal of Speech and Hearing Disorders, 17.

Irvin, O.C., 1948, Infant Speech : Development of Powel Sounds. Journal of Speech and Hearing Disorders, 13.

Jacobs, Roderik A. and Peter S. Rosenbaum, 1968, English Transformational Grammar.

Jacobson, R., 1968, Child Language, Aphasia and Phonological Universals. The Hagne : Mouton.

----------and M, Halle, 1956, Fundamentals of Language. The Hagne : Mouton.

----------, C.G. Fant and M. Halle, 1963, Preliminaries to Speech Analysis. Cambridge : M.I.T. Press.

Jespersen, Otto. Language.

Jettery & Peterson, 1976, Speech : A Basic Text. New York : Harper & Row.

Joos, Martin, 1964, The English Verb : Form and Meanings. Madism : University of Wisconsin Press.

Katz, Jerrold J., 1966, The Philosophy of Language. New York : Harper & Row.

----------, 1972, Semantic Theory. New York : Harper & Row.

----------and J.A. Fodor, 1963, The Structure of a Semantic Theory. Language, 39.

----------and P.M. Postal, 1964, An Integrated Theory of Semantic Descriptions. Cambridge : M.I.T. Press.

Kellogg, Withrop N. and Louise A. Kellogg, 1933, The Ape and the Child. New York : McGraw-Hill.

Keller, F.S., and W.N. Schoenfold, 1950, Principles of Psychology. New York : Appleton-Century-Crofts.

Kendler, H.H. and P. Vineberg, 1954, The Acquisition of Compound Concepts as a function of training. Journal of Exp. Psychology, 48.

---------- and A.D. Karasik, 1958, Concept formation as a function of competition between response produced eves. Journal of Exp. Psy., 55.

Keplan, H.M., 1960, Anatomy and Physiology of Speech. New

York : McGraw-Hill.

Kinch, John W., 1973, Introduction to Social Psychology. New York : McGraw-Hill.

Kiparsky, Paul, 1968, Linguistic Universals and linguistic Change. In Universals of Language. Bach and Horms, eds., New York.

Kisker, George W., 1977, The Disorganized Personality. New York: McGraw-Hill.

Kleinmuntz, B.ed., 1966, Problem Solving. New York : McGraw-Hill.

Kobler, W., 1929, Gestalt Psychology. New York : Liveright.

----------, 1940, Dynamics in Psychology. New York : Liveright.

Krauss, R.M. and S. Glucksberg, 1967, The development of Communication : Competence as a function of age. Child Development, 40.

Krech, D., Crutchfield, R.S., and Ballachey, E.L., 1962, Individual in Society. New York : McGraw-Hill.

Lackoff, George, 1971, On Generative Semantics. In Steiberg and Jacoborils, eds., Semantics, Cambridge.

Lambert, W.E., 1967, A Social psychology of bilingualism. Journal of Sociological Issues, 23.

Landauer, Thomas, 1967, Readings in Physiological Psychology. New York : McGraw-Hill.

Lashley, K.S., 1929, Brain Mechanisms and Intelligence. Chicago: Chicago Univ. Press.

Lawton, D., 1968, Social Class, Language and Education. Routledge and Kegan Paul.

Lehrer, Adnien, 1974, Semantic Fields and Lexical Structure. Amsterdam : North-Holland Publishing Company.

Lennebery, Eric H., 1964, A biological perspective of Language. In Erich H. Lennerberg, ed., New Directions in the Study of Language. Cambridge : M.I.T. Press.

Lewis, M.M., 1963, Language, Thought and Personality. New York : Basic Books.

Lenneberg, Eric H., 1967, Biological Foundations of Language. New York : Wiley & Sons.

----------, 1967, On explaining language. Science, 164.

----------, 1966, The natural history of language. In F. Smith and C.A. Miller, eds. The Genesis of Language, New York : M.

Lett, W.R., 1978, The Creative Artist at Work. Australia : McGraw-Hill.

Liberman, Phillip, 1967, Intonation, Perception and Language. Cambridge : M.I.T. Press.

Logan, V.G., and Logan M.L. A Design for Creative Teaching. Canada : McGraw-Hill.

----------, 1972, Creative Communication, Canada : McGraw-Hill.

----------, 1974, Educating Young Children. Canada : McGraw-Hill.

Lansbury, Floyd., 1963, Linguistics and Psychology. In S. Kock. ed., Psychology, a Study of Science, New York.

Luria, A.R., 1965, Higher Cortial Functions of Man. New York : Basic Books.

Lyons, John, 1963, Structural Semantics. Oxford : Blackwells.

Lyons J., and R.J. Wales. eds. Psycholinguistic Papers. Edinburgh: Univ. of Edinburgh Press.

----------, 1970. The Meaning of Meaning. Times Literary Supplement (London), July, 1970.

Macnamara, John, 1972, Cognitive basis of Language Learning in infants. Psychological Review, 79.

McCawley, James, 1968, 'The role of semantics in a grammar. In Bach and Harms, eds. Universals of Linguistic Theory. New York.

McNeil, Devid, 1966, The Creation of Language by children. In John Lyans and Roger J. Wales, eds., Psycholinguistic Papers. Edinburgh : Univ. of Ede. Press.

----------, 1970, The Acquisition of Language : The Study of